A POPE CHRONOLOGY

Macmillan Author Chronologies

General Editor: Norman Page, Professor of Modern English,
Literature, University of Nottingham

Reginald Berry
A POPE CHRONOLOGY

Edward Bishop
A VIRGINIA WOOLF CHRONOLOGY

Timothy Hands
A GEORGE ELIOT CHRONOLOGY

Norman Page
A BYRON CHRONOLOGY
A DICKENS CHRONOLOGY

F. B. Pinion
A WORDSWORTH CHRONOLOGY

R. C. Terry
A TROLLOPE CHRONOLOGY

Further titles in preparation

A Pope Chronology

REGINALD BERRY
Senior Lecturer in English
University of Canterbury, New Zealand

MACMILLAN
PRESS

First published 1988

Published by
THE MACMILLAN PRESS LTD
Houndmills, Basingstoke, Hampshire RG21 2XS
and London
Companies and representatives
throughout the world

Typeset by Wessex Typesetters
(Division of The Eastern Press Ltd)
Frome, Somerset

Printed in Hong Kong

British Library Cataloguing in Publication Data
Berry, Reginald
A Pope chronology.—(Macmillan author
chronologies)
1. Pope, Alexander—Chronology
I. Title
821'.5   PR3633
ISBN 0–333–39907–2

For Carolynne, Anthea and Aidan

Contents

General Editor's Preface

Most biographies are ill adapted to serve as works of reference – not surprisingly so, since the biographer is likely to regard his function as the devising of a continuous and readable narrative, with excursions into interpretation and speculation, rather than a bald recital of facts. There are times, however, when anyone reading for business or pleasure needs to check a point quickly or to obtain a rapid overview of part of an author's life or career; and at such moments turning over the pages of a biography can be a time-consuming and frustrating occupation. The present series of volumes aims at providing a means whereby the chronological facts of an author's life and career, rather than needing to be prised out of the narrative in which they are (if they appear at all) securely embedded, can be seen at a glance. Moreover, whereas biographies are often, and quite understandably, vague over matters of fact (since it makes for tediousness to be forever enumerating details of dates and places), a chronology can be precise whenever it is possible to be precise.

Thanks to the survival, sometimes in very large quantities, of letters, diaries, notebooks and other documents, as well as to thoroughly researched biographies and bibliographies, this material now exists in abundance for many major authors. In the case of, for example, Dickens, we can often ascertain what he was doing in each month and week, and almost on each day, of his prodigiously active working life; and the student of, say, *David Copperfield* is likely to find it fascinating as well as useful to know just when Dickens was at work on each part of that novel, what other literary enterprises he was engaged in at the same time, whom he was meeting, what places he was visiting, and what were the relevant circumstances of his personal and professional life. Such a chronology is not, of course, a substitute for a biography; but its arrangement, in combination with its index, makes it a much more convenient tool for this kind of purpose; and it may be acceptable as a form of 'alternative' biography, with its own distinctive advantages as well as its obvious limitations.

Since information relating to an author's early years is usually scanty and chronologically imprecise, the opening section of some volumes in this series groups together the years of childhood and adolescence. Thereafter each year, and usually each month, is dealt with separately. Information not readily assignable to a specific month or day is given as a general note under the relevant year or month. The first entry for each month carries an indication of the day of the week, so that when necessary this can be readily calculated for other dates. Each volume also contains a bibliography of the principal sources of information. In the chronology itself, the sources of many of the more specific items, including quotations, are identified, in order that the reader who wishes to do so may consult the original contexts.

NORMAN PAGE

Introduction

In the *Epistle to Dr Arbuthnot*, the poet famously condenses his life into the phrase 'this long disease'. Seen at length in a chronology such as this, the life of Alexander Pope is dominated rather by his dedication to friends and friendship, to the creation of a stable domestic situation for himself, and, centrally, to the discipline of the poet's profession. The evidence of these dominant aspects is found in Pope's correspondence and in the complex publication details of his own works and those of his contemporaries.

The chronology delineates Pope's continuing respect for family values and his pursuit of the quiet country life at his Twickenham villa, with his own landscaped garden. But Pope also spent much time away, visiting with well-to-do friends at their rural estates and commuting to London to deal with the business side of his literary career. Like many writers he spoke infrequently of his works in progress. But he left a detailed record of his intensive participation in the printing and publishing of his works. In two ways represented here, Pope was also fully engaged in a community of writers. On the friendly side, he always sought out the fellowship of men of genius. In particular, because his early participation in the Scriblerus Club (1713–14) so determined his later career, I have included in this chronology selected information about the parallel careers of Gay, Arbuthnot and Swift. On the hostile side, Pope's literary and financial successes (and his often prickly personality) attracted a jealous and vicious crew of detractors, as evidenced by the recurrent appearance in these pages of references to pamphlet and newspaper attacks on the poet, his works, and his character.

More detailed information about these attacks can be found in Guerinot's *Pamphlet Attacks on Alexander Pope* and Rogers' *Major Satires of Alexander Pope*. Full bibliographic descriptions of Pope's works are to be found in Griffith's *Bibliography*. Where works have gone into multiple editions I have not tried to include the dates of all of these, except occasionally to show the popularity of a particular piece, as with *The Rape of the Lock* or *The Dunciad*. In some cases exact publication dates are not available, either because they are unknown or because sources give contradictory dates; some dates, therefore, may be only approximate. In the eighteenth-century book world, the bookseller performed the modern-day function of publisher; here I have used the two terms interchangeably.

A major resource for this chronology has been Pope's *Correspondence*, edited by George Sherburn. Unless otherwise noted, quotations from the letters are from this edition and can be located there according to the date of the entry. Because Pope edited his own correspondence for publication, and the originals for a proportion of the letters do not now exist, not all the information so derived may be accurate. Pope was also notoriously lax or inexact about dating his letters properly, as the extant letters show. And in certain cases, as well, Pope consciously fabricated letters for his own editions (see, for example, 20 July 1705 and 26 July 1734).

The general matter of dating requires a brief explanation. Until 1752, and therefore through the whole of Pope's life, England followed the Julian or Old Style Calendar, whereas most of Europe had adopted the Gregorian or New Style Calendar almost two centuries earlier. The Julian Calendar was eleven days *behind* the Gregorian, and it started the year on 25 March. In this chronology all dates are Old Style, except that the year is taken to begin on 1 January.

The assembly of a chronology implies not only a compiling of dates and events but also an understanding of the life extrapolated upon them. In that regard, I am indebted to the several narratives of Pope's career by Maynard Mack, especially *Alexander Pope: A Life* (1985). More personally, I owe this work to the inspiration provided by Peter Seary and Patricia Brückmann, who in a far-away place first taught me how to read Pope. Here, in another place far away, I have been helped by Helen Deverson, Kate Trevella, Gareth Cordery, Ronys Davey (Waiwetu), Stuart Foster (Matai), and also by Carolynne Berry.

List of Abbreviations

AP   Alexander Pope
Ault   Norman Ault, *New Light on Pope* (London: Methuen, 1949).
CH   *Pope: The Critical Heritage*, ed. John Barnard (London: Routledge and Kegan Paul, 1973).
CIH   Maynard Mack, *'Collected in Himself': Essays Critical, Biographical, and Bibliographical on Pope and Some of his Contemporaries* (Newark, Del.: Delaware University Press, 1982).
Corr.   *The Correspondence of Alexander Pope,* ed. George Sherburn, 5 vols (Oxford: Clarendon Press, 1956).
Mack, *Life*   Maynard Mack, *Alexander Pope: A Life* (New Haven, Conn., and London: Yale University Press; and New York and London: W. W. Norton, 1985).
Mack, *Garden and City*   Maynard Mack, *The Garden and the City: Retirement and Politics in the Later Poetry of Pope, 1731–1743* (Toronto and Buffalo: University of Toronto Press, 1969).
PA   J. V. Guerinot, *Pamphlet Attacks on Alexander Pope, 1711–1744* (London: Methuen, 1969).
Sherburn   George Sherburn, *The Early Career of Alexander Pope* (Oxford: Clarendon Press, 1934).
Spence   Joseph Spence, *Observations, Anecdotes and Characters of Books and Men*, ed. James M. Osborn, 2 vols (Oxford: Clarendon Press, 1966).
TE   *The Twickenham Edition of the Poems of Alexander Pope*, ed. John Butt *et al.*, 11 vols (London: Methuen, 1938–68).

List of Abbreviations

A Pope Chronology

The Childhood Years
(1688–99)

1688 (Mon 21 May) AP born at 6.45 p.m. in the Pope family house at the bottom of Plough Court, Lombard Street, London. In his copy of Virgil AP later recorded 'Natus Maji 21, 1688, Hora Post Merid. 6 3/4.' His father, Alexander, is a merchant; Edith, AP's mother, is his second wife, his first wife having died in 1679. Almost immediately AP is nursed by Mary Beach, who remains with the family until her death in 1725.

During this year, by tradition AP's father is said to have retired from his textile business, with a sizeable fortune, worth at least £10,000. As Roman Catholics, the Popes are affected by King James's second Declaration of Indulgence, ordered to be read from pulpits on 20 May, which decreed official religious tolerance for Catholics and Dissenters. Seven bishops refuse to conform to this decree and are tried for seditious libel. As the crisis of government under James deepens, William of Orange arrives at Torbay (5 November) to begin a Protestant takeover of the nation. On 23 December, King James flees to France. As part of William's new regime, an Act is passed almost immediately requiring papists and reputed papists to leave London and Westminster and reside at least ten miles distant from Hyde Park Corner. The Act is reproclaimed frequently during the next several years; however, the Popes continue to live in the City until 1692.

1689 (13 Feb) William and Mary are offered the Crown of England jointly.

(7 May) England declares war on France: 'King William's War' will last until 1697.

(26 May) Birth of a daughter to the Marquis of Dorchester, later to be Lady Mary Wortley Montagu, AP's friend and adversary after 1715.

(16 Dec) The Bill of Rights is passed in Parliament; the Revolution settlement embodied in this Bill makes England Protestant and includes many other significant governmental reforms.

1

1690 During this year England is under threat of invasion by France. In Ireland, James's forces are defeated at the Battle of the Boyne, whereupon James flees to exile in France. Martha Blount, AP's lifelong friend and principal legatee, born at Mapledurham.

1692 During the summer of this year, the Pope family moves to Hammersmith village, near London, where there is a significant Roman Catholic community. The Plough Court house in London is sold to new owners.

England is once again under threat of French invasion.

1694 (28 Dec) Death of Queen Mary at 1 a.m., leaving William to continue as sole monarch.

1695 At some point before this year AP's half-sister, Magdalen, has married Charles Rackett, son of a well-to-do family of Hammersmith, where the Popes now live. In this year, Rackett purchases a property at Binfield in Berkshire.

(13 Jan) At Dublin, Jonathan Swift is ordained a priest in the Church of Ireland, officially commencing his ecclesiastical career.

(16 Sep) Birth of a daughter to Magdalen and Charles Rackett: the child lives until the following April.

1696 During this year, the Pope family employ a priest, Edward Taverner (alias Banister, alias John Davies), as tutor for AP. AP then briefly attends a Catholic academy at Twyford, three miles from Winchester. After writing a satire on a master there, AP is asked to leave. He then attends Thomas Deane's school at Marylebone, London. In the latter half of 1696, Jonathan Swift begins to compose *A Tale of a Tub*, which will be an archetypal model for his and AP's solo and co-operative satiric enterprises.

1698 (July) AP's father takes over ownership of Whitehill House and fourteen acres of land at Binfield, acquired from son-in-law Charles Rackett.

1699 (30 Nov) Swift's first major work published, an edition of Sir William Temple's letters.

Binfield and London
(1700–9)

During this decade, AP lives at Whitehill House, Binfield, with his parents. From time to time he makes excursions to London, but chiefly his time is devoted to avid reading, writing, and the friendship of neighbouring families and individuals.

1700   During this year, AP purchases, amongst other books, a 1641 edition of George Herbert's poems and the first two volumes of the English translation by Peter Motteux of *Don Quixote*.
(Apr) AP's father conveys the Binfield property to his wife's nephews, the Mawhoods, 'in trust for his only son' (AP) to circumvent the illegality of a Catholic owning property.
(1 May) Death of John Dryden, aged 69, AP's most influential poetic model.

1701   During this year, AP receives as a gift (from Gabriel Young, the previous owner of Whitehill House at Binfield) a copy of the 1598 black-letter edition of Chaucer's *Works*; the volume remains in his library until his death.
(May) Binfield churchwardens notify the Berkshire Archdeacon, during the Visitation at Reading, that AP's father and mother live in the parish as 'Reputed Papists'.
(12 June) The Act of Settlement, necessitated by the death in July 1700 of Princess Anne's only surviving son, is given royal assent. The Act ensures a Protestant succession through Sophia, daughter of Charles I's sister Elizabeth, and secures other political facts and offices.

1702   (8 Mar) Death of King William. The throne is assumed by his sister-in-law Anne (sister of Mary and daughter of James II).

1703   During this year, AP receives from the author a copy of *The Dispensary*, Sir Samuel Garth's mock-heroic satire on apothecaries. He and Garth become good friends.

1704   (10 May) First edition of Swift's *Tale of a Tub* published.
(30 Oct) John Arbuthnot, later to be a charter member of the Scriblerus Club, and close friend of AP, is made Physician Extraordinary to Queen Anne.

1705 (25 Mar) Earliest mention of AP's *Pastorals* ('my green Essays') in his letters (to William Wycherley, who has befriended him).

(20 Apr) Sir William Walsh, man of public affairs and of letters, and member of Parliament, returns the manuscript drafts of AP's *Pastorals* to Wycherley, praising the Preface as 'very judicious and very learned', and wishing to make AP's acquaintance. They will soon become close friends.

(Oct) During this month, AP visits Will's coffee-house, London, in the company of a sometime Binfield resident, Chevalier Charles Wogan.

(19 Oct) Sir William Trumbull (former Principal Secretary of State to William III) returns AP's copy of Milton's shorter poems, with a compliment: 'I know of no body so like to equal him, even at the age he wrote most of them, as your self.' This year sees the beginning of his friendship with AP, who lives only a mile from the Trumbull estate.

(26 Oct) AP now back at Binfield after time spent in London among the wits at Will's coffee-house.

(5 Nov) Wycherley invites AP to visit him in London.

1706 During this year, AP purchases a copy of Charles Cotton's three-volume translation of Montaigne's *Essays* (1685–93), a work which will be central to his reading during the remainder of his life.

(5 Feb) Wycherley praises AP's revision of one of his poems; this is the first reference to AP's editorial work for Wycherley.

(10 Apr) AP writes to Wycherley explaining in detail his corrections and improvements in some of the latter's poems. Revising Wycherley's work is a small project of his at least until 1710.

(20 Apr) Jacob Tonson writes to AP offering to publish the *Pastorals*.

(2 July) Writing from Binfield to Walsh in London, AP rejects the idea of a 'Pastoral Comedy'.

(9 July) Walsh writes to AP suggesting he dedicate the last of the *Pastorals* to 'Mrs Tempest', subject of an earlier eclogue by Walsh.

(22 Oct) AP writes to Walsh on '*English* Versification'. (The letter is likely a fabrication deriving from AP's letter to Cromwell of 25 Nov 1710.)

1707 (1 May) On this day the Union Treaty with Scotland (signed

July 1706) comes into being, uniting the kingdoms of Scotland and England.

(3 July) AP writes to Walsh, hoping to visit him at Abberley (near Worcester), before the end of July. The proposed visit inaugurates a tradition of extended summer visits outside London which AP will carry on for much of his life.

(12 or 13 July) Date of the first extant letter of AP to Henry Cromwell, in verse: 'Dear Mr. Cromwell, – May it please ye!/Sit still a Moment; pray be easy.' Cromwell, thirty years his senior, is one of AP's friends, and a minor poet.

(21 July) Walsh replies to AP's letter of 3 July, promising a 'Coach, or Horses to meet you at Worcester.'

(1 Aug) Possibly on this date, but certainly before the 5th, AP journeys from Binfield to see Walsh at Abberley. During his time at Abberley, he shows Walsh an early draft of lines from the *Essay on Criticism*.

(18 Sep) Sir William Trumbull writes to his nephew, the Revd Ralph Bridges, to say that AP has just returned to Binfield from Walsh's house at Abberley. At this point in his career, AP is resolved 'to go on with translating Homer'.

(28 Oct) First mention of 'verses upon Windsor Forest' by AP, in a letter to Trumbull from his nephew.

(20 Nov) AP returns his edited draft of Wycherley's poem 'Dulness'. During the next several months AP continues his revisions of Wycherley's poems.

1708 (1 Jan) AP confined to his chamber at Binfield with eye trouble, perhaps from excessive reading.

(19 Jan) From Binfield AP sends his Statius translation to Cromwell for collection (published 20 May 1712).

(8 Feb) At the peak of his influence as Secretary of State, Robert Harley is forced to resign under pressure from the Whigs and other Cabinet members. He will later re-emerge as the leader of the government, become Lord Oxford, and be part of AP's circle of friends in the Scriblerus Club.

(3 Mar) In London and frequenting Will's, AP seeks a consultation with Ralph Bridges (chaplain to the Bishop of London at Fulham), probably about his early translations of Homer.

(4 Mar) AP receives his first income from poetry: 10 guineas for the *Pastorals* and the Chaucer translation 'January and May'. The poems are published on 2 May 1709.

(16 Mar) Death of William Walsh, aged 49.

(18 Mar) Back in Binfield after his London visit, AP regrets his country isolation.

(9 Apr) After reading some of AP's early Homer translations, Trumbull encourages him to continue 'to make his works . . . useful and instructive to this degenerate age'. This is the probable beginning of AP's translation of the whole of Homer, which he will complete almost two decades hence.

(28 Oct) Death of George of Denmark, consort of Queen Anne.

(1 Nov) Writing to Cromwell, AP notes that Tonson's *Miscellany* (in which his first published works will appear) has been postponed yet again. The reason for postponement may have been the period of public mourning for George of Denmark.

(13 Nov) AP having spent most of the past year at home at Binfield, probably since April, Wycherley writes to urge a London visit to him this month.

1709 (Jan) During this month, at Wycherley's request, AP visits London, staying in Mrs Bamber's lodging-house, in the chamber next to Wycherley. During the visit he becomes ill and returns to Binfield.

(13 Jan) AP receives 3 guineas from Tonson for his Homer translation 'The Episode of Sarpedon' (published 2 May).

(5 Feb) Failure of John Dennis' play *Appius and Virginia* (see *Essay on Criticism*, l. 585), after its first performance.

(6 Feb) AP ill again at Binfield.

(19 Feb) According to Wycherley, publication of Tonson's *Miscellany* (with Pope's poems) is delayed until three weeks hence (eventually published 2 May).

(9 Apr) Publication of Swift's *Project for the Advancement of Religion and the Reformation of Manners*.

(19 Apr) In *Tatler* no. 4, Richard Steele gives early praise to Charles Jervas, the Dublin-born artist who will soon become AP's tutor in painting and a celebrated society painter.

(30 Apr) Swift's poem 'Description of the Morning' appears in *Tatler* no. 9.

(2 May) AP's first appearance in print: *Pastorals* and 'January and May' in Tonson's *Poetical Miscellanies: The Sixth Part*. AP's *Pastorals* come last in the volume, those by Ambrose Philips at the beginning. In the same volume appears AP's first translation from the classics to

be published, 'The Episode of Sarpedon' (from *The Iliad*, bks xii and xvi), and two poems by Swift.

(7 May) Writing to Cromwell, AP notes the publication of Tonson's *Miscellany*, and sends him more verses for collection. He expects to spend the summer at Binfield. On this same day, Steele, in *Tatler* no. 12, praises Philips' *Pastorals* without mentioning AP's in the same volume.

(17 May) Wycherley writes to thank AP for a copy of Tonson's *Miscellany*, saying that 'all the best Judges . . . like your part of the Book so well, that the rest is liked the worse' and noting the praise of coffee-house readers. He intends to visit Binfield later in the summer.

(26 May) Wycherley assures AP on the *Miscellany* poems: 'the Coffee-house Wits . . . the Criticks, prove their Judgments by approving your Wit'.

(14 June) AP ill again at Binfield.

(10 July) Reviewing his papers, AP finds the 'Ode on Solitude' (published 1717), probably his earliest extant poem, 'written when I was not Twelve years old', and sends it in a letter to Cromwell. Now back at Binfield after a London visit to Cromwell.

(29 Aug) Writing to Cromwell in London, AP inquires of Wycherley (to have visited Binfield earlier), who is ill there.

1710

January
24   (Tues) Death of AP's aunt Elizabeth Turner, according to an entry in the Elzevir Virgil, in which he recorded such family information.

February
9   (Thurs) AP's father makes his will.
14   AP at Binfield, ill with severe head pains.
27   Beginning of the trial of Henry Sacheverell for sedition, after his sermon denouncing the government ministers and bishops (preached 5 Nov 1709).

April
1   (Sat) AP still revising some poems of Wycherley's.

10   Back at Binfield after a brief pre-Easter visit to Cromwell in London (Easter Sunday fell on the 9th), AP sends him some poems together with the Argument to the *Thebaid* translation.

11   Wycherley informs AP that he will visit Binfield a fortnight hence, to stay for the rest of the summer.

27   Wycherley's last extant letter to AP, expressing satisfaction with AP's revisions of Wycherley's poems.

28   Death of Thomas Betterton, the great actor and manager, whose literary works AP will prepare for the press. Chiefly translations of Chaucer, the works will appear in Lintot's *Miscellaneous Poems and Translations*, edited by AP (May 1712).

May

2   (Tues) AP's last extant letter to Wycherley, indicating a temporary halt to editing of Wycherley's poems, after a disagreement over revisions.

17   AP writes to Cromwell, remarking on his own recovery at Binfield from a dangerous illness contracted in London.

June

24   (Sat) In a letter to Cromwell on this day, AP includes the 'Rondeau' ('You know where') without giving a hint of his authorship.

July

31   (Mon) First extant letter of AP to John Caryll. AP suffering from headaches since early July.

August

21   (Mon) AP at Binfield. Complains to Cromwell of his isolation from London friends, including Wycherley.

October

1   (Sun) By this point, AP has completed a draft version of Chaucer's *Hous of Fame*, which he will publish in 1715 as *The Temple of Fame*.

17   Swift's poem 'A Description of a City Shower' published in *Tatler* no. 238.

28   AP comments in a letter to Cromwell on Ambrose Philips' *Pastorals*, 'we have no better Eclogs in our Language. This Gentleman, (if I am not much mistaken in his Talent) is

capable of writing very nobly.' AP is still detached from Wycherley's friendship at this date.

November
25 (Sat) AP writes in great detail to Cromwell about 'the Defect in Numbers of several of our Poets'. The last portion of the letter seems to provide the text of AP's letter to Walsh (22 Oct 1706) in AP's editions of his letters.

December
17 (Sun) AP sends Cromwell a copy of Crashaw's collected poems, together with a critical assessment of the poet.

1711

January
1 (Mon) During this year, Robert Harley establishes the South Sea Company to offset the East India Company and to consolidate part of the national debt.
2 Last issue of Steele's *Tatler* published.
25 Writing to Caryll, AP rejects the vanity of the poet: he is 'that little Alexander the women laugh at'. Acknowledges compliments of Caryll's wife for the gift of one of his own paintings.

February
27 (Tues) Publication of Swift's *Miscellanies in Prose and Verse*, containing 'Baucis and Philemon' and 'An Argument against Abolishing Christianity' amongst other works.

March
1 (Thurs) First issue of *The Spectator*, edited by Joseph Addison and Richard Steele, published this day.
8 A French nobleman in exile, the Marquis de Guiscard, attempts to assassinate the First Minister, Harley.

April
16 (Mon) In *Spectator* no. 40, Addison opposes poetical justice as a principle of tragedy, thereby raising the ire of John Dennis just in advance of the publication of AP's *Essay on Criticism*.

24 In *Spectator* no. 47, Addison quotes a couplet by Dennis, which the latter again takes as a personal insult.

May

10 (Thurs) AP back at Binfield from a visit to London (where he was shown the manuscript of John Dennis' *Reflections* by Lintot; see 25 June) and to Caryll at West Grinstead. During this visit, AP may have met John Gay for the first time.

15 AP's *Essay on Criticism* published, anonymously, by W. Lewis. The *Essay* is AP's first published book.

23 Robert Harley is created Earl of Oxford by the Queen. His official title is to be Baron Harley of Wigmore Castle, Earl of Oxford and of Mortimer. After resigning as Secretary of State in 1708, he has re-emerged as Chancellor of the Exchequer.

25 Robert Harley's Bill establishing the South Sea Company passes its third reading in the House of Commons. The Company is established as a monopoly for South American trade.

29 Harley is appointed Lord Treasurer.

June

10 (Sun) AP returns to Binfield after a visit to London and a brief stay at a near neighbour's, Anthony Englefield, of Whiteknights, about nine miles from Binfield.

18 AP writes to Caryll to refute objections to some parts of the *Essay on Criticism* by strict Catholics.

20 Publication by Lintot of John Dennis' *Reflections Critical and Satyrical, upon a Late Rhapsody, Call'd, An Essay Upon Criticism*, the first public attack on AP's work. Dennis charges AP with Jacobitism, complains he wrote a panegyric to himself under Wycherley's name, and compares him (amongst other personal abuse) to a 'hunch-back'd Toad', all a result of AP's reference to Dennis in the *Essay* (ll. 269–70 and 584–7).

25 AP sends Caryll Dennis' *Reflections* together with a long letter of self-defence: 'I can't conceive what ground he has for [so] excessive a resentment.' AP expecting a visit from Cromwell at Binfield any day.

July

15 (Sun) Cromwell back in London after a fortnight's visit to Binfield. A letter of this date gives AP's earliest reference to

John Gay, and contains lines which clearly refer to *The Rape of
the Locke*.

26 Richard Steele writes to Pope to request a libretto for a
    musical interlude to be performed during the next London
    winter season.

August
2 (Thurs) AP reflecting (to Caryll) on Dennis' attack: 'I shall
   never make the least reply to him . . . if a book can't answer
   for its self to the public, 'tis to no sort of purpose for its
   author to do it.' AP first mentions in his letters Mrs Weston,
   who will become a model for his 'Elegy to the Memory of an
   Unfortunate Lady'.

October
8 (Mon) In the *General Post*, Lintot invites contributions for the
   miscellany which he will eventually publish in May 1712.

November
12 (Mon) AP returns to Binfield from a week's visit to Englefield
    at Whiteknights.
15 In *Spectator* no. 223, Ambrose Philips' *Pastorals* and
    'Winter-Piece' are praised, but no mention is made of AP's
    Pastorals.
27 Swift's political pamphlet *Reflections on the Conduct of the Allies*
    is published on this day, having been commissioned by the
    Tory government in the midst of the peace negotiations.

December
20 (Thurs) In *Spectator* no. 253, Addison praises the *Essay on
    Criticism* as 'a Master-piece in its kind'.
21 Writing to Cromwell from the Blounts' house at Mapledurham,
    AP remarks on his sexual arousal in the presence of the two
    sisters, Teresa and Martha, and laughingly says he will trade
    the *Pastorals* and the *Essay on Criticism* for their maidenheads,
    and by this experience write a tragedy. He also thanks
    Cromwell for sending him his copy of Gay's poem 'On a
    Miscellany of Poems. To Bernard Lintott'.
24 Charles Gildon's first attack on AP appears in the *British
    Mercury*.

29   Upon returning from a visit away from Binfield (to
     Whiteknights?), AP reads the praise of his *Essay on Criticism*
     in *Spectator* no. 253.
30   AP writes to Steele with thanks for commending the *Essay* in
     the *Spectator*.
31   Creation of twelve new peers is announced; Marlborough is
     dismissed from his offices as leader of the British forces and
     as minister.

1712

January
 1   (Tues) During this month, the peace congress begins at
     Utrecht.
     About this date, a second issue of the first edition of the *Essay
     on Criticism* is published, probably the result of Addison's
     praise in *Spectator* no. 253 (20 Dec 1711).
20   Steele writes to AP offering to acquaint him with the real
     author of the praise in *Spectator* no. 253.

March
 4   (Tues) Arbuthnot's first John Bull pamphlet, *Law is a Bottomless
     Pit*, published by John Morphew.
17   Publication of Arbuthnot's second John Bull pamphlet, *John
     Bull in his Senses*.
18   Shortly before this day, AP's 'Sapho to Phaon' is first
     published in *Ovid's Epistles . . . by Several Hands*, issued by
     Jacob Tonson.
21   Lintot pays AP £7 for the two-canto version of *The Rape of the
     Locke* (published 20 May).

April
15   (Tues) Gay's unperformed farce (his first play) *The Mohocks*
     published by Lintot, with an ironic dedication to the critic,
     John Dennis: in the dedication, Gay defends AP's reputation
     as poet and critic.
16   Publication of Arbuthnot's *John Bull still in his Senses*, third in
     the series.

May

9   (Fri) *An Appendix to John Bull still in his Senses* published.

14   AP's 'Messiah: A Sacred Eclogue' appears (anonymously) in *Spectator* no. 378, described by Steele as 'by a great Genius, a Friend of mine, in the country; who is not ashamed to employ his Wit in the Praise of his Maker'.

17   Publication of Swift's pamphlet *A Proposal for Correcting the English Tongue*.

20   Lintot publishes *Miscellaneous Poems and Translations*, which includes the first appearance of the two-canto *Rape of the Locke*. Includes six other poems by AP: his translation of Statius' *Thebaid*, bk I, the 'Fable of Vertumnus and Pomona' from Ovid, 'To a Young Lady with the Works of Voiture', 'On Silence', 'Verses Design'd to be Prefix'd to Mr Lintot's Miscellany', and 'To the Author of a Poem Entitled "Successio"'. The collection also contains Gay's 'On a Miscellany of Poems' (where AP's 'various Numbers charm our ravish'd Ears, / [and] His steady Judgment far out-shoots his Years') and Thomas Betterton's translations of Chaucer's *General Prologue* and *Reeve's Tale*. Betterton died in 1710: these poems were thoroughly revised by AP at the request of his widow. AP seems to have had a large hand in this collection as editor (see Ault, p. 27ff.).

25   AP sends a copy of *The Rape of the Locke* to Martha Blount, 'wherein (they tell me) are some things dangerous to be lookd upon'.

June

During this month, Henry St John is elevated to the peerage as Viscount Bolingbroke; he is angry and distraught that the Queen has refused him an earldom.

1   (Sun) On this day, Steele writes to AP in praise of 'Messiah' (published 14 May): 'I have turn'd to every verse and chapter, and think you have preserv'd the sublime heavenly spirit throughout the whole. . . .'

9   In *Spectator* no. 400, Steele again puffs Ambrose Philips' *Pastorals* without mentioning AP's.

16   *Spectator* no. 406 includes a letter by AP on solitude and tranquillity.

July

15 (Tues) AP writes to Steele, moralising on the theme of sickness in life. The letter is later published in *Guardian* no. 132 (12 Aug 1713).

16 Shortly after this date, AP leaves Binfield to visit John Caryll in Sussex, at West Grinstead. He spends about two months there.

31 Publication of fifth and last of Arbuthnot's series, *Lewis Baboon Turned Honest, and John Bull Politician.*

August

8   (Fri) *Spectator* no. 452 prints a satiric letter, likely by AP, containing a proposal to publish a newspaper for 'Village and Hamlet' news.

14 *Spectator* no. 457 contains a long letter on a newspaper 'project', a *'News-letter of Whispers'*, together with a project to publish *An Account of the Works of the Unlearned*. The letter is likely to be AP's, and if so, initiates the series of Scriblerian works culminating in the *Travels, The Beggar's Opera* and *The Dunciad*.

October

28 (Tues) Thomas Tickell's poem *On the Prospect of Peace* published.

30 Thomas Tickell's poem *On the Prospect of Peace* is praised by Addison in *Spectator* no. 523. The same paper compliments the *Rape*, and the 'late miscellany published by Mr. Pope, in which there are many Excellent Compositions of that ingenious Gentleman'. It also praises Ambrose Philips' *Pastorals* but does not refer to AP's.

November

4   (Tues) *Spectator* no. 527 prints AP's 'On a Fan', an imitation of Waller written in his youth, together with an introductory letter.

7   AP writes to Steele on the subject of Hadrian's last words, enclosing a verse translation from the Latin, and a copy of his *Temple of Fame*.

8   AP's letter to John Caryll, Jr, indicates there is continuing opposition by strict Catholics to some parts of the *Essay on*

Criticism, and to Sir Plume in the *Rape* by the man on whom the character is modelled.

10 Steele prints AP's 7 November letter, without the verses, in *Spectator* no. 532, and comments that AP had also sent 'for my perusal . . . an admirable Poem', presumably *The Temple of Fame* (published 1 Feb 1715).

12 Steele writes to AP on *The Temple of Fame*: '[I] see in it a thousand thousand beauties.' The same letter invites AP's participation in a 'Design', perhaps *The Guardian*, which begins to appear 12 March 1713. *Spectator* no. 534 reveals AP as the author of *Messiah* published in no. 378 (14 May 1712).

16 AP writes to Steele, seeking detailed criticism and correction of *The Temple of Fame*.

27 *The Spectator* advertises the publication this day of a second edition of the *Essay on Criticism*.

29 AP writes to Caryll (who has recently returned from France) commenting favourably on Tickell's verses in *Spectator* no. 532 (10 Nov) and mentioning his own *Windsor-Forest*, a section of which he includes for comparison with Tickell's.

December

4 (Thurs) Steele requests from AP 'an Ode as of a cheerful dying spirit . . . put into two or three stanzas for musick'. In his reply AP includes an early version of 'The Dying Christian to his Soul'.

5 In a letter to Caryll, AP notes his continuing revisions and additions to *Windsor-Forest*.

6 In *Spectator* no. 555, Steele acknowledges his debts for assistance with the periodical, listing AP second in a list of contributors.

21 AP's letter to Caryll indicates his continuing ill state of health, now worsened since the cold weather began.

24 AP congratulates Gay on his recent appointment as domestic steward to the Duchess of Monmouth.

1713

During most of this year AP lives with Charles Jervas at Cleveland Court, behind St James's Palace, London, where he makes a thorough practical study of painting with Jervas.

January

1 (Thurs) The peace negotiations at Utrecht, begun at this time in 1712, continue with further obstacles to signing being discovered.

10 AP writes from Binfield to thank George Granville, Lord Lansdowne, 'for having given my poem of Windsor Forest its greatest ornament, that of bearing your name in front of it'.

13 Publication of Gay's georgic *Rural Sports*, 'inscrib'd to Mr. Pope', whose *Windsor-Forest* was a source and inspiration for Gay's poem.

February

An undated letter to Caryll in this month indicates that AP is now staying in London, presumably at Jervas' in Cleveland Court. He has been reading the manuscript of Addison's *Cato*, and has just sent his *Windsor-Forest* to the press (published 7 Mar). He is still consulting with Steele over *The Guardian*.

2 (Mon) First performance of Nicholas Rowe's *Jane Shore*; the intended epilogue is by AP, but it is not spoken in the theatre (Ault, pp. 133–8).

23 Lintot pays AP £32 5s for *Windsor-Forest*.

March

7 (Sat) Publication of AP's *Windsor-Forest*, dedicated to Lord Lansdowne, just three weeks before the signing of the Peace Treaty at Utrecht.

9 First reference to AP in Swift's correspondence: 'Mr. Pope has published a fine poem, called Windsor Forest. Read it' (*Journal to Stella*).

12 First number of Steele's *Guardian*, successor to *The Spectator*, with AP as a main editorial assistant.

16 AP's first contribution to *The Guardian*, an essay on dedications, appears in no. 4.

24 An essay on 'The Grand Elixir', probably by AP (with Gay?), appears in *Guardian* no. 11.

31 The Treaty of Utrecht is finally signed after fifteen months of negotiations. England makes some colonial gains, France keeps what Louis had won in Lille and Strasbourg, Sicily is acquired by the Duke of Savoy, and Spain's Italian possessions are granted to the Emperor Leopold of Hapsburg.

April

6 (Mon) Appearance of *Guardian* no. 22, first of five essays on pastoral poetry in which Philips' *Pastorals* are equated with those of Theocritus, Virgil and Spenser, and AP's *Pastorals* are not mentioned. Similar essays appear in nos 23 (7th), 28 (13th), 30 (15th), and 32 (17th). All five are probably by Thomas Tickell, AP's later rival in translating Homer.

14 First night (at Drury Lane) of Addison's tragedy *Cato*, with Prologue by AP. The success of the play is considered a Whig triumph, which Lord Bolingbroke tries to overcome by presenting 50 guineas to the actor who plays Cato, for defending the cause of liberty. The play runs for nineteen consecutive performances.

18 Publication of AP's Prologue to Addison's *Cato* in *Guardian* no. 33.

21 Ralph Bridges writes to his uncle, Sir William Trumbull, on AP's reputation after *Windsor-Forest* is published: 'one of the greatest genius's that this nation has bred' (Mack, *Life*, p. 185).

25 Swift created Dean of St Patrick's Cathedral, Dublin, by a warrant signed at London.

27 AP's most famous *Guardian* essay appears in no. 40. The subject is pastorals, and in anger at being ignored in the five previous *Guardian* papers on the subject AP here ironically praises Ambrose Philips' efforts in order to denigrate them. Also on this date is published Addison's *Cato*, including AP's Prologue.

30 AP taking further painting-lessons from Jervas. He reports to Caryll on the partisan reception of Addison's *Cato*, when the 'prologue-writer . . . was clapped into a stanch Whig sore against his will'. He intends to go back to Binfield a week hence.

May

12 (Tues) First night (of two) of Gay's comedy, and second play, *The Wife of Bath*, at the Theatre Royal, Drury Lane. Epilogue by AP. The text is published by Lintot on the 22nd.

21 AP's essay against barbarity to animals published in *Guardian* no. 61.

June

10 (Wed) AP's 'Receit to Make an Epick Poem' published in *Guardian* no. 78.

12 AP still at Jervas', continuing his instruction in painting. Planning to say another fortnight before visiting Binfield.

13 Having arrived from London on the 10th, Swift is formally installed as Dean in a ceremony at St Patrick's Cathedral, Dublin.

23 AP asks Caryll to have his son scrutinise the Pope family investments in Paris.

25 The first part of AP's essay on the Club of Little Men published in *Guardian* no. 91. The second part appears in no. 92 the next day.

July

9 (Thurs) Dennis' *Remarks upon Cato, A Tragedy* published.

13 A letter, possibly by AP (on a dream of a window in his mistress' breast, signed 'Peter Puzzle'), appears in *Guardian* no. 106. The letter has much in common with the five-canto *Rape*, upon which AP is at work at this time.

16 AP's St Cecilia's Day work, the *Ode for Musick*, published by Lintot.

23 AP is paid £15 by Lintot for the *Ode for Musick*.

28 John Morphew publishes AP's satirical pamphlet *The Narrative of Dr Robert Norris, Concerning the Strange and Deplorable Frenzy of Mr JOHN DENN–S*.

August

4 (Tues) Steele conveys to Lintot Addison's disapproval at AP's treatment of John Dennis in the Norris pamphlet.

12 A letter (on sickness) by AP appears in *Guardian* no. 132.

14 AP back with Jervas at Cleveland Court after a brief absence (at Binfield?).

23 In a letter to Gay, AP details his recent attempts to copy portraits by Jervas, and congratulates Gay on the completion of *The Fan*.

September

1 (Tues) Publication of *Guardian* no. 149, by Gay, on 'fashionable dress'.

9 Swift arrives in London from Dublin.

20 AP returns to London after a week's stay at Binfield in the company of Rowe.

24 *Guardian* no. 169 appears, probably written by AP (on nature and death).

28 *Guardian* no. 172 (on the origin of letters), probably by AP, appears this day.

29 AP's last contribution to *The Guardian*, on gardens, appears in no. 173.

October

During this month AP circulates *Proposals for a Translation of Homer's Ilias*.

1 (Thurs) Last number (175) of Steele's *Guardian*.

5 AP receives 15 guineas from Tonson for his translation of 'The Arrival of Ulysses in Ithaca' and 'The Wife of Bath her Prologue' (published 29 Dec 1713).

17 AP writes to Caryll on Steele's discontinuing *The Guardian* for *The Englishman*, after a quarrel with Tonson. Although staying with Jervas, he tells Caryll that he will soon spend a fortnight at Binfield.

21 Lord Lansdowne expresses pleasure with AP's design of translating Homer. AP is by this time promoting the translation by means of subscription.

23 Writing to Gay, AP notes Swift's acceptance of the Scriblerian design for *The Works of the Unlearned*. He expects to go to Binfield in about a month, and will there collect Gay's *Fan*. Working on revised five-canto *Rape of the Lock*.

November

2 (Thurs) Addison compliments AP (still in London) on his Homer design.

December

8 (Tues) Writing from Binfield, AP counters Swift's humorous request to change his religion. He notes that he has finished the revised *Rape*, and expects to stay at Binfield until Christmas. Gay's *Fan* published, as revised by AP. Gay is already at work on *The Shepherd's Week*.

15 AP tells Caryll he has dined with Lady Winchelsea (Anne Finch) earlier in the month. He proposes dedicating the new

Rape to Arabella Fermor, and admits to trembling about his
undertaking to translate Homer.

29 'The Wife of Bath her Prologue', 'The Arrival of Ulysses in
    Ithaca', and several shorter pieces appear in Steele's *Poetical
    Miscellanies, Consisting of Original Poems and Translations* (dated
    1714), published by Tonson.

1714

January
9 (Sat) AP in London determining a subscription list for the
   Homer translation and seeing the new *Rape* through the
   press, with the dedication to Arabella Fermor. He intends to
   stay the winter in London.

February
18 (Thurs) Publication of a miscellany called *The Poetical
    Entertainer*, which includes the first appearance of AP's
    epigram 'On a Lady who P—st at the Tragedy of Cato'.
20 Lintot agrees to publish the new five-canto *Rape*; AP receives
    £15 for the poem.
23 Publication of another of Swift's anonymous political
    pamphlets, *The Publick Spirit of the Whigs*, a defence of Lord
    Oxford's Ministry. Certain seditious statements in it cause a
    price to be put on Swift's head.
25 Advance copies of the *Rape* available: two copies have gone to
    Caryll with a letter asking for names of subscribers for the
    Homer translation. AP expecting to spend the summer at
    Ladyholt, Caryll's Sussex estate.
26 Advance copy of the *Rape* sent to Trumbull (congratulatory
    reply, 6 Mar).

March
2 (Tues) Lintot issues *The Rape of the Lock. An Heroic-Comical
   Poem. In Five Canto's.*
9 Second edition of the *Rape* announced in the *Post-Boy*.
12 AP reports to Caryll (who has not yet received his copies)
    that the *Rape* has sold 3000 copies in four days.
18 Steele expelled from Parliament for publishing a 'seditious'
    pamphlet. AP expects to arrive at Binfield in three weeks.

20 First recorded meeting of Scriblerus Club, held at Arbuthnot's rooms in St James's Palace; present are Lord Oxford, Gay, Thomas Parnell, Swift and AP.

23 AP signs an agreement with Bernard Lintot for a metrical translation of Homer's *Iliad*, from which he is to receive 200 guineas per volume and 750 free copies of the set to distribute to his subscribers, whose subscriptions were his to keep. Lintot retains the copyright and the ability to publish the translation in formats other than quarto starting a month after the appearance of the quartos.

April

6 (Tues) Charles Gildon's *A New Rehearsal, or Bays the Younger* published. The play contains the first published attack on *The Rape of the Lock*, for indecency.

14 Meeting of the Scriblerus Club.

15 Publication of *The Shepherd's Week*, Gay's satiric contribution to the pastoral controversy.

16 Martha Blount contracts smallpox, according to a note in her copy of the breviary.

19 AP asks John Hughes to assist in procuring subscriptions for *The Iliad*. Leaving London for Binfield on the 21st, accompanied by Parnell.

May

1 (Sat) AP at Binfield, 'very busy in my grand undertaking', the *Iliad* translation. Receives a letter from George Berkeley, the philosopher, praising the *Rape*.

15 Proposals for AP's *Iliad* are republished. Included with these is a current list of subscribers to the edition.

31 Thomas Tickell signs an agreement with Jacob Tonson for a rival translation to AP's *Iliad*. Swift prepares to leave London for a retreat at Upper Letcombe (near Wantage, Berkshire). This is his last day in London until 1726.

June

1 (Tues) Swift departs London for Letcombe, frustrated with the current political situation and his inability to reconcile Harley and Bolingbroke. On the way he will stop at Oxford.

5 Meeting of Scriblerus Club, with Swift away at Letcombe.

8 Death of Queen Anne's actual heir, Sophia, mother of George, the Elector of Hanover, following rebukes over her intervention in English politics. AP still in London; according to Gay he has with him the translation of the first book of *The Iliad*, with which he hopes to attract subscribers.

12 Last recorded meeting of the Scriblerus Club; held at the Pall Mall coffee-house at 1 p.m.

14 Gay departs London for Hanover as secretary to the Tory embassy under Lord Clarendon.

18 AP, now in London, writes to Swift at Letcombe of the current political situation and of friendship: 'Of all the world, you are the man . . . who serve your friends with the least ostentation.'

July

4 (Sun) AP and Parnell visit Swift at Letcombe, returning to Binfield on the 11th to continue work on *The Iliad*. AP writes to Arbuthnot proposing a summer vacation for the Scriblerus Club, with revival in the winter.

19 AP suffering severe headache, but working steadily on *The Iliad*.

27 Oxford is forced to give up the position of Lord Treasurer. Third edition of the *Rape* published; copies in print now number above 6000.

30 The Duke of Shrewsbury accepts the office of Lord Treasurer; the Privy Council meets at Kensington, and militia and navy called out to ensure order at the Queen's death, which is expected any day.

August

1 (Sun) Death of Queen Anne. AP goes to London, 'moved by the common curiosity of mankind' (*Corr.*, I, 241). Accession of King George I (Elector of Hanover) proclaimed.

16 Swift leaves England for Ireland. AP writes to Caryll from Binfield on the tense political situation.

20 Jervas writes to AP with a sketched design of the frontispiece for volume I of *The Iliad*.

24 Funeral ceremony for the late Queen, conducted by Francis Atterbury, Bishop of Rochester and Dean of Westminster. Swift arrives back in Dublin.

27 AP just returned from Oxford to Binfield.

30 Bolingbroke forced to resign as Secretary of State. Arbuthnot returns from a short visit to Paris, taking a house in Dover Street, Piccadilly.
31 King George leaves Hanover on his way to London to assume the throne.

September
 2 (Thurs) Parnell and AP at Binfield write to Arbuthnot requesting a continuation of the Scriblerus Club in the winter.
 7 Earliest reference to AP's *Key to the Lock* (see 25 Apr 1715) made by Arbuthnot in a letter to AP.
13 AP at Binfield after a brief visit to the Blounts at Mapledurham.
18 The new King arrives off the English coast.
19 The King steps onto British soil at Greenwich.
23 AP, at Bath with Parnell, writes to welcome Gay back from Hanover.

October
 2 (Sat) AP and Parnell still at Bath. AP plans to be at London or at Binfield after 'the end of next week'.
20 Coronation of King George I. Shortly afterwards, AP writes his 'Epistle to Miss Blount, on her Leaving the Town, after the Coronation'.
26 AP at Binfield now that the Coronation is over. Martha Blount suffering from smallpox. See 'Epistle to Miss Blount, on her Leaving the Town, after the Coronation' (*TE*, vi, 124).

November
19 (Fri) AP in London, at Jervas', informs Caryll that he will visit him at Ladyholt.
24 Parnell *en route* back to Ireland.
29 AP writes to William Broome, his assistant on *The Iliad*, with instructions on critical commentaries, part of the continuing work of the translation.

December
11 (Sat) As part of the programme of national stability, King George directs that preachers should not 'intermeddle in any affairs of state' from the pulpit.
18 In a letter to Barton Booth (repr. in *Remarks upon Mr Pope's . . . Homer* [1717]), John Dennis describes *Windsor-Forest* as a

'wretched Rhapsody' and AP as 'Obscure, Ambiguous, Affected, Temerarious, Barbarous' (*CH*, p. 90).

20   Last number of the Addison-revived *Spectator*.

22   AP journeys with Caryll to Englefield's house at Whiteknights.

30   *The Temple of Fame* ready for publication, according to Gay.

1715

January
16   (Sun) AP back at Binfield after passing a few days with Viscount Bolingbroke, intending to go to London on the 19th.

29   In London, staying with Jervas. The first volume of *The Iliad* is now in the press.

February
1   (Tues) *The Temple of Fame* published by Lintot. AP receives £32 5*s* for the poem. He immediately sends a copy to Martha Blount, together with a letter containing 'To a Lady with the Temple of Fame' (*TE*, VI, 127).

14   AP sends a copy of *The Temple of Fame* to Trumbull. Still in London at Jervas'.

23   First night (of seventeen performances) of Gay's Scriblerian comedy *The What D'Ye Call It*, at the Theatre Royal, Drury Lane. Early reviewers (such as Dennis) assume the play is AP's. Lintot publishes the text on 19 March.

March
1   (Tues) Advertised publication date of AP's *Iliad*. Wet weather prevents the printed sheets from drying fully (the volume finally appears on 6 June).

3   AP writes to Caryll of the success of Gay's *What D'Ye Call It*.

10   Publication of *Aesop at the Bear-Garden: A Vision*, a mock-heroic parody of *The Temple of Fame*.

18   AP, still in London, writes to Parnell in Dublin, promising to send him a parcel of books including *The Temple of Fame*.

23   Lintot pays AP £215 for the first volume of the *Iliad*.

26   Bolingbroke flees London for France to escape arrest as a suspected Jacobite. Soon after he becomes Secretary of State to the Pretender.

April

2 (Sat) *A Complete Key to . . . The What D'Ye Call It* published. Implies AP's collaboration with Gay in the play.

25 AP (using the pseudonym Esdras Barnivelt) publishes *A Key to the Lock*, his burlesque explication of the *Rape*.

30 AP receives £12 10s. from Lintot for the *Key to the Lock*. Publication by Lintot of Nicholas Rowe's tragedy *Lady Jane Gray*. After the Epilogue there appears a second Prologue, possibly by AP.

May

2 (Mon) Samuel Garth's Preface to his poem *Claremont*, published this day, praises AP's *Windsor-Forest*.

6 Thomas Burnet, in *The Grumbler* no. 14, accuses AP ('Arch Wag') of authorising both *A Key to the Lock* and *A Complete Key to . . . The What D'Ye Call It*.

19 At some point between this date and June 12th, AP composes 'A Farewell to London. In the Year 1715'.

21 Publication announced (in *The Post-Man*) of AP's sermon–pamphlet *The Dignity, Use and Abuse of Glass-Bottles*.

30 Thomas Burnet and George Duckett's anonymous *Homerides: Or, A Letter to Mr Pope* published (earlier issue on 7 Mar). Designed to appear just before AP's *Iliad*, it attacks AP for 'greed' and for his religion.

31 Second edition of AP's *Key to the Lock* published, with the addition of four of his poems addressed (under pen names) to the author (AP himself). Volume I of *The Iliad* announced in the press to be published on 6 June.

June

3 (Fri) AP writes from Binfield to Martha Blount, mentioning work on the second volume of *The Iliad*, and promising a special copy of volume I for her father.

4 The *Weekly Journal* comments (anonymously) on the forthcoming rival translations of Homer, blaming Addison's Whig clique at Button's for 'violent Incursions into all the Provinces of Literature, [where] they have laid waste all good Sense as well as Honesty'.

6 First volume (bks I–IV) of AP's *Iliad* translation issued for the subscribers by Lintot in quarto (folio copies on fine paper

would be published later). Lintot may actually have issued some copies on 4 June.

8 Tickell's rival translation, *The First Book of Homer's Iliad*, published by Tonson.

10 Lintot writes to AP with the news that Tickell's rival *Iliad* translation has met with no success while his has been extremely well received. On this day Harley is indicted by the Whig government, who wish revenge for his conduct during the reign of Queen Anne.

11 Support for AP's *Iliad* translation in the *Weekly Journal*: 'as HOMER was accounted most ingenious among the Greek Authors, so Mr. *POPE'S* Translation has the Reputation of coming next to it: And as all Authors agree that HOMER was Blind, so Mr. *Tickel* is said to have imitated him in that Respect' (Sherburn, p. 143). In *Mist's Weekly Journal*, authorship is said to be shared by Tickell and Addison. As of this date, AP has returned from London to Binfield to continue work on the second volume of *The Iliad*.

12 According to Jervas, Gay is currently at work on *Trivia*.

16 Robert Harley, Earl of Oxford, is committed to the Tower, while he awaits trial for high treason.

28 Swift, writing to AP from Dublin, on *The Iliad*: 'if it pleases others as well as me, you have got your end in profit and reputation: Yet I am angry at some bad Rhymes and Triplets. . . .' In a letter to Tickell, Edward Young (the poet) comments that 'the University almost in general gives the Preference to Popes translation' (Sherburn, p. 144).

30 *The Post-Man* announces the publication of Lintot's regular folio edition of the first volume of AP's *Iliad*; the subscribers' editions have appeared on 6 June.

July

1 (Fri) The Riot Act introduced to Parliament in light of continuing Jacobite demonstrations; royal asssent is given on the 20th.

4 AP visiting Trumbull at Easthampstead, just south of Binfield. He is at work on the second volume of *The Iliad* (bks v–viii).

23 AP writes to the Blount sisters with much confidential news of Jacobite political matters. First mention of Lady Mary Wortley Montagu in AP's letters. He has presumably met her shortly before this.

27 In the wake of the Jacobite rebellion, all Catholics are ordered to withdraw from London beyond a ten-mile radius.

31 Jervas has completed his portait of AP, and now supervises its engraving by George Vertue.

August

1 (Mon) AP at Binfield. Nicholas Rowe made Poet Laureate.

7 Writing to George Duckett, Thomas Burnet praises Tickell's translation but calls AP's 'only like a smooth soft Poem, rather of Dryden's than Homer's Composing' (*CH*, p. 120).

14 AP at Binfield, preparing to journey to Bath with Arbuthnot and Jervas. The journey is deferred and soon after AP goes up to Oxford with Arbuthnot.

23 Lintot publishes George Vertue's engraving of Jervas' portrait of AP.

September

6 (Thurs) The Earl of Mar launches the Jacobite rebellion at Braemar in Scotland.

October

8 (Sat) In the *Daily Courant* and other journals, Lintot announces the publication of the second (and last) edition of *The Temple of Fame*, and the fourth edition of *The Rape of the Lock*.

11 AP back at Binfield after several weeks at Bath with Gay and William Fortescue. The second volume of *The Iliad* is now so advanced that he intends delivering it to Lintot in the next several weeks.

November

13 (Sun) Defeat of the Jacobite forces at Preston, Lancashire, and the beginning of the end of the Jacobite rebellion.

December

1 (Thurs) During this month, Lady Mary Wortley Montagu contracts smallpox.

6 AP in London, probably seeing *The Iliad* (vol. II) through the press. He expects to leave for Binfield in a week, to spend Christmas there.

22 As the Jacobite rebellion sputters to a close, James lands at Peterhead in Scotland. He will embark for France on 4 February, in utter defeat.

31   Death of William Wycherley, aged 75. AP attends him twice
     during his last days.

1716

January
 5   (Thurs) AP associated with Jacobite sympathies in a burlesque
     ballad ('The Raree-Show') published in *The Flying-Post*.
10   AP reports (to Caryll) that Gay's *Trivia* is 'just on the brink of
     the press'.
16   Deadline for Roman Catholics to take oaths of obedience to
     the Crown when registering their estates. No evidence
     survives to show whether AP took the oath or refused.
26   Publication of Gay's mock-georgic *Trivia: or, The Art of Walking
     the Streets of London*. Subscriptions for the poem were greatly
     increased through the efforts of AP and the other Scriblerians.

February
 9   (Thurs) For the second volume of *The Iliad*, AP receives £215
     from Lintot.

March
 6   (Tues) Royal assent given to 'An Act for the Speedy and Easy
     Tryal of the Rebels' (i.e. those captured in the Jacobite
     uprising).
20   Publication of Richard Graham's (the second) edition of Du
     Fresnoy's *Art of Painting* as translated by Dryden. AP edited
     the Dedication (to Lord Burlington) and contributed the poem
     'To Mr Jervas, with Fresnoy's Art of Painting'. On the same
     day, AP writes to Caryll from 'Windsor Forest, which I am
     come to take my last look and leave of'. The Popes are
     leaving Binfield out of fear of the laws against the purchase of
     land by Catholics.
22   Lintot publishes volume II of the *Iliad* (bks V–VIII).
24   By this date the Popes' Binfield property is sold; they will
     move to Chiswick.
26   Edmund Curll publishes the unauthorised volume of *Court
     Poems* ('The Toilette' by Gay and two satirical poems by Lady
     Mary Wortley Montagu), imputing authorship to AP.

28 Supposed date of Curll's poisoning by AP in revenge for publishing *Court Poems*.

31 On or just before this date is published AP's *A Full and True Account of a Horrid and Barbarous Revenge by Poison on the Body of Mr Edmund Curll*.

April

1 (Easter Sunday). Writing to Martha Blount from Binfield just prior to this, AP notes that he is at work on 'Eloisa to Abelard'.

7 *The Flying-Post* advertises publication, by Curll, of 'The Second Part of Mr Pope's *Popish* Translation of Homer' together with 'The Catholick Poet'. Edward Wortley Montagu, husband of AP's friend, Lady Mary, appointed Ambassador to the Court of Turkey.

10 Another advertisement by Curll in *The Flying-Post* threatens the publication of 'Homer defended: Being a Detection of the many Errors committed by Mr. *Pope*, in his pretend translation of *Homer*'. The work is never published.

19 The Popes are finally settled at Chiswick at 110 Chiswick Lane, in Mawson's New Buildings, just a few steps from Lord Burlington's Chiswick House.

May

1 (Tues) Curll, unauthorised, publishes AP's satire *To the Ingenious Mr Moore, Author of the Celebrated Worm-Powder*. Given its republications during the next forty years, this is probably AP's most popular poem during his own time.

5 The *Weekly Journal* reprints AP's satire on Moore.

7 In *The Freeholder* no. 40, Addison praises the published parts of AP's translation of Homer, which 'give us reason to think that the *Iliad* will appear in English with . . . little disadvantage to that immortal Poem'.

19 In a collection called *State Poems*, AP accused of Jacobitism (*PA*, pp. 34–5).

29 Publication of Thomas Burnet and George Duckett's *Homerides: Or Homer's First Book Moderniz'd* in a new expanded edition (see 30 May 1715).

31 Publication of John Oldmixon's *The Catholick Poet*, a burlesque ballad attacking AP's politics and his *Iliad* translation: 'Mr *Pope* doth not understand *Greek* thoroughly, for he was never

at any *University'* (*PA*, p. 40). On this same day appears John Dennis' *A True Character of Mr Pope and his Writings*, a pamphlet accusing AP of being a Jacobite and Catholic, of writing libels, and of being 'a Lump Deform'd and Shapeless' (*PA*, pp. 40–5).

June
1 (Fri) Thomas Burnet writes to George Duckett on the relationship between Addison and AP: 'It has very often made me smile at the pitifull soul of the Man, when I have seen Addison caressing Pope, whom at the same Time he hates worse than Belzeebub & by whom he has been more than once lampooned' (*PA*, p. 36).
23 The bill obliging Catholics to register names and estates passing through Parliament; royal assent given on the 26th. The Popes are renting the Chiswick house, having sold the Binfield property.
28 Curll publishes *A Roman Catholick Version of the First Psalm . . . By Mr. POPE* without AP's authorisation.

July
12 (Thurs) Protest in *The Flying-Post* over Pope's *First Psalm* (published 28 June): 'an unparallel'd Piece of Impiety'. After reprinting AP's poem, it prints an 'Eccho to Pope's Drury-Lane Ballad'.
28 In an equivocal advertisement in *The Post-Man*, AP disowns the *First Psalm* as published under his name by Curll.

August
1 (Wed) Lady Mary Wortley Montagu leaves England for Constantinople, where her husband is to be Ambassador to Turkey.
7 Writing to Teresa Blount, AP admits that the *First Psalm* is his, and that in the Advertisement of 28 July 'I have not told a lye . . . but equivocated pretty genteely.' At this time AP is planning a ramble into the north country with Burlington, but defers it until September.
18 AP's first letter to Lady Mary Wortley Montagu after her departure for Constantinople.
30 Swift writes to AP suggesting that Gay might try a set of 'Quaker-pastorals', for 'the Pastoral ridicule is not exhausted'.

His other idea, of 'a Newgate pastoral, among the whores and thieves there', looks forward to *The Beggar's Opera* (first produced 29 Jan 1728).

November

7 (Wed) AP's single-sheet squib, *God's Revenge against Punning*, is issued on this day; it will later appear in *Miscellanies. The Third Volume* in 1732.

10 Writing to Lady Mary, AP notes that he has just visited both York and Bath with Lord Burlington in the space of a fortnight; he is now probably at Chiswick, working ahead on the *Iliad* translation.

29 AP just returned from a ramble to Oxford, where he has spent some time in the company of George Clarke, Fellow of All Souls, who was an early patron of Jervas.

December

1 (Sat) By this date AP has completed and polished the Preface to his *Works*, published in June 1717. At about this time he publishes his second anti-Curll lampoon, *A Further Account of the Most Deplorable Condition of Mr Edmund Curll*.

12 After this date and before 18 January 1717, AP writes his humorous *Court Ballad, to the Tune of 'All you Ladies now at Hand'*.

1717

January

5 (Sat) Lewis Theobald applauds AP's *Iliad* translation in *The Censor*: 'the Spirit of *Homer* breath[e]s all through this Translation' (*CH*, p. 122).

16 First night (of seven performances) of *Three Hours after Marriage*, the Scriblerian farce written by Gay in collaboration with Arbuthnot and AP. Published by Lintot on the 21st. Some early response implicates AP as sole author, until Gay acknowledges the collaboration in the printed text.

17 Audience reception of *Three Hours* very mixed, but on the third night (18th) it is greeted by a 'numerous and polite audience with general applause! as for my own particular part, I was extremely delighted' – anonymous author of *A*

Key to the New Comedy in *A Supplement to the Works of AP* (Dublin, 1758).

18 King George lands at Margate, returning from a visit to Hanover.

21 Lintot issues octavo copies of *Three Hours after Marriage*.

22 A broadside, *The Drury-Lane Monster*, published this day, reveals the identities of the three collaborators in *Three Hours after Marriage*, including AP.

31 AP's *Court Ballad* published anonymously, and probably unauthorised, as a broadside, perhaps with the connivance of Curll as publisher.

February

2 (Sat) Appearance of the pseudonymous pamphlet *A Complete Key to the New Farce, call'd Three Hours after Marriage*, which outlines AP's hand in the play.

12 Writing to AP from Belgrade, Lady Mary Wortley Montagu continues *en route* to Turkey.

18 AP has been suffering a 'very severe Fit of Illness' for the previous fortnight, but continues work on the third volume of the *Iliad* translation (bks IX–XII).

28 Appearance of Dennis' *Remarks upon Mr Pope's Translation of Homer, with Two Letters concerning Windsor Forest and the Temple of Fame*, published by Curll. Another literary and personal harangue by AP's critical enemy.

March

1 (Fri) Appearance of a pseudonymous *Letter to Mr John Gay, Concerning his Late Farce* attacking AP's role in writing *Three Hours after Marriage*.

7 Appearance of Leonard Welsted's *Palaemon to Caelia, at Bath; Or, The Triumvirate*, outlining AP's collaboration in *Three Hours* and other Gay plays. A second edition appears on the 12th.

10 AP arranges by formal contract to pay Teresa Blount an annuity of £40 for six years or until she marries; the annuity is probably meant to supplement her intermittent income from the Mapledurham estate managed by her brother.

20 Lintot advertises the publication 'in a few days' of AP's *Works*, although they do not appear until June. AP still fussing with details of the poems.

26 Volume II of Sir Richard Blackmore's *Essays upon Several Subjects* published. Blackmore attacks AP's 'shameless Immorality' in *Three Hours* and the *First Psalm*.
30 Publication of John Breval's play *The Confederates: A Farce*, charging AP, Gay and Arbuthnot with packing the house for *Three Hours*, and describing AP as a monkey and a toad. All three writers appear as characters.

April
1 (Mon) Lady Mary has reached Adrianople, from which she sends AP some translations of Turkish poetry she has made.
15 Addison appointed Secretary of State.

May
16 (Thurs) Lintot publishes Parnell's *Homer's Battle of the Frogs and Mice*, the work seen through the press by AP.
30 AP at Chiswick, planning to go up to London and afterwards to Caryll's by way of Binfield.

June
1 (Sat) AP in London to oversee publication of *The Iliad* (vol. III) and the *Works*.
3 Both volume III of the *Iliad* translation and AP's first collected *Works* appear on this day. New pieces published in the *Works* include the 'Elegy to the Memory of an Unfortunate Lady', 'Eloisa to Abelard', the 'Discourse on Pastoral Poetry' (prefixed to the *Pastorals*), and his long Preface to the *Works*, amongst others. Both volumes are issued in quarto, folio, and large folio formats. Several friends contribute congratulatory poems to the *Works*: the Duke of Buckingham, Parnell, Wycherley, Fenton and Lady Winchelsea.
7 With the *Works* and *Iliad* (vol. III) both published, AP is already thinking about the fourth volume of *The Iliad* as well as correcting the proofs for Lintot of the miscellany he has edited, *Poems on Several Occasions* (published 13 July). He hopes to spend part of the summer with Caryll at Ladyholt, working on Homer.

July
1 (Mon) Publication of Garth's edition of Ovid's *Metamorphoses*, which assembles parts previously translated by others,

including Dryden and Addison. Gay contributes most of book IX, surrounding AP's 'Fable of Dryope'.

6   AP writes to Parnell seeking continued assistance with the *Iliad* translation.

12 First advertisement (in the *Daily Courant*) of AP's miscellany *Poems on Several Occasions*, published the next day.

13 Lintot issues the miscellany *Poems on Several Occasions*, anonymously edited by AP. Fifteen poems by him appear here for the first time, all of them juvenile works, together with additional poems by him and by many other writers. AP's poems include the 'Ode on Solitude', 'Of a Lady Singing to her Lute' and 'Verses in Imitation of Waller', 'Verses in Imitation of Cowley', 'On the State of Cleopatra', 'Psalm XCI', 'Stanza's from the French of Malherbe' and 'From Boethius'.

17 First performance of Handel's *Water Music*, at a river party in honour of George I.

30 After this date, the Blount sisters reside with their mother in Bolton Street, London, having left Mapledurham in 1716 on the marriage of their elder brother.

August

6   (Tues) For the previous fortnight (after Parliament adjourned on 15 July), AP has been visiting friends' houses, including those of Lord Burlington, the Duke of Shrewsbury, the Duke of Argyll, Lady Rochester, Lord Percival, Mr Stonor, Lord Winchelsea, Kneller, and the Duchess of Hamilton. This has delayed his visit to Caryll.

9   Payment for volume III of *The Iliad*; AP receives £215 from Lintot.

22 AP in London writes to Caryll requesting assistance with an investment and twelve dozen bottles of good French wine.

September

6   (Fri) AP sets off from Chiswick on a ramble towards Oxford. His first stop is Hampton Court, where he dines with two maids of honour.

8   AP arrives at Hallgrove from Staines.

10 AP *en route* to Thomas Dancastle's near Binfield.

12 AP arrives at Thomas Stonor's house at Wattleton Park in Oxfordshire, but leaves immediately when he discovers no one is home. Reaches Oxford late the same night.
13 AP now at Oxford, probably the guest of Dr Abel Evans at St John's College. In a letter to the Blounts, AP encloses a short verse reminiscence of his early days, 'A Hymn Written in Windsor Forest'.
25 AP heading back to Chiswick from Oxford, expecting to arrive the next day.

October
18 (Fri) AP finishes his translation of *The Iliad*, book xv.
23 AP's father dies suddenly of a heart-attack during the night at the Chiswick house: 'I have lost one whom I was even more obliged to as a friend, than as a father' (*Corr.*, I, 448).
26 AP's father buried in the churchyard of the Chiswick parish church.

November
 2 (Sun) Writing to AP from Naples, George Berkeley describes finding the Italian writer, Salvini, reading AP's *Iliad*: 'he liked the Notes extremely, and could find no other fault with the version, but that he thought it approached too near a Paraphrase' (*Corr.*, I, 447).
 8 AP in London, staying at Jervas', attending to his father's estate. The senior Pope's will is proved this day; apart from small bequests to his wife, daughter and son-in-law, the entire estate is left to AP. Atterbury, the Bishop of Rochester, writes to ask AP to consider converting to the Anglican church now that he is the head of his family.
10 AP invited to the Blounts' in Bolton Street, London.

December
 6 (Fri) Colley Cibber's Whiggish adaptation of Molière's *Tartuffe*, titled *The Non-Juror*, has its first night.
31 Evidence of a disagreement with Teresa Blount, resulting in a temporary estrangement.

1718

January

2   (Thurs) The text of Cibber's play *The Non-Juror* is published.
18 Death of Samuel Garth, one of AP's early mentors and models. AP is at Chiswick, 'immersed in books', working on the *Iliad* translation.

February

4   (Tues) AP, in receipt of the French wine requested of Caryll, asks for two or three dozen more of 'the other sort'. He has been working on the subscription list for *The Iliad*; all but ten of the original subscribers have continued.
15 AP's anonymous pamphlet attack *A Clue to the Comedy of the Non-Juror* is mistakenly published by Curll.
18 AP visiting Lord Allen Bathurst in London.

March

Composition of AP's short 'Epistle to James Craggs, Esq; Secretary of State' occurs during his month. The poem is eventually published in AP's *Works*, volume II, in 1735.

3   (Mon) Lintot pays AP £210 for volume IV of the *Iliad*.

April

6   (Palm Sunday) Caryll's son and AP's friend John Caryll, Jr, dies of smallpox.
10 Charles Gildon's *Memoirs of the Life of William Wycherley*, published by Curll on this day, criticises AP for his flattery of Wycherley, his vanity, and for allegedly writing Wycherley's verses in praise of him. AP is described as a 'little Aesopic sort of an animal'.

May

1   (Thurs) During this month AP makes two visits, to Oxford and to Lord Bathurst's seat at Cirencester.
18 Publication of the revised second edition of Edward Bysshe's *Art of English Poetry*, with frequent quotations from AP's works.

June

1 (Sun) AP writes Caryll, noting his intention to spend the summer at Lord Harcourt's house at Stanton Harcourt, near Oxford.

14 Volume IV of the *Iliad* translation appears. About this date, Charles Gildon's handbook *The Complete Art of Poetry* is published, with frequent quotation of AP's poems.

July

5 (Tues) AP arrives in London after a visit again to Lord Bathurst at Cirencester and probably also to Stanton Harcourt. He is settling accounts with Lintot and investigating a site for a house in London, a property belonging to Lord Burlington behind Burlington House. Eventually he decides against building here, and settles on Twickenham. Also on the 5th, Lady Mary Wortley Montagu and her husband leave Constantinople to return to England.

8 Revival of the Scriblerus Club at the Ship Tavern, Charing Cross, with Oxford, Parnell, Gay and Pope. Swift (in Dublin) and Arbuthnot are absent.

31 Death by lightning of the Stanton Harcourt lovers, the event giving rise to AP's three epitaphs for them.

August

6 (Wed) AP at Stanton Harcourt writes to Martha Blount with the story of the two lovers struck by lightning, and includes his epitaph for them (*TE*, VI, 197–8).

16 AP and his mother still visiting at Stanton Harcourt, planning to stay another month or six weeks.

September

1 (Mon) Writing to Lady Mary Wortley Montagu, AP relates the story of the Stanton Harcourt lovers, including his second epitaph on them (*TE*, VI, 199–200) with the first. AP is at work on the fifth volume of *The Iliad* (bks XVII–XX).

8 AP still at Stanton Harcourt.

12 In a letter to AP, Atterbury praises the 'Epitaph on John Hewet and Sarah Drew' and suggests revisions.

20 First public appearance of AP's second epitaph for the Stanton Harcourt lovers, in the *White-hall Evening-Post*.

October

2 (Thurs) Lady Mary Wortley Montagu arrives in London, at the end of her journey from Constantinople.

8 AP now at Lord Bathurst's 'Oakley-Bower', just west of Cirencester.

11 The *Weekly Packet* prints AP's second epitaph for the Stanton Harcourt lovers. AP complains to Burlington of being 'miserably chained down to finishing Homer'. He hopes to have finished volume v in a week's time.

18 AP back in Chiswick, having returned with his mother from Stanton Harcourt via Oxford.

24 Parnell buried at Chester, having taken fatally ill as he is returning to Ireland.

25 AP has spent the past week visiting the neighbouring villages before winter sets in.

December

4 (Thurs) Giles Jacob's *Poetical Register: Or, The Lives and Characters of the English Dramatic Poets*, published by Curll on this day, includes a sketch of AP's life and writings which may have been written and/or revised by AP himself.

6 Death of the Poet Laureate, Nicholas Rowe, at age 44. His successor will be Laurence Eusden.

12 Writing to Jervas, AP notes that he is this day writing an epitaph for Nicholas Rowe's tomb in Westminster Abbey.

1719

During this year, AP is much preoccupied with completing the *Iliad* translation and with the acquisition and refurbishing of his new house at Twickenham to which he moves in March. He has little time either for letters or for original poems. Also during this year Mme Anne Dacier publishes her 'Réflexions sur la première partie de la Préface de M. Pope' in *L'Iliade d'Homère*. AP had used her prose translation for his effort; here she reacts with hostility to his prefatory remarks, disputing that the poem is a 'wild Paradise' (*CH*, p. 131).

February

2 (Mon) AP's letter to Burlington indicates his final decision not to build a house in town.

March

17 (Mon) Matthew Prior's *Poems on Several Occasions* are published this day (but dated 1718). The poem 'Alma', first printed here, contains brief praise of 'Eloisa to Abelard'.

22 News arrives from AP's sister, Mrs Rackett, that her young daughter has died of a violent fever.

May

2 (Fri) On this day or just before, Lintot issues the sixth edition of the *Essay on Criticism*.

19 AP advertises in the *Evening Post* that he will publish the final volume of *The Iliad* at beginning of the next winter. Both volumes v and vi are finally published in May 1720.

June

1 (Mon) During the next three months, Gay rambles unaccompanied through Belgium and France.

10 Government forces defeat a Jacobite expeditionary brigade of Spaniards and Scots in the Scottish highlands: this is the last military threat to the Hanoverian succession until 1745.

16 Godfrey Kneller writes to AP with news of a house he is renting and furnishing near Twickenham, for the Wortley Montagus.

17 Death of Addison.

July

26 (Sun) Dr Abel Evans writes to AP, thanking him for his hospitality at Twickenham; he is the earliest known recipient of that at AP's new house.

27 Book xxi of *The Iliad* just about completed in transcription for the press by Thomas Dancastle at Binfield, who has been assisting AP in providing fair copy.

August

1 (Sat) AP invites his sister to visit him at Twickenham, promising to send a 'chariot' to fetch her.

September

13 (Sun) From Twickenham, AP writes to Lord Bathurst about the Royal Gardens at Richmond, now being renovated by the Prince of Wales.

October

10   (Sat) William Melmoth writes to a friend on the Homer
     translation: 'Mr. Pope seems in most places to have been
     inspired with the same sublime spirit that animates his
     original' (*CH*, p. 135).
13   The second edition of 'Eloisa to Abelard' is published by Lintot
     in a volume with 'Verses to the Memory of an Unfortunate
     Lady' and poems by several others.
15   Lintot issues AP's *Ode for Musick on St Cecilia's Day* in its third
     edition.
18   Lintot pays AP £210 for volume v of *The Iliad*.
29   Lord Mayor's Day. Ostensible date of action in *The Dunciad*.

November

 9   (Mon) AP writes to Thomas Dancastle about his recent
     acquisition of two acres of land across the highway from the
     new Twickenham house (the grotto will connect the
     properties). 'As to my poetical affairs, they lie neglected
     enough of conscience, yet not so totally forgot, but that I
     hope to finish the whole [*Iliad*] by Christmass.'

December

31   (Thurs) AP writes to William Broome to notify him of the safe
     arrival of the Eustathius gloss for *The Iliad* and to invite him to
     Twickenham in January, before AP gets in the rush of reading
     proofs. AP praises his new situation: 'The place I am in is as
     delightful as you can imagine any to be, in this season; the
     situation so very airy, and yet so warm, that you will think
     yourself in a sort of heaven . . . .'

1720

This year sees the inflation and deflation of the South Sea Bubble,
the stock-market crisis in which AP and many others lose large sums
of money. James Craggs, Secretary of State and AP's Twickenham
friend and neighbour, is implicated in allegations of corruption in
the Bubble. AP continues to refurbish the gardens and interior of his
Twickenham villa, spending most of the year there.

January
1 (Fri) Stocks in the South Sea Company quoted at £100, as the price begins to rise.
5 Intending to go up to London, AP is delayed at Twickenham until the 10th, when he will go to Jervas'.
22 Back at Twickenham, AP is in bad health, which prevents him from working on the Homer translation and from providing a Prologue to John Hughes's play *The Siege of Damascus*.

February
During this month, AP reviews a draft of Matthew Prior's poem 'Conversation', but suggests no amendments or revisions. He is also continuing to invest in South Sea Company stock.
17 (Wed) First night of John Hughes's *Siege of Damascus*.
18 AP still at Twickenham, unwell, and unable to attend the première of *The Siege of Damascus*. Hughes dies of consumption about this time.
26 Lintot pays AP £210 for the sixth and final volume of *The Iliad*. AP sends condolences to Jabez Hughes on the death of his brother.

March
1 (Tues) South Sea stock quoted at £175–8.
2 AP continues to speculate in South Sea stock. He intends to go up to London in the next few days. He thanks Aaron Hill for sending him a long poem (*The Creation*) and an apology for attacking AP in a previous work.
3 AP projects a further fortnight's work with Homer, and is now directing the masons on the construction of a portico and the grotto for his villa.
12 AP in London, where he purchases on credit £500-worth of South Sea stock at £180 a share.
16 AP finds a suitable house for the Wortley Montagus to lease in Twickenham.
24 AP writes from Twickenham to Broome with profuse thanks for help with the index (and all) of the *Iliad* translation. Mrs Lepell (who will marry the future Lord Hervey in April), recuperating from a severe illness, is staying with the Popes.

April
1 (Fri) South Sea stock now risen to £304–10.
12 On or just before this date appears AP's third lampoon against Curll, *A Strange but True Relation how Edmund Curll . . . was Converted from the Christian Religion . . . by Jews.*

May
1 (Sun) AP notes that *The Iliad* has received only two of the intended four indexes and that he has left unfinished two essays on the theology and morality and on the oratory of Homer. South Sea stock now up to £335 per share.
5 AP informs Elijah Fenton that he has arranged for him to be tutor to James Craggs, Secretary of State, who will move into a house at Twickenham in three weeks; Fenton will stay with AP until then.
12 The end of AP's *Iliad* labours is marked this day by Lintot's publication of volumes v and vi of the translation.
20 Gay's first major collection, *Poems on Several Occasions*, published by Jacob Tonson, earning the poet £1000.
24 On or shortly after this date, Swift publishes (anonymously) his pamphlet containing *A Proposal for the Universal Use of Irish Manufacture*, the earliest of his satirical works on political economy.

June
During this month, Sheffield, Duke of Buckingham, takes AP to Tunbridge Wells to take the waters.

July
13 (Wed) Curll publishes Giles Jacob's *Historical Account of the Lives and Writings of our Most Considerable English Poets*, which includes a full-page portrait and seven-page biography of AP. The assumption made by Curll and others is that AP wrote the complimentary account of himself.

August
During this month, AP consults with Atterbury (as Dean of Westminster) over a suitable monument for Dryden. AP writes (now?) a couplet epitaph for it which is not used. He also borrows a copy of Chapman's Homer, indicating that he is already

considering translating *The Odyssey*. Also during August, the stock market begins to slide. Share prices in the South Sea Company drop from about £1000 this month to £130 later in the year. Gay, like many others, loses hundreds of pounds; AP's losses are much smaller.

22 (Mon) AP, at Twickenham, still speculating in South Sea stock, and advising Lady Mary on it, even though the price has begun to slide.

September
 2 (Fri) The slide continues: South Sea stock quoted at £780 a share.
19 Writing to Caryll, AP alternately is absorbed by his house renovations and worried by the slump in South Sea stocks.
23 AP now fully aware of the Bubble disaster, and writes philosophically of his losses to Atterbury.
27 South Sea stock now at £340 a share.
28 Atterbury sends AP a Latin inscription for Dryden's monument; it is not used.

October
15 (Sat) South Sea stock slides even lower: now at £190 a share.
26 Lintot publishes a fourth edition of *Windsor-Forest*.

December
 1 (Thurs) During this month South Sea stock hits bottom, at £130 a share. Despite the pricking of the Bubble, AP seems to have emerged from this stock speculation with no great losses.
11 AP reports bad flooding of the Thames in front of and even around his house, which is 'exactly like Noah's Ark in every thing, except that there's no propagation of the Species in it'.

1721

Except for a September visit to Oxfordshire and Gloucestershire, AP spends most of this year at Twickenham, where he is enlarging his villa. His literary work is largely editorial: the Shakespeare edition, Parnell's posthumous *Poems* and Buckingham's *Works*.

February

16 (Thurs) James Craggs, Secretary of State, dies of smallpox, in the midst of the South Sea scandal.

24 Death of John Sheffield, Duke of Buckingham.

March

15 (Wed) Following charges against him in the wake of the South Sea Bubble, the Earl of Sunderland is acquitted of corruption. Shortly after this he is released as first Lord of the Treasury and is replaced by Sir Robert Walpole, who also becomes Chancellor of the Exchequer.

16 Death (in circumstances suggesting suicide) of the Postmaster-General, father of James Craggs, in the wake of the South Sea scandal.

26 Atterbury receives from AP an early version of the 'Epitaph on Simon Harcourt'; AP's friend had died in France, 1 July 1720.

April

15 (Sat) In a letter to his friend Charles Ford, Swift makes his earliest reference to *Gulliver's Travels*, 'which will be a large volume, and gives account of countries hitherto unknown'.

May

1 (Mon) During this month Richard Morley's anti-Catholic pamphlet-fiction, *The Life of the Celebrated Mrs Elizabeth Wisebourn*, is published. In it AP is abused as the alleged lover of the Duchess of Buckingham; further, the 'Unfortunate Lady' of his elegy on the same is said to have committed suicide for love of him.

21 AP signs a contract with Jacob Tonson, Jr (nephew of the older Jacob Tonson), to edit Shakespeare's *Works* for a fee of £100.

August

During this month, while AP remains at Twickenham, Gay visits Bath with Lord Burlington.

September

3 (Sun) AP now visiting Oxford, where he is staying with George Clarke at All Souls. He writes to Jacob Tonson, Jr, about

leaving the business side of the *Works* of Buckingham to Alderman John Barber, and about the division of scenes for the Shakespeare edition.

6 AP on his way to visit Lord Bathurst at Cirencester.
15 AP's last extant letter to Lady Mary Wortley Montagu, about his failure to obtain the loan of a harpsichord for her.
25 First draft of AP's 'Epistle to Robert, Earl of Oxford' completed by this date. Tonson's memorial edition of Addison's *Works* (4 vols) begins to appear. AP's Prologue to *Cato* is reprinted here.
26 AP writes to Joseph Bowles, Bodley's Librarian at Oxford, about the final two volumes of *The Iliad* which he has sent to the Library.

October
3 (Tues) AP visiting Edward Blount at Rentcomb, Gloucestershire, just north of Cirencester.
21 AP back in residence at Twickenham. He writes to Robert Harley, Earl of Oxford, with a printed copy of his 'Epistle to Robert, Earl of Oxford', asking permission to include this as preface to his edition of Parnell's *Poems*. In the *Evening Post* AP advertises for help in obtaining 'old Editions of single Plays' in connection with the Shakespeare edition.

November
6 (Mon) Lord Oxford writes to AP with permission to print his Epistle: 'I am contented to let the World see, how well Mr. Pope can write upon a barren Subject.'

December
7 (Thurs) The *White-hall Evening-Post* advertises Lintot's publication of Parnell's posthumous *Poems on Several Occasions*, as edited by AP.
12 With Parnell's *Poems* published, AP writes to Oxford in gratitude for his permission to print the Epistle.

1722

In this year, AP is engrossed with editing the works of Buckingham and Shakespeare and with translating *The Odyssey* (with the help of Fenton and Broome). Most of his time is spent at Twickenham.

January

1 (Mon) Atterbury writes to AP with the first of several letters on literary subjects, enclosing a translation of Horace by his son.

27 AP back at Twickenham after a brief visit to London, where with Jervas he consulted the Italian sculptor who created Buckingham's monument.

February

6 (Tues) AP writes to Edward, Lord Harley, with word that the Duchess of Buckingham has asked AP to send him Buckingham's tragedies in advance of publication of the *Works*.

10 Lord Harley responds to AP with a promise not to reveal the tragedies to anyone. AP writes to Broome with more editorial requests for the Shakespeare edition and the *Odyssey* translation.

26 Atterbury requests a complete copy of AP's verses on Addison (the 'Atticus' portrait).

March

14 (Wed) AP just returned from London, where he has visited Jonathan Richardson but missed Atterbury. AP stays two nights at Atterbury's deanery.

April

2 (Mon) AP, in London, writes to Caryll to say that a visit to Ladyholt or any long absence from Twickenham is impossible because of his mother's feebleness.

6 Atterbury writes to AP on the imminent death of his wife, postulating a visit after the event to Twickenham.

7 AP now back at home at Twickenham.

26 Death of Atterbury's wife.

May

5 (Sat) AP advertises in the *Evening Post* to borrow old editions of Shakespeare's *Tempest, Macbeth, Julius Caesar, Timon of Athens, King John* and *Henry VIII.*

16 At some point after or just before this date, AP has Atterbury and two servants as house-guests for a week. Following this he will go up to London to supervise a group of friends to help collate the several editions of Shakespeare's plays.

23 Having finished translating *Odyssey* book I, Fenton is about to begin work on book IV.

25 Atterbury now back at Bromley after visiting AP at Twickenham.

June

15 (Fri) Atterbury writes to AP with unasked-for literary advice, such as for AP to polish Milton's *Samson Agonistes.*

16 Death of the Duke of Marlborough, Commander-in-Chief of the Army.

July

9 (Mon) AP continues at Twickenham, complaining of general illness for the past month, which has inhibited work on *The Odyssey.*

12 The patent for William Wood's copper coinage for Ireland is signed, as authorised by Walpole. The scheme will bring forth Swift's *Drapier's Letters* in 1724.

27 AP writes ironically to Atterbury that he will attend the Duke of Marlborough's funeral in London: 'I intend to lye at the Deanery, and moralize one evening with you on the vanity of human Glory.'

August

1 (Wed) During this month, Gay goes down to Bath alone, probably on the strength of profits from his panegyric to the late Duke of Marlborough, *An Epistle to Henrietta, Duchess of Marlborough*, published 11 July.

9 Funeral of the Duke of Marlborough, conducted at Westminster Abbey by Atterbury. AP probably attends, although he continues unwell during this summer.

24 Atterbury arrested on suspicion of treason in support of the Jacobite opposition to the Crown and imprisoned in the Tower.

September

11   (Tues) In London, AP writes to Gay (at Bath) showing great concern at Atterbury's imprisonment.

22   AP attempts to use his contracts to get a performance of the Duke of Buckingham's *Julius Caesar* tragedies at the Theatre in Drury Lane.

30   AP at Twickenham, continuing unwell: to Gay, he writes, 'I have never been in a worse state in my life.'

October

18   (Thurs) AP writes to Judith Cowper complaining of his 'Ugly Body' and constant infirmities.

November

5   (Mon) By this date, the Shakespeare edition is about one quarter printed; AP conjectures the finished set to be ready a year hence.

24   AP visits Atterbury in the Tower. He is still revising the 'Epitaph on Simon Harcourt'.

December

15   (Sat) First known public appearance of the 'Atticus' lines, AP's portrait of Addison (later to appear in the *Epistle to Dr Arbuthnot*), in a pseudonymous letter to the *St James's Journal*.

22   Gay, with AP looking over his shoulder, writes to Swift in Dublin to reopen a correspondence which has been silent for several years.

1723

During this year AP continues his work on the Shakespeare edition and the *Odyssey* translation. Unlike in recent years, he makes frequent visits to London, where he now customarily stays with Lord Peterborough.

January

5   (Sat) In the *London Journal*, a prose pamphlet, *Annus Mirabilis* (published Dec 1722), is ascribed to AP; it is 'a Performance full of Wit'.

10   At a private performance (at Buckingham House) of the Duke's musical version of *Julius Caesar*, AP's 'Two Chorus's to the Tragedy of Brutus' heard for the first time.

22   Curll advertises (in the *Daily Journal*) the imminent publication of *The Works of John Sheffield, Duke of Buckingham*.

23   In a committee of the House of Lords, Curll reveals that his edition of Buckingham's *Works* is unauthorised.

24   On this date *The Works of John Sheffield, Earl of Mulgrave, Marquis of Normanby, and Duke of Buckingham* is published. AP selected the works and prepared them for publication, receiving profits of over £200. By the King's authority, certain offensive political passages were cancelled in volume II.

27   Officials from the Secretary of State's Office (at the instigation of AP's Whig enemies) seize the copies of Buckingham's *Works*, which contains passages of Jacobite sympathy. AP has just arrived in London, and is anxious to see Viscount Harcourt.

31   The House of Lords forbids publication 'without consent' by Curll of Buckingham's *Works* and of 'any Lord of this House'.

February

 3   (Sun) Gay writes to Swift in Dublin mentioning AP's engagement to translate *The Odyssey*, 'I believe rather out of a prospect of Gain than inclination. . . . He lives mostly at Twickenham, and amuses himself in his house and Garden.'

12   By this date, AP has read the revised second edition of Anne Dacier's 1719 French translation of *The Iliad*, where AP's Preface to *The Iliad* is attacked.

13   In the wake of the Buckingham suppression, AP accepts Lord Harcourt's advice to suspend solicitation for *Odyssey* subscriptions. A satirical letter, as if by AP, in *Pasquin* (a newspaper) aligns AP with Buckingham's Jacobitism.

16   AP writes to Lord Carteret, Secretary of State, to deny that he had suppressed Buckingham's Jacobite writings in order to obtain a licence for the *Works*.

19   Publication of the *Memoirs of the Life of Scriblerus*, as if by Swift, under the imprint of A. Moore. The book is likely a forgery, and not by any member of the Club, although it is similar in aim to the real *Memoirs* later published by AP.

20   AP staying put at Twickenham because of his mother's ill health and the Buckingham controversy. A second satirical letter, as if by AP, in *Pasquin*, has AP confess to withholding

Buckingham's Jacobite pieces in order to have his *Works* licensed.

22 First night (of seventeen) of Fenton's play *Mariamne*, with Prologue by Broome. AP had been asked for a prologue but declined.

March
1 (Fri) During the spring, Gay gains a sinecure (worth £150 per year) as commissioner of the State Lotteries and moves into lodgings in the Gatehouse in Whitehall.

9 The *London Journal* reports that AP is re-editing Buckingham's *Works* in order to remove the prohibition on their publication.

April
6 (Sat) Curll issues *Cythereia: Or, New Poems upon Love and Intrigue*, which includes AP's 'Atticus' portrait of Addison (first published in 1722).

10 Atterbury writes secretly from the Tower to thank AP and Arbuthnot for their services.

May
During this month Parliament passes the Black Act, which creates many new capital offences, including poaching in the royal forests.

6 (Mon) Beginning of the trial of Bishop Atterbury, on charges of treason, before the House of Lords.

8 AP is called to testify at Atterbury's trial. In spite of his nervousness in advance, the questions concern matters of fact and make no reference to his religion or his edition of Buckingham's *Works*. During the trial AP lodges with Lord Peterborough.

11 Final day of defence in Atterbury's trial. At last he speaks in his own defence.

13 At the climax of the trial, Walpole takes the stand to refute Atterbury's self-defence.

14 Still awaiting a vote on Atterbury, AP dines with William Fortescue, his lawyer friend.

16 The House finally votes against Atterbury, sealing his fate. He is ordered into perpetual exile, never to return to England.

17 A bill for added taxes on Catholics passes in the Commons;

final passage is given in the Lords on the 22nd. AP now back at Twickenham.

20 AP's brother-in-law, Charles Rackett, arrested with his son and two servants for deer-stealing in Windsor Forest. He is scheduled to appear in court on the 25th. His son Michael apparently flees the country.

23 Having been pardoned in May, Bolingbroke arrives back in England from his French exile.

June

2 (Sun) Death of Swift's 'Vanessa', Esther Vanhomrigh.

15 At Twickenham, AP writes a short birthday poem for Martha Blount ('Oh be thou blest with all that Heav'n can send!').

17 AP has a final interview with Atterbury, who gives him an inscribed Bible.

19 Date of Atterbury's departure into exile in France.

25 After this date, open correspondence with Atterbury is officially forbidden.

July

12 (Fri) AP unwell for the past two weeks. His earliest extant letter to Hugh Bethel is written this day.

August

14 (Wed) AP has just finished entertaining his friend Robert Digby for several days at Twickenham.

21 AP comes to London so that Kneller can finish the portrait of him.

22 Kneller's third portrait of AP, painted for Lord Harcourt, is finished. AP writes to Harcourt with thanks for the honour, and is back at Twickenham.

September

20 (Fri) Swift writes to AP at Jervas' house, relating his four-month absence from Dublin and his daily activities.

26 AP writes to Judith Cowper to commend descriptive poems which mix vision and morality, as in three or four poems by Chaucer.

29 Just before this date AP has gone up to see Lord Harley in London about the posthumous edition of Prior's poems. Ill, he returns to Twickenham, where his 'Head & eyes are yet

extremely disordered by the straining & Vomiting for 9 or 10 hours yesterday.'

October

3 (Thurs) Fenton is about to go into the employ of Lady Trumbull, a position arranged by AP.

19 Probable date of Sir Godfrey Kneller's death. Atterbury's son-in-law, returned to London after seeing the Bishop in exile, seeks an immediate meeting with AP.

21 Lord Bathurst writes to request that AP visit him at Riskings (his house at Cirencester) early in November (4th or 5th).

November

4 (Mon) The appointment of Jervas as Portrait Painter to His Majesty, following the death of Kneller, is announced in the press.

December

24 (Tues) AP has received the sixth book of *The Odyssey* as translated by Broome.

1724

During this year, AP continues to work towards completing both the Shakespeare edition and the *Odyssey* translation, and stays mostly at home at Twickenham, confined by work and the ill health of both himself and his mother.

January

15 (Wed) First night (of seven) of Gay's tragedy *The Captives* at Drury Lane, earning him more than £1000 in author's benefits (two nights) and gifts.

19 Swift, in Dublin, has finished writing book IV of the *Travels* (the voyage to the Houyhnhnms) and is now working on the flying-island section of book III.

23 Publication of Gay's tragedy *The Captives*, with an Epilogue probably written partly and revised by AP.

30 AP has been in London and visits Fenton, who is at Lady Trumbull's in Leicester Fields.

February
Early in this month, AP asks Fortescue to draw up a contract with Lintot for printing *The Odyssey*.

18 (Tues) In a long letter, Bolingbroke advises AP on his future career: 'you must not look on your Translations of Homer as the great Work of your Life. You owe a great deal more to your self, to your Country, to the present Age, and to Posterity . . . after translating what was writ three Thousand Years ago, it is incombent upon you that you write . . . what will deserve to be translated three Thousand years hence.' On the same date an indenture signed by AP and Lintot allows for £315 copy money for AP and 750 copies of *The Odyssey* translation for his own 'use and benefit'.

25 By this date, printing of *The Odyssey* has begun in Lintot's establishment.

29 AP's edition of Buckingham's *Works* is finally republished, a year after the initial prohibition.

March
During this month, Swift anonymously issues the *Letter to Shopkeepers, Farmers, and Common-People*, the first of the *Drapier's Letters*, on the subject of Wood's copper coinage.

1 (Sun) About this date, AP is expected in London, during which time he is invited to dine with Craggs's sister.

23 A few days before this, AP has been ill with a severe fever.

April
3 (Fri) By this date, the first thirteen books of *The Odyssey* are completely translated into verse, and the notes are done for only the first two books.

9 AP replies to Bolingbroke's letter of 18 March to say that he is unfit to renovate English poetry, as Bolingbroke has suggested. AP has just finished reading Voltaire's poem *La Ligue*.

23 The gathering of *Odyssey* subscriptions goes on; AP's friend Mrs Caesar has by this date secured seventeen for him.

24 AP complains to Broome that Fenton's notes for *Odyssey* book IV are not forthcoming, and the printing must stop. Book V goes to press in about a week.

May

2 (Sat) AP in London for a brief visit on *Odyssey* business, staying at Lord Digby's in St James's Street.

21 Death of Robert Harley, Earl of Oxford, former Lord Treasurer and member of the Scriblerus Club.

22 AP arrives in London, learns of Lord Harley's death and writes immediately to his son Edward, who will now be the second Earl of Oxford.

31 Fenton, now at Easthampstead with Lady Trumbull, has finally finished book IV of *The Odyssey*, which he sends to AP this morning.

June

15 (Mon) AP has set off on a ramble towards Lord Digby's at Sherborne, Dorset; Martha Blount is staying with Mrs Pope at Twickenham.

27 AP safely back at home in Twickenham.

July

9 (Thurs) AP engaged by his friend Mrs Newsham to obtain an appropriate monument for her brother, James Craggs, to be placed in Westminster Abbey.

19 By this date Fenton has finished translating the nineteenth book of *The Odyssey* and has almost completed the index for AP's Shakespeare edition.

August

6 (Thurs) Publication of Swift's second pamphlet in the *Drapier's Letters* series, *A Letter to Mr Harding the Printer*.

16 AP suffering ill health, which makes writing almost impossible. He has just been working on book XIV of the *Odyssey* translation.

September

1 (Tues) Dr Arbuthnot and Gay heading off to Bath for a fortnight; AP still at Twickenham.

5 Swift's third *Drapier's Letter* published, the *Letter to the Nobility and Gentry*.

7 AP in London, partly in connection with Craggs's monument.

12 After the brief visit to London, AP is back home. His health is

improved enough for him to lay out a design for Mrs Howard's ornamental garden at Marble Hill. He finds the translation of *Odyssey* book xiv especially heavy-going.

17 The printing of *The Odyssey* has now reached book viii. AP is planning a fortnight's ramble to see Lord Oxford and Lord Cobham in the country.

29 His mother having taken ill, AP must postpone his visit to Lord Oxford at Wimpole.

October

8 (Sun) With his mother still too ill to be left, AP cancels his visit to Lord Oxford's. He has at last finished book xiv of *The Odyssey*, which completes the third volume of the translation.

17 First publication, simultaneously in the *London Journal*, the *St James's Evening Post*, and the *White-hall Evening-Post*, of AP's 'Epitaph on Simon Harcourt'.

21 Swift's fourth *Drapier's Letter* appears, *A Letter to the Whole People of Ireland*. A reward is offered by the Irish Privy Council for discovering the author of the seditious pamphlet.

26 Between the 22nd and this date, AP speaks to Lord Harcourt to recommend Lord Percival's chaplain as next preacher to the Charterhouse.

31 AP about to correct Broome's translation of *Odyssey* book xi. The Shakespeare edition is finally complete, as AP has just written the Preface.

November

During this month AP writes to press Broome into sending the notes for *Odyssey* book xi, the verse of which is half printed, and to hurry with verse and notes for book xii, next to be printed. His mother continues gravely ill.

14 (Sat) First publication of AP's birthday poem to Martha Blount ('Oh be thou blest with all that Heav'n can send!'), in the *British Journal* and the *White-hall Evening-Post*.

18 Subscriptions for AP's Shakespeare edition first solicited, in the *Daily Post*.

20 Death of John Kyrle, AP's 'Man of Ross', aged 87 years (see *Epistle to Bathurst*, ll. 250ff.).

28 Gay's ballad 'Newgate's Garland' sung in John Thurmond's pantomime *Harlequin Sheppard*. The political satire foreruns that of *The Beggar's Opera*.

December

4   (Fri) AP finally receives Broome's notes on *Odyssey* book xi,
    but without the verse for book xii. AP claims he will reveal
    the collaboration of Broome and Fenton when the *Odyssey*
    proposals are published.

12 AP writes to Lord Oxford requesting that he subscribe for
    five sets of *The Odyssey*.

17 Lord Oxford subscribes for ten sets of *The Odyssey*, his wife
    for five, and their daughter for one set.

22 AP's mother now recovered. AP writes to Lord Oxford with
    thanks for his generous subscription, and comments on the
    work: 'I have made this Translation more exact than that of
    The Iliad. And indeed I was sensible it would be a much more
    difficult task to make the Odyssey appear in any Splendor.'

23 Jacob Tonson, Jr, sends AP proofs of the Shakespeare Preface
    and of George Vertue's engraving of the Shakespeare
    monument in Stratford Church.

1725

January

At some point, likely during the middle of the month, AP spends
a few days in London attending to business in connection with
the Shakespeare edition and *Odyssey* printing, both about to be
announced in the daily press. While there, he stays with Lord
Peterborough.

7   (Thurs) Bernard Lintot himself has just finished transcribing a
    fair copy of *Odyssey* book xiv, for AP's revisions before
    printing.

10 In the separately printed proposals for publishing a translation
    of *The Odyssey* AP finally acknowledges (vaguely) the
    assistance of Broome and Fenton (see *Dunciad*, 1729, pp. 10–
    11).

18 In the *Daily Courant*, Jacob Tonson's advertisement of
    'Proposals for Mr. Pope's Edition of Shakespeare' is published,
    seeking subscribers for Tonson's own benefit.

20 From Twickenham, AP sends instructions that an
    advertisement of his 'Proposals for a Translation of Homer's
    Odyssey' be published in the *Gazette* and *Daily Courant*.

21 AP's translation of *The Odyssey* first announced in the *White-hall Evening-Post*. Neither here nor in the published proposals does AP credit his collaborators, Broome and Fenton.

25 AP's proposals for the *Odyssey* translation published in the *Gazette* and the *Daily Courant*. The same advertisement appears in the issues for the 27th, 28th and 29th, and in other journals.

26 Lintot advertises in the *Evening Post* that he is selling (for his *own* benefit) cheaper editions of AP's *Odyssey*. These are the 'trade' editions. The announcement annoys AP greatly.

February

13 (Sat) AP in London again on publishing-business, chiefly that of completing *The Odyssey* (with text and notes up to the end of book XIV) for the press. He warns Broome against Lintot: 'you cannot imagine what a scoundrel [he] is in all respects'.

20 AP receives 210 guineas from Mrs Caesar for the seventy subscriptions she has secured for *The Odyssey*.

March

 5 (Fri) AP still in a great hurry of business as the Shakespeare edition is just about to appear. He is also still revising Broome's notes on *Odyssey* books XIII and XIV.

12 Tonson publishes AP's edition of *The Works of Shakespear*, in six quarto volumes. According to Samuel Johnson, AP received £217 12s (but see 21 May 1721). 750 copies were printed, and 140 still left unsold in 1767. In total 411 subscribers bought 417 of the copies at a guinea a volume.

18 Worn out by publishing-business, AP has been ill but is now recovered. He seeks Fortescue's advice on Lintot's two-faced dealings with the *Odyssey* edition.

20 A lengthy critical article on AP's Shakespeare appears in *The Weekly Journal, or Saturday's Post*. The edition is attacked for its price (5 guineas) and for encroaching on the rights of the playwright. A similar article appears on the 27th in the same journal.

22 By this date Bolingbroke has settled into his new residence at Dawley Farm, just south-east of Uxbridge.

30 AP attending to company at Twickenham, but still fussing over delivery of subscribers' sets of *The Odyssey*, **due** imminently.

April

8   (Thurs) AP promises to send Broome his sets for the eight subscribers he has secured. After this date he also sends a copy to Mrs Caesar, whose name is printed in capitals and prefixed by a star in the subscribers' list.

13 The *Gazette* advises that subscribers may pick up their copies of *The Odyssey* at Jervas' house in advance of regular publication (on the 23rd).

23 The first three volumes of AP's translation of *The Odyssey of Homer*, published by Lintot, are finally made available. In total 610 subscribers purchased 1057 sets. Edward Harley, Earl of Oxford, took sixteen of these. AP received free from Lintot all the subscribers' copies together with £600 for the copyright, and grossed at least £4500 from the edition.

29 In the Treasury's Civil List AP is granted £200 for his work in translating *The Odyssey* into English verse.

May

1   (Sat) Thomas Cooke's *Battle of the Poets. An Heroick Poem*, published during this month, has AP as a poetical general who loses in the wars to Ambrose Philips.

3   *The Plain Dealer* no. 116 complains that the seventh volume (edited by George Sewell) of AP's Shakespeare must be purchased separately.

25 Broome has just returned from staying with AP at Twickenham; AP again encourages him to send in his poems so that they can be published in a proposed fifth edition of Lintot and AP's *Miscellaneous Poems and Translations*.

June

Towards the end of the month, AP is involved in controversy over the placing of a monument to Sir Godfrey Kneller in the parish church at Twickenham (*Corr.*, II, 300–1), which will mean demolition of AP's father's monument.

2   (Wed) In a letter to Edward Blount, AP makes his first reference to his grotto at Twickenham, describing it at length about five years since beginning work on it, and enclosing the two-couplet 'Inscription' ('Nymph of the Grot, these sacred Springs I keep').

10 On his way back from the Duchess of Buckingham's at Leighs in Essex, AP calls at Jonathan Richardson's in London. He is out, but AP writes to invite him to stay at Twickenham.

29 By this date AP has well begun the second half of the *Odyssey* translation, having completed the verse of books xv and xvii. (Broome will be working on book xvi.) He regrets the increased pace: 'my cares are grown upon me, and I want relaxation. . . . Hurry, noise and observances of the world, take away the power of just thinking or natural acting' (*Corr.*, II, 302).

July

3 (Sat) In a long letter to Lord Harcourt, AP details the current controversy over the proposed monument to Sir Godfrey Kneller in the Twickenham parish church.

6 AP writes similarly to the Earl of Strafford on the Kneller monument, this time enclosing a mock epitaph on Lady Kneller ('One day I mean to fill Sir Godfrey's tomb').

17 A letter to the *London Journal*, signed 'Homerides', attacks AP's concealment of assistance on the *Odyssey* translation, and his avarice in taking subscriptions for his own benefit.

30 Having been in town briefly, AP is now back home, and invites Lord and Lady Oxford to visit him before they go to Down Hall, in Essex.

31 Writing in *Applebee's Original Weekly Journal*, Daniel Defoe defends AP's *Odyssey* translation as a collaborative enterprise appearing only under AP's name.

August

4 (Wed) Late in the day, AP visits the Harleian Library in Lord Oxford's Dover Street house in London, where he converses with the Librarian, Humphrey Wanley.

12 AP again writes to the Earl of Strafford on the legal aspects of the Kneller monument controversy: 'the Suit continues gloriously'. He is now back home after several days' ramble in Buckinghamshire and Oxfordshire.

14 In a letter to Charles Ford, Swift announces that he has finished composing the *Travels*, and is now transcribing them: 'they are admirable things, and will wonderfully mend the world'.

September

2   (Thurs) Dr Arbuthnot very ill with 'distemper'; Gay is attending to him just before setting off to Amesbury, Wiltshire, with the Duke and Duchess of Queensberry.

12 AP ill with a short but severe fever.

14 AP writes to Swift to express pleasure at the latter's forthcoming visit to England: 'after so many dispersions, and so many divisions, two or three of us may yet be gather'd together; not to plot, not to contrive silly schemes of ambition, or to vex our own or others hearts with busy vanities . . . but to divert ourselves, and the world too if it pleases'. AP has just received more *Odyssey* material from Broome; he is revising the draft translation on a daily basis.

23 Gay staying with AP at Twickenham. At some point just before this date, Sir Robert Walpole, the Prime Minister, has paid a visit to AP at home.

29 Writing from Dublin to AP, Swift outlines the philosophical basis of his *Travels* in the celebrated formulation: 'I have got Materials Towards a Treatis proving the falsity of that Definition *animal rationale*; and to show it should be only *rationis capax*. Upon this great foundation of Misanthropy (though not in Timon's manner) the whole building of my Travells is erected' (*Corr.*, II, 325).

October

2   (Sat) First collected edition of Swift's *Drapier's Letters* published by George Faulkner in Dublin.

5   AP relates to the Earl of Strafford the state of play in the Kneller monument controversy, which may be concluded by the end of this month. Meanwhile AP continues 'as busy in three inches of Gardening, as any man can be in threescore acres'.

10 Mrs Pope again very ill, and AP confined to home by a fever and an 'impertinent Lameness'.

15 Responding to Swift's letter of 29 September, AP lists the friends who await him in London, and notes that he is working on a new satire, which is probably *The Dunciad*.

November

2   (Tues) AP writes to Broome in agitation: his mother is suffering from jaundice, and Mary Beach, his old nurse, is on

her deathbed. Yet he still remembers to request Broome's draft translation of *Odyssey* book XVIII.

5 Death at age 77 of Mary Beach, AP's nurse, who had resided with the family since 1688. AP later commemorates her with a memorial stone in the parish church at Twickenham.

7 If he can find an attendant for his mother, AP plans to go up to London to see Lord Oxford four or five days hence.

10 By this date, AP has received the complete draft translations of books XVI and XVIII of *The Odyssey* from Broome; he now writes to request the notes for books XXII–XXIV, having decided to leave books XVII–XIX to the end.

11 In *The Adventures of Pomponius*, published this day by Curll, a special digression on AP refers to his *Odyssey* translation as a 'Jobb of Journey-Work', and his Shakespeare as a 'mutilated Edition'. Both works are 'wretched Performances' by a poet who 'crawls under the *Toilet* of every *Court-Lady*; and . . . flatters every brocaded *Fop* of *Distinction*'.

20 Fenton writes to Broome to arrange a convenient time for settling the *Odyssey* business with AP.

23 Worn out by the illness of his mother, the death of his nurse, and *The Odyssey*, AP writes to Caryll, 'when I translate again I will be hanged; nay I will do something to deserve to be hanged, which is worse, rather than drudge for such a world as is no judge of your labour'.

December

1 (Wed) In response to Fenton's letter of 20 November, Broome decides that a joint meeting with AP over *The Odyssey* is pointless: 'I fear we have hunted with the lion. . . . Be assured Mr. Pope will not let us divide – I fear not give us our due share of honour. He is a Caesar in poetry, and will bear no equal' (*Corr.*, II, 345).

21 Just before this date AP has asked Fenton to get the remainder of *The Odyssey* notes from Broome; without them, the printing cannot continue.

25 AP writes to Caryll to refute allegations that he and Martha Blount 'lived 2 or 3 years together since in a manner that was reported to you as giving scandal to many'. Martha Blount is Caryll's god-daughter.

27 AP writes to arrange a week's stay with Lord Oxford at Down Hall.

30 AP reports to Broome that *Odyssey* book xxiii is just going through the press.

1726

January
1 (Sat) AP staying at Hoddesdon, north of London, where he is met by Lord Oxford's horses and chariot to take him to Down Hall.
2 Broome writes exultantly to AP that the *Odyssey* notes are at last finished for all twenty-four books.
7 AP staying at Lord Oxford's house in Dover Street, London, on his way back to Twickenham from Down Hall.
13 AP has just met with Fenton, who writes to Broome requesting that he send the remainder of the *Odyssey* notes immediately, and that they decide on how they wish to be mentioned in the edition as AP's assistants.
18 AP receives the last packet of *Odyssey* notes from Broome.
19 Writing to Caryll, AP notes that he has been very ill since his return home from Lord Oxford's in Essex.
20 AP writes to Broome to request that he acknowledge his debts to Dacier's notes for his own in *The Odyssey*.
29 Fenton writes to Broome to say that AP has just agreed to a meeting of the *Odyssey* collaborators.

February
26 (Sat) First publication of AP's 'Rondeau' ('You know where'), in *Mist's Weekly Journal*. It had originally appeared in AP's letter to Cromwell, 24 June 1710.

March
During this month, Lewis Theobald brings out his *Shakespeare Restored . . . A Specimen of the Many Errors . . . by Mr Pope in his Late Edition*. AP's edition is thoroughly devastated as a reliable text, although Theobald asserts 'so great an Esteem for Mr. *Pope*, and so high an Opinion of his Genius and Excellencies, that I beg to be excused from the least Intention of derogating from his Merits'. Theobald nevertheless becomes the main victim of the satire in the first *Dunciad*.

3 (Thurs) AP is engaged in writing the Postscript to the *Odyssey* translation at about this time; a summary of his ideas he sends to Caryll in a letter on this day.

6 Swift leaves Dublin, on his first visit to London since 1714. He carries with him the manuscript of *Gulliver's Travels*.

10 Lord Oxford writes to AP that he has discovered in some of his father's papers an early version of AP's translation of one of Donne's satires.

15 About this date Swift arrives in London, to arrange the publishing of the *Travels*, to visit old friends and to prepare materials for a life of Robert Harley, Earl of Oxford. He lodges in Bury Street.

22 AP has just spent two days in London with Swift. He would like to accompany Swift to Down Hall but a printing-deadline for *The Odyssey* makes this impossible.

26 Swift goes to stay a few days with Bolingbroke at Dawley Farm.

April

2 (Sat) Swift now at Twickenham with AP.

3 AP has now learned that printing of *The Odyssey* cannot be finished until the end of the month.

16 Greatly fatigued, AP has completed the writing of the *Odyssey* Postscript. To Broome he comments, 'it is not to be imagined with what sickly reluctance I have at last finished [it]'. Broome is spared the preparation of the index, but AP urgently requests the complete list of errata.

19 Death of AP's friend and correspondent the Hon. Robert Digby.

May

20 (Fri) Fenton, in Cambridge with the son of Lady Trumbull, reports that there is as great a clamour there against AP and the *Odyssey* translation as there had been last winter in London.

June

1 (Wed) During this month Joseph Spence publishes his *Essay on Mr Pope's Odyssey*, which both compliments and criticises AP's translation. Spence will later become a close friend of AP and recorder of much personal detail about him.

4 Writing to Broome, AP describes both his work on the Postscript to *The Odyssey* and his well-being: 'I have had a long and troublesome disorder upon me of the piles, which has put me more out of humour than out of health.' By this date, AP has seen a copy of Spence's *Essay*, which he recommends to Broome.

10 The *Daily Post* announces that volumes IV and V of AP's *Odyssey* translation will (at last) be published during the next week. Fenton sends Broome a copy of Spence's *Essay* on or just before this date.

26 At Lord Burlington's house at Chiswick, AP witnesses Burlington's formal presentation to Swift of a copy of Fréart de Chambray's *Parallèle d'architecture antique et de la moderne*.

July

3 (Sun) AP, Gay, and Swift at Lord Bathurst's in London.

5 Gay and Swift dining with company at AP's house.

14 Curll brings out a collection called *Miscellanea. In Two Volumes.* The first volume contains the unauthorised publication of correspondence between AP and Henry Cromwell, which Curll has obtained from Mrs Thomas, who was Cromwell's former lover.

17 Death of AP's friend Edward Blount.

August

3 (Wed) AP ill and unable to dine in company with Swift, Lord Peterborough and others, at the farewell dinner for Swift.

4 Swift gathering up his luggage, in preparation for his return to Ireland.

7 Fenton writes to Broome in obvious annoyance that the latter has publicly revealed his contribution to the *Odyssey* translation.

8 Swift, in London, makes secret arrangements for the anonymous publication of *Gulliver's Travels*.

15 Swift leaves London and Twickenham (where he gives AP a set of inscribed silver cups), heading back to his deanery in Dublin, arriving there on the 22nd. AP sends Lord Oxford a manuscript copy of Swift's *History of the Four Last Years of the Queen* (published 1758).

22 AP writes to Swift in Dublin with humble thanks for his

parting gift of silver cups and to say that 'you have used me more cruelly than you have done any other man; you have made it impossible for me to live at ease without you'.

23　AP informs Broome that he can now collect the £100 owing to him for his *Odyssey* subscriptions (he had received £500 for translating), and that he will look over Broome's collection of miscellany poems.

September
5　(Mon) Between this day and the 11th AP is injured in a serious coach accident, coming back to Twickenham from Bolingbroke's estate at Dawley, four miles away. The coach is overturned into the river at Whitton (a mile from AP's house), AP is trapped inside, and in being rescued, receives a serious gash in the hand; the gash severs tendons in two fingers of his right hand.

11　Gay visits AP and learns of the coach accident.

16　Gay writes to Swift in Dublin with news of AP's coach accident and injury.

17　Starting today, Gay intends to stay with AP at Twickenham to help him recover from the coach accident.

21　AP still suffering severe pains in his right arm and hand.

23　In a copy of his *Odyssey*, AP writes the 'Presentation Verses to Nathaniel Pigott' ('The Muse this one Verse to learn'd Pigot addresses'), to whose house he is taken after the coach accident.

29　AP arranges for Lord and Lady Oxford to visit him at Twickenham on this day.

October
22　(Sat) Gay writes to Swift explaining that he has attended AP as amanuensis at Twickenham for the past month.

26　In a letter to Thierot, Voltaire praises AP ('the best poet in England, and at present in the world') and his poems (*CH*, p. 153).

28　On or about this date Benjamin Motte issues *Gulliver's Travels* in two octavo volumes (priced at 8*s* 6*d*). Although Swift is displeased with unauthorised changes to the text, the book is wildly popular. By December a third (reprint) edition is required, of a further 2500 copies.

November

16 (Wed) AP writes to Swift with congratulations and news about the reception of the *Travels*, which 'I prophecy will be in future the admiration of all men.' Indeed he has just recently gone up to London to see the public's response.

22 During the previous two weeks, AP (in London) has visited Broome three times.

December

3 (Sat) Publication of a key to Swift's *Travels*, *Gulliver Decypher'd*, published by J. Roberts. Written in a style imitating *A Tale of a Tub*, the key takes potshots at Arbuthnot, Gay and AP.

5 AP has just finished entertaining John Caryll and his wife at Twickenham. At this point in his career, perhaps spurred by Curll's *Miscellanea* (26 July), AP tells Caryll that he intends to call in all his papers and letters which friends have preserved, to vet them for potential scandal, and then return them. AP's hand has now recovered enough for him to write, as he does to Broome on this day.

6 First number appears of *The Craftsman*, the long-running journal of opposition comment directed initially at Walpole and his Ministry. AP may have been an occasional anonymous contributor to the journal.

17 Fenton urges Broome not to continue seeking public recognition for their part in the *Odyssey* translation, 'unless you resolve to break all measures with [AP]' (*Corr.*, II, 423).

20 AP's and William Pulteney's *The Discovery: Or, The Squire Turn'd Ferret. An Excellent New Ballad* published (a second edition appears on the 24th); the ballad is their humorous account of Mary Toft, the celebrated 'Rabbit-woman' of Surrey.

1727

January

5 (Thurs) Caryll repays the £200 he has borrowed from AP's father in 1710. On this date appears the collection *Atterburyana*, which contains the second appearance (the first is an undated broadside) of AP's 'Receipt to make Soup. For the Use of Dean Swift'.

20   AP orders for himself a copy of Arbuthnot's recently published *Tables of Ancient Coins*, and ten copies for Lord Oxford.
27   First night of James Moore Smythe's comedy *The Rival Modes* (published by Lintot in Feb), with a Prologue by Lewis Theobald. AP first allowed then withdrew permission for Smythe to use six lines of his in the play. Smythe used them anyway and inaugurated a feud that would continue for several years.

February
Early in this month, and in late January, Walter Harte's *Poems on Several Occasions* is being printed (published in May). The collection was probably corrected by AP.
17   (Fri) A cold prevents AP from dining with Arbuthnot and Swift's friend James Stopford, who is heading off to Dublin; AP promises to send him a large paper copy of *The Odyssey*. Stopford is to ask Swift whether 'Cadenus and Vanessa' should be inserted in the new miscellany collection AP is planning. In the letter to Swift which Stopford is carrying, AP notes that the 'Miscellany is now quite printed. I am prodiguously pleased with this joint-volume, in which methinks we look like friends, side by side, serious and merry by turns, conversing interchangeably, and walking down hand in hand to posterity.' AP also mentions the planning of the 'Third' volume and his commendatory verses for the *Travels*, and comments on his unusual good health at this season.
25   On this date is published *Some Memoirs of the Life of Lewis Maximilian Mahomet*, which includes in a postscript the first separate printing of AP's 'Epitaph on James Craggs', which had originally been for the end of AP's 'Verses Occasion'd by Mr Addison's Treatise of Medals'.

March
 1   (Wed) AP asks Lord Harcourt to intervene in the case of John Hope, who is about to be bounced by the Privy Council as Governor of the Bermudas.
28   AP writes to Caryll to propose a small pension for his schoolmaster at Marylebone, London, Thomas Dean, getting Lord Dormer also to contribute. During this day he goes to Easthampstead to visit Fenton.

29 AP signs an agreement with Benjamin Motte for the publication of the *Miscellanies*.

April

9 (Sun) Swift leaves Dublin for an extended stay in England, chiefly at AP's Twickenham estate.

18 AP sends the quarto *Odyssey* set, with inscription, to his friend William Cleland, Commissioner of Taxes in England.

22 Swift reaches Twickenham at the beginning of his five-month visit to England.

24 AP arranges for Swift and him to dine this day with Lord Oxford in London, but the meeting must be put off for about a week because of Swift's 'great Businesses'.

26 AP writes to Broome with mixed praise for his recently published *Poems* ('one or two little things I thought too puerile') and to encourage him to defend the *Odyssey* collaboration publicly. AP denounces the methods and behaviour of Lintot.

May

6 (Sat) William Congreve writes to AP that he is glad to have his company in Curll's publishing-lists; he suggests AP administer another emetic, recalling AP's trick (and pamphlet) of a decade earlier. At some point just prior to this date Motte issues *Several Copies of Verses on Occasion of Mr Gulliver's Travels*, which contains the first publication of four of AP's poems on the *Travels*: 'To Quinbus Flestrin', 'The Lamentation of Glumdalclitch', 'To Mr Lemuel Gulliver', and 'Mary Gulliver to Captain Lemuel Gulliver'. The variant issue of *Several Copies* adds another *Travels* poem by AP, 'The Words of the King of Brobdingnab'. When Motte publishes the 'Second Edition' of the *Travels* shortly after this date, he includes the poems as prefatory verses.

10 AP's mother has been seriously ill with an intermitting fever, preventing AP from his normal work and correspondence.

11 After this date Motte adds AP's *Gulliver* burlesque poems to some copies of the new edition of the *Travels* which had been advertised on the 4th.

16 Swift still with AP at Twickenham, as AP continues to attend his mother in her long illness.

June
3   (Sat) King George leaves London for a summer trip to Hanover.
11 At Osnabrück, *en route* to Hanover, George I dies unexpectedly, leaving the throne to his son, who becomes George II.
15 Swift comes up to London from AP's Twickenham house to begin a trip to the Continent, but is forced to delay it, then cancel it, following the King's death.
24 Publication by Benjamin Motte of first and second volumes of *Miscellanies in Verse and Prose*, by AP, Swift, Gay and Arbuthnot (first advertised on 15 June in the *Evening Post*). Volume II contains AP's revised edition of Arbuthnot's John Bull pamphlets. AP's mother has now recovered, unexpectedly.
27 Cromwell's former lover, Mrs Thomas, writes to him to have him pronounce the AP–Cromwell letters to be her legal property and not stolen. Curll had published them in *Miscellanea* (1726), and 'surely Mr. Pope ought not to resent the publication, since the early pregnancy of his Genius was no dishonour to his character' (*Corr.*, II, 438).
30 By this date AP and Swift are busy with the proofs of the 'Last' volume of the *Miscellanies*. At this point AP is planning to have 'The Progress of Dulness' (later *The Dunciad*) end the volume, and is preparing for a fourth volume of prose in which '*Peri Bathous*' is planned to appear.

July
6   (Sat) Henry Cromwell writes to AP to admit that he gave their letters to Mrs Thomas (who gave them to Curll), but also refused to write anything about them for Curll.

August
During this month is published an 'improved' edition of Joseph Spence's *Essay on Mr Pope's Odyssey*, sometimes called the second part.
1   (Tues) A further letter of apology from Cromwell to AP over the Curll publication of their letters.
5   AP has just returned to Twickenham after a three weeks' ramble to Cambridge and to Lord Oxford's at Wimpole, amongst other places. On the way back he visits Sir Robert

Walpole in London. On this ramble AP is accompanied by Swift for part of the time. Swift's complaint of deafness reappears as he and Lord Oxford reach London.

12 Writing from AP's house to Thomas Sheridan in Dublin, Swift complains of severe 'Giddiness', resolving to leave Twickenham for somewhere else if it continues. He is still expecting to leave for Ireland on 15 September.

15 AP writes to Lord Oxford, worried about Swift's health; Arbuthnot has been asked down to examine him.

25 After two days of recovery, Swift's condition is again very bad, and AP writes in concern to Lord Oxford.

31 Swift leaves AP's Twickenham house to go to his cousin Lancelot's in London, feeling acute embarrassment over his frequent attacks of deafness and vertigo; AP continues to see him regularly.

September

6 (Wed) Swift's health improved, but not enough (in AP's opinion) for him to journey home to Dublin.

18 Swift sets off from London (from an inn in Aldersgate Street) to return to Dublin, at the end of his summer's visit with AP and others.

October

Just before the beginning of this month and after Swift's departure (18 September), AP spends several days in London, being ill for two of them.

4 (Wed) After a long trip with many delays (including a week at Holyhead), Swift finally arrives back in Dublin.

5 AP now himself in a 'very ill state of health, which increases daily; my old complaints of the stomach are turned into an inveterate cholic, which seldom leaves me in any lively sensation of life for two days together' (*Corr.*, II, 449).

7 Mather Byles writes from Cambridge, Massachusetts, in praise of AP, and encloses a copy of his own verses which contain forty lines of tribute to AP.

12 Gay is finally gazetted as gentleman usher to the Princess Louisa, but turns down the £150 a year to continue his writing-career with *The Beggar's Opera* (produced in Janaury 1728). Swift writes to AP to announce his safe arrival, his resignation at having to live in Ireland rather than England,

and his reliance on God to improve his health enough for a
return visit to AP.

16 AP writes to Gay, congratulating him on his refusal of the
court post, and condemning the corrupt practices of patronage.

22 Gay and AP write to Swift in order to reveal that they know
what passed on his return trip (probably from Thomas
Sheridan). Gay announces that he has finished *The Beggar's
Opera*; AP has evidently finished most of *The Dunciad*.

30 AP has just returned from Lord Burlington's, where he has
overseen the carving of some statuary.

November

8 (Wed) Isaac Newton's literary executor, John Conduitt, sends
AP a copy of his Dedication to Newton's *Chronology of Ancient
Kingdoms Amended*, asking him to revise it.

10 AP writes back to Conduitt with detailed revisions of the
Dedication, many of which Conduitt accepts. The work is
published in 1728.

24 For a second time, AP sends a copy of the inscription to be
placed on Craggs's monument in Westminster Abbey, with
which the monument will be complete.

December

13 (Wed) Just prior to this date AP has been to London for a
day, during which he tries to see Lord Oxford.

26 AP at Twickenham, celebrating Christmas with friends.

28 AP writes to Lord Oxford with Christmas greetings and a
brief sketch of his health: 'I am in a very indifferent state of
health & afraid to go to Town as yet.'

1728

January

During this month AP is working on his 'Chef d'oeuvre, the
Poem of Dulness, which after I am dead and gone, will be printed
with a large Commentary, and lettered on the back, *Pope's Dulness*'
(*Corr.*, II, 468). Gay's *Beggar's Opera* is being prepared for its
first performance, on the 29th.

9 (Tues) AP writes to Broome to patch up a disagreement over
the latter's poems caused by the publisher, Lintot.

28 Death of Swift's 'Stella', Esther Johnson, in Dublin. On this evening, Swift begins to write his narrative *On the Death of Mrs Johnson*.

29 First night of *The Beggar's Opera*, at Lincoln's Inn Fields. Gay's masterpiece runs for an unheard-of sixty-two nights, inaugurates the fashion for ballad opera, and contributes to the decline in audiences for Italian opera.

February

During this month, AP makes a brief visit to stay with Lord Bolingbroke at Dawley Farm, and to London, where *The Beggar's Opera* 'succeeds extremely' (*Corr.*, II, 473).

5 (Mon) *The Dunciad* now becoming known beyond AP's circle: the poet Edward Young writes to Tickell about it, having seen it in manuscript.

26 Swift writes to Gay to discover if, and when, AP will publish *The Dunciad*.

March

8 (Fri) Publication by Benjamin Motte of *Miscellanies*, the third volume here titled 'The Last Volume'. The book begins with *'Peri Bathous'* (first published here) and a dozen smaller minor works. *'Peri Bathous'* takes the intended position of *The Dunciad*, which will be published separately, and anonymously, two months hence.

12 Benjamin Motte's letter of this date (*Corr.*, II, 477) indicates that Curll intends to publish a pamphlet reprisal for Motte's publishing of the *Miscellanies*.

16 John Oldmixon's rambling prose *Essay on Criticism* hits at AP for his unoriginality in his poem of the same title. But, although he frequently objects to AP's diction in the Homer translations, he calls the effort an 'excellent Performance . . . of the most pure and harmonious Diction and Versification'.

19 Swift publishes his pamphlet analysis of Ireland's economic woes, *A Short View of Ireland*.

20 By this date, *The Beggar's Opera* has been acted thirty-six times, all to full houses. Gay has made £700–800, and Rich, the theatre-manager, has netted £4000.

23 Writing to Swift, AP confesses that one motivation for *The Dunciad* is 'to rid me of these insects', the Grub Street hacks; and notifies him of a title change from 'The Progress of

Dulness' to *The Dunciad*, in part so that the brief title would not become 'Pope's Dulness'. He encloses a copy of the *New England Weekly Journal* sent to him by Mather Byles, 7 Oct 1727), which mentions a real-life Captain Jonathan Gulliver.

28 In a letter to Gay, Swift summarises the successes by the three central Scriblerus Club members twenty years on: 'the Beggars Opera hath knockt down Gulliver, I hope to see Popes Dullness knock down the Beggars Opera, but not till it hath fully done its Jobb'.

30 *Mist's Weekly Journal* prints 'An Essay on the Arts of a Poet's Sinking in Reputation', an attack on AP's *'Peri Bathous'* from the 'Last' volume of the *Miscellanies*.

April

3 (Wed) Fenton mentions to Broome that AP is being criticised severely in the weekly journals.

5 The *Daily Journal* prints 'An Auction of Goods at Twickenham', a satiric list of awkward epithets from AP's works.

7 Fenton has not yet seen AP's *'Peri Bathous'*, where (Broome complains) some of Broome's poetry has been mentioned and jokingly illustrated. He advises Broome 'not to remain passive under such a provocation' (*Corr.* II, 488).

18 Sections of a folio pamphlet published this day, *A Collection of Several Curious Pieces Lately Inserted in the Daily Journal*, accuse AP of plagiarising James Moore Smythe and Nicholas Rowe.

May

During this month, Gay heads off to spend the summer at Bath in the company of William Congreve and the Duchess of Marlborough. While there he works on *Polly*, his sequel to the *Beggar's Opera*.

3 (Fri) Broome still furious with AP for his inclusion in *'Peri Bathous'*: 'he has used me ill, he is ungrateful. . . . I often resemble him to an hedgehog; he wraps himself up . . . and sets his bristles out against all mankind. . . . I wonder he is not thrashed: but his littleness is his protection; no man shoots a wren' (*Corr.*, II, 489).

6 AP, whose health has been poor all winter and spring, remains at home, 'immers'd in the Country & in Books' (*Corr.*, II, 489).

10 Swift writes to AP; he is impatient to see *The Dunciad* published.

11 In the Preface to the playscript of *Penelope, A Dramatic Opera* (by Thomas Cooke and John Mottley), published this day, AP is said to have shown Homer as the father of farce through his translation. On this same day, a letter to the *Daily Journal*, probably by John Dennis, reviews AP's career and ridicules the forthcoming *Dunciad* by 'this little turbulent Creature [who] has endeavoured to decry and calumniate every Author who has excelled him' (*CH*, p. 157).

13 In a letter to *Mist's Weekly Journal*, Theobald says he hopes that by publishing his *Shakespeare Restored* he has provoked AP into a more accurate second edition of the Shakespeare edition. His own further *Remarks* on all of Shakespeare will contain 'about *five hundred* more fair *Emendations*' for AP to consider. On the same day, *The Twickenham Hotch-Potch*, by 'Caleb D'Anvers', appears; mostly attacking *The Beggar's Opera*, it also lashes AP's Shakespeare and the *Miscellanies*.

17 AP sends part of a manuscript copy of Swift's *History of the Last Four Years of the Queen* to Lord Oxford for copying.

18 Writing again from Harvard College in Cambridge, Massachusetts, Mather Byles lists AP's works he has read in the College Library, not including *The Dunciad. An Heroic Poem*. The first edition of the first form of *The Dunciad* appears this day. This edition has a frontispiece featuring an owl on a pedestal of books. A second edition and a third appear by the 24th, all published as from 'Dublin and reprinted in London for A. Dodd'. From this point on, the publishing-record of the poem becomes exceedingly complex, with many variant issues in different sizes together with significant additions to the original poem in 1729 and 1742.

25 In the third number of his own paper, *The Intelligencer*, Swift replies to critics of Gay's Scriblerian production *The Beggar's Opera*, defending it against charges of immorality and subversion.

28 By this date Curll publishes *A Compleat Key to the Dunciad*, in which he supplies names for the 1728 text's asterisks. By the way he abuses AP as a dunce himself and the poem as a 'Patch-Work Medley'. (A second enlarged and corrected edition appears on 4 June.) Lord Oxford has seen the *Key* advertised, and several of his friends have asked for copies.

29 A letter in *Mist's Weekly Journal* takes issue with literary aspects of *The Dunciad*, claiming the poem as beneath that of 'so great a Genius' as AP (*CH*, p. 208).

30 On this day, the printer James Bettenham enters a claim for copyright of *The Dunciad*, depositing nine copies with the Stationers' Company. It is likely that the real copyright-owner was AP. AP is now visiting London. He visits the daughter of Earl Cowper, the Lord Chancellor, in order to get Walter Harte recommended for a fellowship at Exeter College, Oxford.

June

1 (Sat) The famous pamphlet attack *A Popp upon Pope* published in response to *The Dunciad*. In this fantasy AP is birched by two assailants, producing blood which is yellow with gall, and is rescued by Mrs Blount. Swift reports to AP that *The Dunciad* has been very well received in Dublin.

8 *Mist's Weekly Journal* prints parodic accounts of a cabal, 'The Knights of the Bathos', brought together to attack *The Dunciad* and AP.

13 AP requests a copy of the Preface from Caxton's Virgil from Lord Oxford; this means that he is already preparing *The Dunciad Variorum* (1729), where the Preface appears as Appendix III.

14 In an advertisement in the *Daily Post*, AP denies the truth of the birching-incident in *A Popp upon Pope* of 1 June.

15 Publication of *The Progress of Dulness*, yet another work in response to *The Dunciad*; AP's *Rape* is here called 'Mushroom Fictions', *Windsor-Forest* a 'String of Verses . . . without any Connection . . . [which] with most *Seraphic Emptiness* . . . roll,/Sound without Sense, and Body without Soul' (*PA*, p. 92). A further account of the 'Knights of the Bathos' appears in *Mist's Weekly Journal*, and *A Compleat Collection of All the Verses, Essays, Letters, and Advertisements, which Have Been Occasioned by the . . . Miscellanies, by Pope and Company* is published, a compendium of newspaper items abusing AP, his friends and his works. Broome's letter of the same date to Fenton shows that he is still brooding over the perceived injustices AP has dealt him.

17 AP writes to Hugh Bethel, seeking the return of his previous letters, supposedly to prevent any future scandal.

25   AP sends Lord Oxford the manuscript of the second part of
     Swift's *History of the Four Last Years of the Queen* for copying.
     He has just been up to London for a few days, where he
     missed seeing Lord Oxford.
26   Publication of James Ralph's satirical poem *Sawney*, occasioned
     by *The Dunciad*.
27   Publication of a satiric pamphlet, *An Essay on the Dunciad*, in
     which the poet is accused of blasphemy, disloyalty,
     ingratitude, and ill-nature: it is difficult to believe that 'Mr.
     POPE, who is the Honour of our *English* Nation, was the
     Author of such a notorious Libel' (*CH*, p. 217).
28   AP at Dawley with Lord Bolingbroke, who has just returned
     from Bath. AP writes to Swift to say that *The Dunciad* is to be
     expanded with ironically elaborate scholarly apparatus, and
     invites him to contribute material.
29   Arising from the *Miscellanies* controversy, there appears on
     this day *An Essay upon the Taste and Writings of the Present
     Times*, in which AP is routinely attacked.

July
 1   (Mon) AP asks Lord Oxford to have his amanuensis transcribe
     a fair copy of what will become the 'Letter to the Publisher' in
     The Dunciad Variorum. The letter is perhaps by AP's friend
     William Cleland.
 2   Curll's *Popiad* published, a collection of miscellaneous reprints
     of earlier attacks on AP, including Dennis' 1717 Homer
     Remarks.
 5   His death having occurred a few days earlier, the will
     is proved of Henry Cromwell, AP's early friend and
     correspondent.
 6   Gay reports to Swift that AP is 'in a state of Persecution for
     the Dunciad[;] I wish to be witness of his fortitude, but he
     writes but seldom' (Gay, *Letters*, p. 76).
16   Swift responds with suggested revisions and additions to *The
     Dunciad*, including indexes, notes on the poem's verbal
     parodies, and an account of the scribblers' works. He also
     recommends that real names be used.
17   Lord Oxford's scribe is busy making a fair copy of *The Dunciad
     Variorum* for AP, who will send the second book in a week's
     time.
18   Dennis' *Remarks on Mr Pope's Rape of the Lock* published, a

thoroughly detailed critical reading of the poem from AP's most celebrated enemy. Also on this day appears Jonathan Smedley's *The Metamorphosis: A Poem. Shewing the Change of Scriblerus into Snarlerus.*

25 AP sends the remainder of the notes for book II of *The Dunciad Variorum* for Lord Oxford's scribe to write out in fair copy.

August
2 (Fri) Gay writes to AP, admiring his fortitude in the public controversy following publication of *The Dunciad*.

3 Bishop Atterbury writes to his son-in-law, noting that in *The Dunciad* AP has engaged in troublesome and improper scuffles with his inferiors.

8 Publication of a miscellaneous reprint collection, *The Female Dunciad*, probably from Curll's hand, with the usual array of charges against AP, including sexual dissoluteness. One section is 'The New, Surprizing Metamorphosis; or Mr. Pope Turn'd into a Stinging-Nettle'.

11 Thomas Cooke writes to AP to disavow authorship of recent attacks on him, although he admits conversing with some of the authors of those attacks. AP will ask Lord Oxford for advice in dealing with the man (17 Aug).

12 Another reply to the Pope–Swift *Miscellanies* published. Jonathan Smedley's *Gulliveriana* attacks AP personally and widely misreads many of his works.

16 Matthew Concanen's *A Supplement to the Profound* published, in response to AP's *'Peri Bathous'*. Concanen attacks the Homer translations for departing from the original.

17 AP is just setting out for a journey to Bath, where he will stay for about ten weeks. During the next two weeks, on the way, he visits Lord Cobham at Stowe, Colonel Dormer at Rousham, Mr John Howe of Stowell, and Sir William Codrington together with Hugh Bethel's sisters at Dodington, where he is made to take physic in preparation for his stay at Bath.

29 Anonymous publication of *Characters of the Times*, a hack defence of men allegedly attacked by AP in the *Miscellanies*.

September
2 (Mon) AP attempts to visit Lord Bathurst at Cirencester, but

finds he is away; instead he goes to stay with John Howe at Stowell.

4 AP writes to Martha Blount, who is attending his mother during his absence. He has just arrived in Bath.

5 Curll publishes *Codrus: Or, The Dunciad Dissected*, mostly a personal attack on AP: 'A little scurvy, purblind-Elf . . . a proud, conceited, peevish Creature'.

14 After two weeks of consuming the Bath waters, AP claims (to Lord Oxford) that he can feel little effect on his health, except giddiness.

16 Thomas Cooke sends another apologetic letter to AP (see 11 Aug) in which he promises to omit in his forthcoming *Poems* a passage critical of AP; AP puts him into *The Dunciad Variorum* (II.130).

October

12 (Sat) AP comments on *Gulliveriana* (see 12 Aug), by 'that Fool, Smedley'. He asks Thomas Sheridan to collect any Irish notices or responses to *The Dunciad*, and adds (thinking of Swift's exile), 'were I my own Master (which I thank God I yet am, in all points but one, where Humanity only constrains me) I would infallibly see *Ireland* before I die' (*Corr.*, II, 524). On or about this day, AP leaves Bath, possibly with Gay as companion.

15 On or about this day, AP safely reaches home at Twickenham.

November

4 (Mon) Tonson issues the second edition of AP's *Works of Shakespear. In Eight Volumes*, with a ninth volume of attributed plays. For this edition, AP took account of the suggestions made by Theobald in *Shakespeare Restored* (1726).

7 AP writes to Lord Bathurst with complaints about his violent headaches, which the Bath waters did nothing to alleviate. Since returning from there three weeks ago AP has been to London once, remaining at home otherwise. Her husband (Charles Rackett) having recently died, AP's sister, Magdalen, is granted letters of administration in her husband's estate.

9 AP having trouble over payment for the *Miscellanies*. He writes to Motte, the publisher, to remonstrate.

27 AP in London to confer with Lord Oxford and Samuel Wesley, possibly over the problem with Thomas Cooke.

December

A letter (to Fortescue) possibly of this month demonstrates AP's health at this late stage of the year: 'I am in the condition of an old fellow of Threescore, with a Complication of Diseases upon me; A constant Headake; ruind Tone of the Stomach; the Piles; a Vomiting and Looseness; & an Excess of Wind . . . upon the whole I am in a very uncomfortable way' (*Corr.*, II, 530).

12 (Thurs) *Polly*, Gay's sequel to *The Beggar's Opera*, suppressed by the Lord Chamberlain, probably at Walpole's urging. In his verse pamphlet *Durgen. Or, A Plain Satyr upon a Pompous Satyrist*, Ned Ward attacks AP's *Dunciad* and Homer translations.

23 AP thanks Lord Bathurst for arranging the *Dunciad* papers to be vetted by a lawyer for possible libels. Mrs Pope is very ill, 'tho' not quite yet at the point of expiring'.

28 AP has been ill since Christmas Day; his mother is still gravely ill, but no worse.

1729

January

6 (Mon) AP writes to Samuel Wesley proposing that Thomas Cooke publicly recant his aspersion on AP, and asking Wesley to return to him Cooke's letters. AP's mother continues very ill.

14 AP still having trouble with Motte over the financial agreement for the three volumes of *Miscellanies*; he wishes to publish a fourth volume (eventually called the 'Third') but will wait.

19 Death of William Congreve, playwright and AP's early friend.

20 Lord Oxford reports to AP that Gay, who has been ill for several months with asthma and pleurisy, has now almost recovered. AP's mother continues very ill, and he is unable to leave her.

February

3 (Mon) In a letter of self-defence to Caryll, AP reports that he has been charged surgeon's expenses after the death of Mrs Cope (in France), a woman to whose welfare he has generously contributed; and he explains the reasons for the interruption of his correspondence.

4 AP entertains the Earl of Oxford and others (possibly including Samuel Wesley) at home.

14 AP himself is very ill, but his mother is now recovering; her long illness has affected her memory. Lord Oxford sends two of AP's ballads and two epigrams as AP is collecting material for the fourth volume of the *Miscellanies*.

16 AP advises Caryll that two sets of the *Odyssey* translation are waiting for him, but that he could find, so long after publication, only one quarto set of *The Iliad*, for which Lintot was asking £10.

20 AP's mother is well enough to be left alone, but only for one day. He contemplates a visit to London to see Lord Oxford and others.

March

2 (Sun) On this day (or possibly the 9th), AP ventures to Chiswick with an advance copy of *The Dunciad Variorum* for Lord and Lady Burlington.

12 In an amazing piece of real-life irony, Sir Robert Walpole presents a copy of *The Dunciad Variorum* to the King and Queen at St James's Palace.

13 AP writes to Lord Oxford that the King and Queen have received his presentation copy of *The Dunciad Variorum* 'by the hands of Sir R[obert] W[alpole]'. He now will allow Lord Oxford to distribute the copies he has sent him previously.

25 Gay publishes the text of *Polly* at his own expense, making almost £1200.

27 AP requests Lord Oxford to send twenty copies of *The Dunciad Variorum* to be sold (but not by booksellers) at Cambridge. Lord Oxford (with others) is performing the duty of distribution because AP has avoided legal responsibility for the potentially libellous aspects of the poem by disavowing authorship.

28 AP writes to accept a quarto set of *The Iliad* which Motte has obtained for him.

29 In *The Weekly Journal or British Gazetteer* no. 201 appears an anonymous and abusive poem on Michael Rysbrack's bust of AP ('half Man, half Monkey . . .').

31 Probably on this date AP composes his retort to the verses on his bust by Rysbrack ('Well, Sir, suppose, the Busto's a

damned head'), incorporated into *The Dunciad Variorum*, octavo edition (see 26 Nov).

April

8 (Tues) AP writes to inform Caryll that his *Odyssey* set is waiting for him at Jervas' house, together with a presentation copy of *The Dunciad Variorum*. By this date Lord Bathurst has given consent that booksellers may now offer the book in their shops.

10 Publication announced in the *Daily Post* of *The Dunciad Variorum. With the Prolegomena of Scriblerus*. The title-page vignette has the famous ass laden with remaindered books. Although the name 'A. Dod' appears on the title-page, the real publisher was Lawton Gilliver. Many variant issues and at least one pirated edition (by Curll) follow in the next few weeks.

12 *The Flying-Post: Or, Weekly Medley* prints two of AP's epigrams (on Roome and on Moore Smythe). The two are later incorporated into *The Dunciad*.

18 In light of possible litigious responses by scribblers mentioned in *The Dunciad Variorum*, AP asks Lord Oxford (together with Lords Burlington and Bathurst) to sign an acknowledgement of publication and distribution, so as to shield AP from legal attacks.

30 Curll's *Curliad* appears, in response to *The Dunciad Variorum*. Mostly rehashes familiar charges against AP.

May

During this month the Duke and Duchess of Queensberry take Gay to Edinburgh for a four weeks' visit.

8 (Thurs) AP sends Motte a draft agreement for payment and ownership in the matter of the three volumes of *Miscellanies*. The projected fourth volume is to remain the property of Swift and AP (see 1 July). At this time AP seems to be spending more time in London than he has done for months.

13 Publication of *Pope Alexander's Supremacy and Infallibility Examin'd*. Written in response to *The Dunciad Variorum*, with the usual charges against AP and his poetry, this pamphlet also contains the famous frontispiece with a monkey – AP perched on a column (see *PA*, p. 166).

14   Appearance of *Tom o' Bedlam's Dunciad; or Pope Alexander the Pig. A Poem.*

16   AP has now seen *Pope Alexander's Supremacy*, which is 'so false and scandalous that I think I know the Authors, and they are of a Rank to merit Detection'. He thus asks Lord Oxford to have a man secretly buy a copy from Lintot, and the same man is then to go to James Roberts (the publisher) 'and threaten him, unless he declares the author'. AP suspects Thomas Burnet, George Duckett and 'a Person who has great obligations to me' (could this possibly be Broome?).

30   AP has just had a visit at home from John Caryll, to clear up their earlier misunderstanding over correspondence. AP has given him a *Dunciad*, on which he comments, 'there is such an edifying mixture of roguery in the authors satirised there'. This day AP leaves for a week's visit to Essex (his exact destination is not known).

June
Returning to London from the Edinburgh visit, Gay discovers that his Whitehall lodgings are occupied by another, a result of the *Polly* débâcle. Hereafter he resides with the Queensberrys. Their London residence is in Burlington Gardens; summers are spent first at Middleton Stoney in Oxfordshire in 1729, and afterwards at Amesbury, Wiltshire.

 9   (Mon) Arbuthnot reports to Swift that AP has had an injunction against the printers of a pirated edition of *The Dunciad*, but it is dissolved for lack of proof of property or authorship.

24   Writing to Broome, Fenton reports seeing AP recently in London. He has heard of only two persons writing in defence of AP and *The Dunciad*, and reports that AP in future 'intended to write nothing but epistles in Horace's manner' (*Corr.*, III, 37).

26   The *Evening Post* prints AP's epigram on Burnet and Duckett ('Burnet and Ducket, friends in spite'), which is later incorporated into *The Dunciad*.

July
 1   (Tues) AP pays Motte £25 as an abatement for money due for the three volumes of *Miscellanies* already published. This agreement allows AP to regain publishing-rights to the three

volumes in preparation for publishing a fourth volume (see 8 May).

7 Appearance of Dennis' *Remarks upon Several Passages in the Preliminaries to the Dunciad*, a logical but wrong-headed critical essay, part of which argues that *The Dunciad* is not an epic. On the same day appears Ned Ward's further revenge on AP in *Apollo's Maggot in his Cups*.

8 AP has spent the preceding three weeks reviewing his correspondence from the past twenty years; some of his letters have now been returned to him, and he may be preparing them for deposit in the Harleian Library.

9 AP helping his sister, Mrs Rackett, with investment advice.

20 AP reports to Caryll on problems in the Blount family, including Teresa's alleged 'intrigue' with a married man for the past six months.

August

11 (Mon) Swift writes from Dublin to be remembered to all his and AP's friends, since he is not visiting England this summer. His health is tolerable except for his old complaint of giddiness.

14 AP, having just returned from visiting Lord Oxford (in London?), has been miserably ill with a 'violent Fit of the Headache and Cholick' for the past three days.

26 The *Evening Post* publishes an epigram, probably by AP, 'On J. M. S. Gent.' ('To prove himself no Plagiary, MOORE').

30 Still concerned over the possible loss of reputation in the Blount family, AP urges Caryll to write frankly and forcefully to Teresa Blount.

September

8 (Mon) AP working on revisions to his 'Epitaph on the Monument of the Hon. Robert Digby and of his Sister Mary' (*TE*, vi, 313). Mary Digby had died on 31 March.

13 Writing to Fortescue, AP notes that Gay is now completely in the orbit of the Duchess of Queensberry. AP has met with Walpole once during the past months.

15 AP has been ill, but writes to Lord Oxford at Wimpole to request that he be allowed to deposit some of his letters and manuscripts in the Harleian Library in London; the recent publication of posthumous works by Wycherley (in 1728) has made this request necessary.

October

5 (Sun) After several weeks in France, Bolingbroke returns to Dawley Farm, from where he immediately visits AP.

6 By now it is clear that AP is intending to publish a second volume of Wycherley's posthumous papers, which will include some of AP's letters. He again writes to Lord Oxford for permission to lodge the originals in the Harleian Library.

9 Lord Oxford writes with permission for the AP–Wycherley letters to be kept in his library.

14 About this date, AP is in London, where he dines with the son and daughter-in-law of his friend Mrs Caesar. He is also attending to publishing-business connected with *The Dunciad* and with Wycherley's *Posthumous Works*.

16 Lord Oxford, Lord Burlington, and Lord Bathurst, representing AP who wishes to remain anonymous, formally assign copyright of *The Dunciad* to Lawton Gilliver. AP writes to Lord Oxford on his plans to give reference to the placement of the original letters (in the Harleian Library) in the Preface to his edition of Wycherley's *Posthumous Works*. He is also having other manuscripts transcribed for deposit there.

17 Around this date Lady Mary Wortley Montagu writes twice to Arbuthnot to deny any part in a lampoon (possibly *One Epistle to Mr Pope*, published April 1730). She accuses AP of contriving the whole mess to blast her reputation.

19 AP and his mother both unwell.

23 Appearance of John Roberts' *Answer to Mr Pope's Preface to Shakespear*, which criticises AP's knowledge of the Elizabethan theatre and players.

29 AP writes urgently for Lord Burlington to sign the agreement with Gilliver for the next *Dunciad* edition, as Lords Oxford and Bathurst have already done so. AP has been confined for four days at London and for the past three at home with a cold and fever. He has arranged for a copy of his edition of Wycherley's *Posthumous Works* and the new *Dunciad* edition to be sent to Lord Oxford.

31 Just before this date is published Swift's *Modest Proposal*, his fiercely ironic attack on programmes to improve the chronically bad economic state of Ireland. Swift writes to AP that he has received five copies of *The Dunciad*, not one, but that there is already an octavo edition in Ireland, in advance of the one about to appear in London.

November

2 (Sun) AP sends Lord Burlington the *Dunciad* indenture to be signed, which he does, sending it back (with AP's messenger) with a promise to see AP at Twickenham in the next two days.

4 Publication of the 'Second Volume' of *The Posthumous Works of William Wycherley*, edited by AP; the first volume had been edited by Theobald in 1728. AP's volume contains letters between himself and Wycherley and some early poems. It sold poorly, and AP bought up the unsold copies and held them for future use.

9 Gay expects to return to London (to the Duke of Queensberry's in Burlington Gardens) in a week, having been absent for three months in the country. At this date he is rewriting his comedy *The Wife of Bath*.

13 AP is in London, to visit friends and attend to publishing business.

19 Writing to Swift, Bolingbroke notes that AP is at work on the *Essay on Man*.

20 Atterbury complains directly to AP that he has (in *The Dunciad*) wasted his 'precious moments and great talents on little men and little things'. Writing to Caryll, AP affirms that he will not change his marital status (nor his religion), even in regard to Martha Blount, whom he visits this day.

21 Lawton Gilliver enters the octavo edition of *The Dunciad Variorum* in the registers at Stationers' Hall.

22 AP thanks Lord Oxford for his annual Christmas gift of a collar of brawn, recently received.

26 Gilliver issues the octavo ('second') edition of *The Dunciad Variorum*.

28 AP's year-end summary to Swift includes the notice that both *The Dunciad* and the *Drapier's Letters* are republished of late, that his mother's health decays perceptibly, and that he is working on 'a system of Ethicks in the Horatian way'.

December

12 (Fri) AP has just done a favour for young David Mallet, by sending the manuscript of his tragedy *Eurydice* to Lord Burlington, who will speak to the Lord Chamberlain about it.

21 AP reports to Mallet that the Lord Chamberlain's response to his play has been favourable.

24   AP closes his year's correspondence with a letter
     ('Compliments of this Season') to Lord Oxford.

1730

In a cumulative list compiled in this year of members of the Lodge
of Freemasons (meeting at the Goat Tavern in the Haymarket,
London), AP's name appears. He may have been a Mason since
1726, the year of the visit by Swift, who may also be a member.

January
16   (Fri) Just before this date AP has been in London, trying to
     speak to Lord Burlington in person about David Mallet's
     play. Failing to meet him there, AP has also unsuccessfully
     sought him at home in Chiswick before returning to
     Twickenham.
19   Gay's heavily revised second version of *The Wife of Bath* (the
     first version appeared in 1713) performed at Lincoln's Inn
     Fields, with little success.
22   Lawton Gilliver publishes Edward Young's *Two Epistles to Mr
     Pope, Concerning the Authors of the Age.*
29   AP ill at Twickenham, but plans to see Lord Oxford on
     Monday (1 Feb), in London.

February
 6   (Fri) Swift reports to AP from Dublin that Motte has finally
     paid him for his share of the *Miscellanies.*
 9   Swift's *Libel on D[octor] D[elany] and a Certain Great Lord*
     published; AP is highly praised in ll. 71–110.
12   AP has just returned from a short visit to London. Intending
     to see Caryll at Covent Garden, he has been disappointed. At
     present he is very ill.
20   AP writes to Fortescue, upset over Swift's verses on Dr
     Delany, 'which has done more by praising me than all the
     Libels could by abusing me. . . . I can hardly bring myself to
     think it his, or that it is possible his Head should be so
     giddy.'
26   Swift reports to AP from Dublin that the *Libel* may cause the

printer to be prosecuted and the matter discussed in the
House of Lords.

28 First performance of James Thomson's *Tragedy of Sophonisba,*
with Prologue by AP.

March

 1 (Sun) On or about this date, AP visits Gay, who is staying in
town with the Queensberrys.

 4 AP writes to Swift to request his help in obtaining subscriptions
for Samuel Wesley's commentary on Job, and to complain
ironically about the *Libel*: 'we have here some verses in your
name, which I am angry at. Sure you wou'd not use me so ill
as to flatter me? I therefore think it is some other weak
Irishman.'

12 Publication of James Thomson's *Tragedy of Sophonisba,* with
AP's Prologue ('When learning, after the long *Gothic* night').

22 Fenton reports to Broome that he has heard (a month since)
while in London that AP and Broome have no further
correspondence with each other.

April

 4 (Sat) Aaron Hill's *The Progress of Wit* published, a fantasy
poem which covertly attacks AP for obscenity and malice.

 9 AP writes to Swift to forgive him (jocularly) for praising him
in the *Libel,* and remarks that he might assemble their
correspondence in a volume, perhaps to be published.

21 The *St James's Evening Post* prints the public version of AP's
'Epitaph on Sir Godfrey Kneller', a transcription of the
engraved version just being put up in Westminster Abbey.

24 AP sends directions to the publisher (D. Lewis) that the
'Epitaph on the Monument of . . . Robert Digby' may be
printed if the third and fourth lines are cancelled.

28 Appearance of Leonard Welsted and James Moore Smythe's
One Epistle to Mr A. Pope, a compendium of charges (plagiarism
and libel) against AP and many of his works.

May

At some point during this month, AP makes his first revelation of
what will be the *Essay on Man,* by showing the first fragments of it
(and other projects) to Joseph Spence.

 2 (Sat) As AP's letter of this date shows, he has resumed

correspondence and friendship with Broome after their earlier misunderstanding over *'Peri Bathous'* and *The Odyssey*. AP reveals that he has come across *One Epistle to . . . Pope*, 'a lie' just published about him. He claims that quoting Broome in *'Peri Bathous'* was a case of faulty memory.

3   Death of Arbuthnot's wife.

5   In the publisher David Lewis' *Miscellaneous Poems, by Several Hands* appear AP's Hadrian pieces, 'The Heathen to his Departing Soul' and 'The Dying Christian to his Soul', together with the epitaphs on Elizabeth Corbet and Robert Digby.

18   AP entertains Lord Oxford at Twickenham for lunch. On this same day, AP's friend Lord Burlington is elected a Knight of the Garter.

22   AP sends his formal congratulations to Lord Burlington upon having been elected a Knight of the Garter.

June

2   (Tues) AP 'very sick' at Twickenham.

3   On this day, Arbuthnot allegedly flogs with his cane James Moore Smythe, assumed to be the author of *One Epistle to . . . Pope*.

7   Evidently well again, AP is preparing to entertain a rash of early summer visitors to his villa.

11   An account is given in the *Grub-Street Journal* of Arbuthnot's caning of James Moore Smythe.

14   AP is invited to dine on this day at Sir Robert Walpole's house in London; he asks Fortescue to meet him there.

16   AP writes to Broome with a fulsome repetition of pleasure at resumption of friendship: 'you and I shall never quarrel'. He again reiterates that his inclusion of Broome's work in *'Peri Bathous'* was inadvertent. AP intending to visit young Edward Caryll (John Caryll's third son) and his wife at Whitton, near Twickenham.

25   The *Grub-Street Journal* prints AP's epigram 'On Mr M—re's Going to Law with Mr Gilliver'.

30   On this day appears George Lyttelton's *Epistle to Mr Pope, From a Young Gentleman at Rome*. AP is compared to Virgil, urged to drop satire, and urged to undertake 'thy country's praise' (*CH*, p. 39). Lyttelton (later Lord Lyttelton) is Lord Cobham's nephew.

July

2 (Thurs) A second epigram on Moore Smythe ('A gold watch found on Cinder Whore'), probably by AP, appears in the *Grub-Street Journal*.

6 At the 'Publick Commencement' at Cambridge, AP's rewritten *Ode for Musick on St Cecilia's Day* is given its first performance, with a musical setting by Dr Greene.

13 Death of Fenton, while at Lady Trumbull's home in Easthampstead.

16 Already published in the *Present State of the Republick of Letters* for the month of June, AP's 'Epitaph for Isaac Newton' ('Nature, and Nature's Laws lay hid in Night') appears in the *Grub-Street Journal*.

18 AP preparing to go to Lord Bathurst's place, at Richings, so that he is unable to see Lord Oxford on this day.

22 AP visiting friends in the neighbourhood.

23 AP in London, where he hopes to meet Lord Oxford. The *Grub-Street Journal* publishes a mock 'Epitaph on James Moore Smythe' ('Here lyes what had nor *Birth*, nor *Shape*, nor *Fame*'), probably by AP.

28 AP dines with Edward Caryll. During this summer he often travels about the countryside, for his mother's improved health allows her to be left, but he seldom stays away for more than two days.

30 AP writes to John Knight, having missed him on a recent trip to London; his letter includes his epigram 'When other Ladies to the Groves go down'.

August

1 (Sat) During this month, Matthew Concanen's pamphlet *The Speculist* attacks several of AP's works.

4 Lord Oxford comes down from London to see AP at Twickenham.

17 Broome, writing from Pulham in Dorset, has just recently heard the news of Fenton's death. He urges AP to make a suitable memorial of him in an elegy or epitaph.

18 AP writes to thank Caryll for his gift of a haunch of venison from the Ladyholt stock. His sister, Magdalen Rackett, is staying with him.

22 AP has just been to visit Mrs Howard at Marble Hill in the company of Lord and Lady Burlington.

24 Fortescue is very seriously ill; AP sends a worried note.
29 AP writes to Broome on Fenton's death, including his praise
   for this 'Amiable, quiet, deserving, unpretending, Christian
   & Philosophical character', which he will draw in an epitaph.

September
6 (Sun) Fortescue is now recovered sufficiently to be out of
   danger.
11 Joseph Spence writes to AP to introduce his discovery of the
   'Thresher Poet', Stephen Duck.
27 Death of the Poet Laureate, Laurence Eusden.

October
During this month, perhaps during the first half, AP's mother
almost meets her end. Having fallen asleep in her chair by the
hearth, she falls into the fire, which burns her clothes but not her
body. She recovers gradually from the shock of the fall.
1 (Thurs) For the past few weeks, AP has been putting his
   library in order and enlarging the chimney in it, he tells Gay;
   he is also taking Martha Blount's advice and spending more
   time writing and reading. He has been once to London
   recently, when he went to see Atterbury's son-in-law, just
   going over to visit the exiled Bishop.
8 Lord Bolingbroke is planning to dine with AP at Twickenham
   tomorrow.
22 AP's 'Epitaph on Mr Elijah Fenton' ('This modest Stone what
   few vain Marbles can') appears in its first published version,
   in the *Daily Post-Boy*.
23 AP writes resignedly to Gay on the dismal state of taste in the
   land: 'the whole age seems resolv'd to justify the *Dunciad'*.
   For him Eusden (the late Poet Laureate) represents 'inspiration'
   and Stephen Duck (the 'Thresher Poet') emblematizes 'Pains
   and Labour'.

November
3 (Tues) Lord Oxford has just sent AP and his mother his
   annual gift of a collar of brawn. AP asks Oxford to
   recommend, by letter, the son of his friend William Cleland
   to some of the worthy men of his college; he hopes Oxford's
   Christ Church connections will find a position for the young
   man.

12 The *Grub-Street Journal* publishes an epigram 'On the Candidates for the Laurel' ('Shall Royal praise be rhym'd by such a ribald'), possibly by AP.

16 AP asks Lord Oxford for another favour, this time to help his Catholic nephew (Henry Rackett) gain admission to the bar, without taking the usual religious oath for attorneys.

19 Swift writes to the Duchess of Queensberry and Gay that he has heard in London of AP's being 'at present the cheif poeticall favorite; yet Mr. Pope himself talks like a Philosopher and one wholly retired'. In the *Grub-Street Journal* appears a second epigram on the Laureateship ('Behold! ambitous of the British bays'), probably by AP.

December

2 (Wed) About this date, AP writes to Lord Oxford with thanks for agreeing to assist his nephew. The plan has not succeeded, and Henry Rackett is unable to practise law. AP also notes that he is well at work on the *Essay on Man*: 'it will consist of nothing but such Doctrines as are inoffensive, & consistent with the Truest Divinity and Morality'.

3 Colley Cibber, the actor and playwright, is appointed Poet Laureate, following the death of Eusden in September.

6 AP now writes to Caryll in hopes that he can find Henry Rackett a position as a steward or estate-manager. He also speaks confidently of the *Essay on Man*: 'I have many fragments which I am beginning to put together, but nothing perfect, nor finished; nor in any condition to be shown, except to a friend at a fireside.'

14 AP writes to Broome, enclosing a copy of the 'Epitaph on Mr Elijah Fenton', recounting his mother's narrow escape from the fire, and commenting obliquely thereby on the argument of the *Essay on Man*: 'I think there are many reasons to believe as well a particular as a general providence, and the effect of such a belief is of singular use in our life and conduct.'

17 AP's 'Epitaph on General Henry Withers' ('Here Withers rest! thou bravest, gentlest mind') first appears, in the *Grub-Street Journal*.

18 AP hints in a letter that he projects writing an epistle to Burlington, as a poetic memorial of their friendship.

24 In the *Grub-Street Journal* appears an epigram, possibly by AP, on the Lord Chamberlain's choice of Cibber as Poet Laureate.

29   AP has been away from home for six days, visiting friends.
      He tells David Mallet that *Eurydice* has been shown to the
      Queen, as an excellent play recommended by AP himself. He
      adds that he is 'sorry, not surprised' that Cibber has been
      made the Poet Laureate.

1731

January
7   (Thurs) On this day appears Walter Harte's *Essay on Satire,
      Particularly on the Dunciad*, which praises AP for having taught
      'old Satire nobler fruits to bear, / And check'd her Licence
      with a moral Care' (*CH*, p. 234).
17   AP in London for three days, staying with Lord Peterborough
      in Bolton Street. His mother's health is well enough now for
      her to be left.
18   Aaron Hill sends AP a complimentary two-volume set of the
      Plain Dealer, his periodical, together with a gentle complaint
      about his inclusion in the *Dunciad* footnotes, but says nothing
      about his previous published attacks on AP.
26   AP replies to Hill's compliments and complaint with a peevish
      self-defence in the matter of *The Dunciad*, adding that 'I was
      never angry at any Criticism, made on my Poetry, by
      whomsoever.'
28   Hill replies to AP with a long, tiresome analysis of his
      behaviour and AP's, and indicates that he is preparing a long
      essay on the propriety and impropriety of the design, thought
      and expression of AP's poetry.

February
5   (Fri) AP is visiting Lord Peterborough at his house in Parson's
      Green; while there he writes a very long conciliatory letter to
      Aaron Hill.
6   AP returns home to Twickenham.
9   *An Epistle to Mr Pope, on Reading his Translations of the Iliad and
      Odyssey* (by Walter Harte?) argues that AP was not qualified
      to translate Homer but did so for money and praise.
10   Hill responds fervently (and politely) to AP's conciliatory
      letter of the 5th. Lord Burlington is visiting AP at home.
11   AP has been suffering violent rheumatic pain in his left arm,
      and so must postpone seeing Lord Oxford in London.

15   AP's rheumatic pain now gone, and he is able to thank Hill
      for the generous statements about him in Hill's *Advice to the
      Poets*, which will soon be printed.

25   AP again suffering from severe rheumatic pain in his arm and
      unable to write.

March

5   (Fri) Gay and Lord Oxford dine with AP at Twickenham.
      Lord Oxford returns to London the same evening.

13   Intending to stay with Lord Oxford in Dover Street, London,
      AP is unable to find a convenient vehicle to take him to town.
      Instead he intends to be there in two days' time.

19   Recovered from his rheumatic attack, AP is in London, where
      he dines with Lord Oxford, Lord Bathurst, Jacob Tonson (the
      elder) and Gay.

20   With Bolingbroke, AP writes to Swift about their recent
      activities. AP is undertaking a cure for his medical problems
      which includes asses' milk, plenty of rest and no study or
      exercise. He urges Swift to help with the subscription for
      Nathaniel Hooke's *Roman History*.

26   First recorded public performance of Gay's pastoral
      entertainment *Acis and Galatea*, with musical score by Handel,
      at Lincoln's Inn Fields. Gay had probably known Handel
      since 1713; they collaborated on the earliest version of *Acis* for
      the Duke of Chandos, performed privately in 1718.

April

3   (Sat) AP back at home (and ill) after a visit to Lord Oxford in
      London. While there he has been making transcripts of letters
      and organising his correspondence (and others'). He has
      apparently also been ill while staying in London.

4   From Twickenham, AP sends Lord Burlington a manuscript
      copy of his *Epistle to Burlington, Of Taste*, suggesting that it
      could be prefixed to Burlington's folio of Palladio's architectural
      designs. He also asks Burlington not to show the poem to
      anyone, as he will continue to revise it.

20   Swift sends a long summary letter to AP on health matters,
      his wish to visit England again, and his failure to get
      subscribers for Hooke's *Roman History*, since AP has given
      him insufficient details about it.

22   AP sends a poem (the *Epistle to Burlington*?) to be transcribed

by Lord Oxford's amanuensis. He is still continuing his regimen of asses' milk.

27 AP invites Lord Oxford to dine on 2 May, so that they may look over some of his recent work. AP has also recently dined in London with Lord Oxford.

May

During the first three weeks of this month, AP is staying with Lord Bolingbroke at Dawley Farm so that he can continue his consumption of asses' milk. He makes a few day visits home to check on his mother, and at least one visit to London.

1 (Sat) AP asks Fortescue to act as trustee in some financial affairs of his sister's estate. He writes also to Hugh Bethel, who is travelling to Yorkshire.

5 AP is unable to entertain Lord Oxford at home this day, but suggests that tomorrow would be better.

13 AP has just arrived back at Twickenham after being in London, and has narrowly missed seeing Broome.

June

During this month AP's friend Mrs Howard becomes the Countess of Suffolk, when her husband succeeds his brother to the earldom.

1 (Tues) AP expects to visit Lord Burlington at Chiswick, but Burlington's coach cannot be sent to fetch him and he must postpone the visit.

2 AP in London this day and the next.

5 AP has been reading the manuscript of Aaron Hill's tragedy *Athelwold*, which he returns with general praise and a few suggested revisions.

15 AP seems to have been at Dawley Farm for a few days just prior to this date.

20 About this time, AP is trying to get David Mallet placed as tutor to his friend John Knight's step-son.

22 Writing in the *Hyp-Doctor* no. 29, 'Orator' Henley attacks *The Dunciad* as a revenge on Theobald: AP 'wrote [it] to blacken all that knew he was prov'd an *Ignoramus*, that is, all Mankind'.

29 Swift writes (unhappily) to Gay to announce the return of a lawsuit, and his old complaint of giddiness, which will prevent him from visiting England, as he seems about to have done.

July
During this month, AP spends part of his time visiting friends in the country. He makes a visit to John Knight at Gosfield, north-west of Colchester. The *Gentleman's Magazine* for this month prints AP's epigram 'On Dennis' ('Shou'd D——s print how once you robb'd your Brother').

28 (Wed) AP writes to Hugh Bethel that he has 'just finished an Epistle in Verse, upon the Nature & Extent of Good nature & Social affection; & am going upon another whose subject is, The True Happiness of Man . . . you should pull off your hat to me, for painting You as the happiest man in the Universe'. Thus AP has just finished epistle III of the *Essay on Man*, and is working on the fourth; Bethel is praised in IV, 123–30. AP's friend, William Cleland, has just stayed with him for two days.

August
2 (Mon) In a very long letter to Swift, Bolingbroke discourses on the progress of AP's *Essay on Man* (three epistles complete) but also explains that the poem is only the first part of a much larger project for moral poetry. Bolingbroke writes with pride of his and AP's strength in the face of 'volumes of scurrility' (*Corr.*, III, 214).

15 AP visiting Lord Cobham at Stowe, in company with Brigadier James Dormer; he plans to return to London in two days' time.

23 AP still with Lord Cobham at Stowe. He is about to move on to Lord Peterborough's house at Southampton and to Dormer's at Rousham, Oxfordshire.

30 AP has recently returned from visiting Lord Oxford at Down Hall. He writes to return a borrowed book and a copy of Persius' *Satires*.

September
1 (Wed) Back at home, AP has just read, and now returns, David Mallet's epitaph on William Aikman, with praise for his restraint: 'the best way I know is to be very modest & reserved in the Commendation that it may be believed not to be *Hired*, or not to be *Partial*'. AP also writes to Aaron Hill with sympathy at the death of his wife, Miranda. AP has been promoting Hill's *Athelwold* at Drury Lane.

2 AP attempting to assist his sister in the complex legal arrangements for renting the Racketts' house at Hallgrove, now that Magdalen Rackett lives in Bloomsbury with her son Henry.

3 AP's mother now very ill; he fears she is on her deathbed, and thus he cannot entertain friends. In a letter to Hill, he encloses a version of the final lines of the *Epistle to Dr Arbuthnot*, sections of which he has begun working upon.

8 Gay visiting AP at Twickenham. AP writes to Hugh Bethel that he is adding more characters and facts to the *Essay on Man* (epistle IV), and reminds him that he has seen a preliminary part of the *Epistle to Bathurst* (to become the third of the *Moral Essays*), where AP celebrates the 'Man of Ross' (ll. 249–84).

25 AP invites Aaron Hill and his daughter to visit him at Twickenham. AP has again been supporting Hill's tragedy amongst his friends.

October
During this month, Gay is staying both at Twickenham and at Dawley Farm, so that he can see both AP and Bolingbroke.

3 (Sun) AP sends Jonathan Richardson an edition of Milton, and agrees to look over the latter's notes on *Paradise Lost* (published as *Explanatory Notes and Remarks on Paradise Lost* in 1734).

4 It is now too late for Hill to visit AP, who has been ill. The *Essay on Man* he is still revising, and he has no thought of publishing it yet. AP also intends to show Hill's *Athelwold* to two celebrated actors, Mr Booth and Mrs Porter.

8 William Cleland staying with AP at Twickenham.

28 Lewis Theobald and Jacob Tonson, Jr, sign articles of agreement to publish Theobald's edition of Shakespeare.

29 Hill sends AP a revised manuscript of *Athelwold*, with added scenes and announces that it will be performed before Christmas. AP has arranged for the Countess of Suffolk to receive the play.

30 Hill sends a copy of his tragedy to the Countess of Suffolk.

November
1 (Mon) AP visiting Lord Burlington at Chiswick. He recommends Lawton Gilliver to Hill as publisher of *Athelwold*; Gilliver eventually brings out the play.

2 AP engaged to dine with the three defence attorneys in the *Craftsman* libel trial which results from Bolingbroke's piece on 2 January, but he is ill. He arranges for Jonathan Richardson to send him the *Paradise Lost* notes in exchange for the Milton edition.

7 AP reports to Lord Oxford on the fire in the Cotton Library, in the Earl of Ashburnham's house, pretending to blame Richard Bentley. He notes obliquely that he has included a compliment to Oxford in the *Epistle to Burlington* (ll. 243–8).

9 At this time, negotiations are beginning for AP to write an epitaph for the sixth Earl of Dorset (who died in 1706). It is eventually published ('Dorset, the Grace of Courts, the Muses Pride') in 1735.

11 The *Grub-Street Journal* reprints a *Daily Journal* item announcing Theobald's edition of Shakespeare's plays, to be published by Jacob Tonson, Jr, in six octavo volumes. AP writes to Tonson to warn against including personal attacks on him in Theobald's edition.

13 Tonson explains the Theobald Shakespeare edition to AP.

14 AP writes back to Tonson, reiterating his concern about personal comments by Theobald, and about damage to sales of the second edition of AP's own *Works of Shakespear*. He also writes to Jacob Tonson, Sr, with similar concerns, and with a request for specific information on the 'Man of Ross', which will go in the *Epistle to Bathurst*. AP has been reading Gilbert West's poem *Stowe: The Gardens of the . . . Viscount Cobham*, which West has dedicated to AP.

19 AP in London, and visits Lord and Lady Oxford, where he discovers that Lady Margaret (their daughter) has been extremely ill. He has just received his annual gift from them of a collar of brawn.

23 Atterbury writes to AP to justify his *Vindication . . . Relating to . . . Lord Clarendon's History*, enclosing a copy each for him and Swift. This is Atterbury's last extant letter to AP.

December

1 (Wed) AP ill with constant headaches, which he endures. Gay is staying with him at this time. In Dublin, Swift is now writing *Verses on the Death of Dr Swift*, in which he mentions AP.

2 Publication of Atterbury's *Vindication . . . Relating to the*

Publication of Lord Clarendon's History in an English translation (originally published in France) is announced in the *London Evening Post*.

9   AP writes to tell Aaron Hill that he will attend the first performance of his play, together with Gay, Lord Bathurst and Lord Burlington.

10 Aaron Hill's *Athelwold* first performed. It closes after three performances.

11 AP writes to Hill with praise for *Athelwold*, which he prefers to read rather than see. He asks Hill to get a box at the theatre for Martha Blount. Today he leaves London to attend to his mother, who is taken ill again.

14 Lawton Gilliver issues AP's *Epistle to the Right Honourable Richard Earl of Burlington*, the first published but eventually to be the fourth of the *Moral Essays*. The original title reads *Of Taste*, but this is subsequently changed to *Of False Taste* in the second edition.

16 A letter appears in the *Daily Post-Boy* strangely defending AP's *Epistle to Burlington* as non-personal satire and disavowing any connection (as in current rumours) between the satire on Timon's villa and the character of the Duke of Chandos. Although the letter is later attributed to William Cleland, AP is probably the author.

17 Hill writes to AP praising the *Epistle to Burlington*, suggesting *Of False Taste* as an appropriate title.

21 Since his return home from London ten days ago, AP has been confined at home by his mother's illness, and claims just to have heard of the uproar following publication of the *Epistle to Burlington*. He writes to Lord Burlington to refute the Chandos–Timon connection: 'nothing is so evident, to any one who can read the Language, either of English or Poetry, as that Character of Timon is collected from twenty different absurditys & Improprieties: & was never the Picture of any one Human Creature'.

22 AP writes to Hill, having just read his *Athelwold* for a sixth time. He also again defends his sincere intentions in the *Epistle to Burlington*: 'I lament the Malice of the Age, that studies to see its own Likeness in every thing; I lament the Dulness of it, that cannot see an Excellence.'

23 The *Grub-Street Journal* advertises Lawton Gilliver's publication of *A Collection of Pieces in Verse and Prose . . . on the Occasion of*

the Dunciad (edited by Richard Savage and AP?); this is a collection of unsold sheets for several complimentary works.

24 Hill has just read 'Cleland's' letter in the *Daily Post-Boy*; he admits to AP that he too has connected Chandos with Timon in the *Epistle*.

27 James Brydges, Duke of Chandos, writes to AP. He is troubled by the town's reading of the satire on Timon's villa in the *Epistle to Burlington* as upon his seat at Cannons, but absolutely absolves AP of blame.

1732

During this year, AP is confined to the villa at Twickenham, both by his literary work and the deteriorating health of his mother, except for day trips to London and the neighbourhood.

January
During the first ten days of this month, Gilliver issues the second edition (*Of False Taste*) of the *Epistle to Burlington*, and the dunces' campaign against AP begins to heat up. Also published during this month is Richard Bentley's edition of Milton's *Paradise Lost*, with his extensive revisions and cuts.

 3 (Mon) Prompted by the *Epistle to Burlington*, Leonard Welsted issues *Of Dulness and Scandal. Occasion'd by the Characters of Lord Timon*, which charges AP with ingratitude, writing in a 'self-applauding Strain', and satirising the Duke of Chandos.

15 Matthew Concanen's pamphlet *A Miscellany on Taste* published, with the usual charges against AP. This collection also contains important notes on the *Epistle to Burlington* and a satirical frontispiece in which AP is shown whitewashing the gateway of Burlington's house.

18 AP visiting Gay in London, to consult with Burlington on the repair of the Dublin monument to Burlington's ancestor (the first Earl of Cork) in St Patrick's.

20 Third edition of the *Epistle to Burlington* published. AP adds to it a formal letter to Burlington emphasising that the Timon character is a general one. The title has now become *Of False Taste*.

22 Lines from the 'Sporus' portrait (to appear in the *Epistle to Dr Arbuthnot* in 1735) appear in the *London Evening Post*. Yet

another hack attack from Grub Street appears: *Of Good Nature*
vilifies AP's supposed ingratitude to the Duke of Chandos.
AP informs Lord Oxford that the fuss over the *Epistle to
Burlington* has caused him to suppress the publication of
what will be the *Epistle to Bathurst*. Also in the *London Evening
Post*, AP's verses 'Horace, Satyr 4. Lib. I. Paraphrased' ('The
Fop*, whose Pride affects a *Patron*'s name') appear. These lines
are later revised and incorporated into the *Epistle to Dr
Arbuthnot* (ll. 291–304).

February
During this month, Fortesque visits AP at Twickenham, then
takes AP to London, and is having one of the epistles of the *Essay
on Man* transcribed in a fair copy. In town AP obtains another
edition of Milton for Jonathan Richardson, and Jacob Tonson, Jr,
shows him Bentley's edition (with extensive notes) of Milton.

3   (Thurs) Another of Leonard Welsted's poem attacks on AP
    published: *Of False Fame* claims that AP favours fraud and
    libel, and that his reputation is undeserved.
5   AP has just received a translation by Dr William Cowper of
    the 'Elegy to the Memory of an Unfortunate Lady' into Latin
    hexameters; AP thanks Cowper, and recommends 'Eloisa to
    Abelard' as a subject, 'since it has more of that Descriptive, &
    . . . Enthusiastic Spirit, which is the Character of the Ancient
    Poets.' He also writes to Hill to say that following Hill's hint
    he has changed the *Epistle to Burlington*'s title to *Of False Taste* in
    the second edition.
8   Publication of an attack *On P[ope] and W[elsted]. Occasion'd by
    their Late Writings*.

March
During this month, Gay visits AP at Twickenham. Fortescue's
amanuensis is transcribing epistle III of the *Essay on Man*.

4   (Sat) Death of Atterbury, sometime Bishop of Rochester, in
    exile in France.
13 Gay back in London, where AP, in good health, is visiting
    him. While there, AP suffers from a fever, but recovers well
    after four days at Lord Oxford's house.
16 AP, back at home, commiserates with Lord Oxford over the
    news of Bishop Atterbury's death, which he has recently
    heard.

29 Writing to Caryll, AP is still worried about the Chandos–
Timon controversy: 'I don't yet now the effect it will have on
my conduct, – whether so great a stupidity . . . should give
me such a pique to the world's malice, as to never publish
anything, or such a contempt of its judgment as to publish
everything. . . .' He is also still worried about the condition
and conduct of the Blount sisters.

April
During this month, AP makes at least one visit to London, staying
alone in Lord Oxford's house, as the Harleys are at Down Hall.
His mother's health prevents long absences from Twickenham.
5 (Wed) *Mr Taste, The Poetical Fop* published, a comedy possibly
by Eliza Heywood. The play is founded on AP's rejection by
Lady Mary Wortley Montagu (Alexander Taste and Lady
Airey), with much venom shed on AP's works; the Homer
translation is a 'Piece of Patch-Work . . . an inhuman Murder
committed upon the Prince of Poets, and the *Greek* Tongue'.
29 Atterbury's body and personal effects are landed at Deal, in
Kent. His papers are immediately seized and examined by
customs officers, but nothing of a Jacobite nature is found.

May
During this month, AP makes at least one visit to London,
spending two days there. He misses meeting Fortescue, Lord
Peterborough (at Parson's Green), and Lord Burlington (at
Chiswick). He is also conducting some investment business for
Martha Blount.
4 (Thurs) AP expecting a visit from Caryll at home.
17 Gay heading off to Amesbury with the Queensberrys. He is
just now working on a second collection of *Fables*, and is
thinking about another dramatic work (possibly *Achilles*).
20 AP now at Whitton, visiting Edward Caryll.
23 Atterbury's body finally buried in the family vault at
Westminster Abbey, with only his son-in-law and two former
chaplains in attendance.

June
7 (Wed) Still working on revisions to the 'Man of Ross' portrait,
AP thanks Jacob Tonson, Sr, for verifying details of the life.
In light of the Chandos–Timon uproar, he has no present

thoughts of publication, and will possibly wait until the *Epistle* is accompanied by others. Within the last week AP has sent a portrait of himself (by Michael Dahl, 1727) to Tonson's nephew.

12　Writing from Dublin, Swift lists his works for which AP has asked for a fourth volume (the 'Third') of *Miscellanies*, to be published in October. He recommends to AP a young clergyman named Matthew Pilkington, who is desirous of seeing AP in person.

16　AP arranging the legal niceties for allowing some of his copper-type ornaments, initials and tailpieces from the Homer translations (designed by William Kent) to be used in Samuel Buckley's edition of Thuanus (published in Oct).

July

9　(Sun) In a week's time (about the 16th to the 22nd) AP expects to entertain William Cleland and his wife. Lord Bathurst has just sent AP a haunch of venison.

10　Swift, having contemplated yet another possible visit to England (dividing his time between Amesbury, Dawley Farm and Twickenham), is forced by illness to stay in Ireland.

20　Lord Bathurst invites AP to meet him at Oxford and travel back to Cirencester with him, to stay for a week. He also sends a 'half a buck' (of venison) for AP's use in entertaining the Clelands.

24　AP now preparing some of his and Swift's materials for the October volume (the 'Third') of the *Miscellanies*.

28　AP plans to see Lord Burlington tomorrow, but is obliged to see Lady Bolingbroke at Dawley instead. By letter he asks Burlington's help in obtaining some of Henry Savile's (Marquess of Halifax) papers.

August

16　(Wed) In the midst of tangled negotiations for the publication of the 'Third' volume of *Miscellanies* AP grants Motte a share of the book with Lawton Gilliver.

28　Gay informs Swift of the current tangled state of publishing-rights for the 'Third' volume of the *Miscellanies*.

September

19　(Tues) AP writes to Lord Burlington to compliment him on

his new Assembly Room at York. AP is working (for a proposed edition?) on the papers of Henry Savile, Marquess of Halifax, who was Lady Burlington's grandfather, together with the papers of her father, the second Marquess. Together, William Kent and AP have designed a new portico and basement waterfall for the Twickenham house, and are now putting it into real terms. AP has just finished writing his occasional poem 'On the Countess of B[urlington] Cutting Paper'.

22 AP has recently spent four days in London, in part with Lord Oxford, who has just left for the country. On this day he sends him a manuscript copy of the *Epistle to Bathurst*, which contains lines praising Lord Oxford (ll. 243–8).

27 AP informs Caryll of his publishing- and writing-programme, all directed 'to a good end, the advancement of moral and religious vertue, and the discouragement of vicious and corrupt hearts'. He expects to publish the *Epistle to Bathurst* next winter: 'I shall make living examples, which inforce best, and consequently put you once more upon the defence of your friend against the roar and calumny, which I expect, and am ready to suffer in so good a cause.' The death of Robert Wilks on this day leaves Colley Cibber 'absolute and perpetual dictator of the stage' at Drury Lane.

October

2 (Mon) AP informs Gay that the 'Third' volume of the *Miscellanies* is now publishing, 'which concludes all our fooleries of that kind'. He urges Gay to write some flattering verses on the Queen to re-establish himself at court.

4 Motte issues *Miscellanies. The Third Volume*, containing several prose pieces and some minor poems and epigrams by AP. Although designated the 'Third', it is in fact the fourth volume, as the so-called 'Last Volume' (8 Mar 1728) had been third in the series.

7 Gay now back in Amesbury after a visit to Somerset. In his last extant letter to AP he rejects AP's suggestion that he write panegyric verse to restore his standing at court.

17 AP has come to London (to Lord Oxford's in Dover Street), where he expects to meet Matthew Pilkington, a young friend of Swift's. Instead Pilkington has gone by mistake to Twickenham. Pilkington, acting in Swift's interest, has

conducted negotiations for the 'Third' volume of *Miscellanies* with the printer Bowyer, despite the fact that Motte and Gilliver have already printed the volume.

23　Lord Oxford, just returned from a ramble in Norfolk, writes humbly to thank AP on his inclusion in the *Epistle to Bathurst*.

November

2　(Thurs) AP informs Jonathan Richardson of Mallet's satirical poem *Of Verbal Criticism*, which Mallet inscribes to AP, without permission, although AP praises it.

3　Lord Lansdowne has just ordered to be sent to AP the second volume of his *Genuine Works in Verse and Prose*, together with an attack on Lansdowne by one of the dunces. He asks AP to provide an honest critique of his play *Once a Lover*.

6　AP writes to Lord Burlington about his work on Lady Burlington's family papers, suggesting the arrangement of possible volumes. AP has recently written a 'Dialogue' about the architectural work of William Kent, which Kent has kept completely secret; it is now not extant.

7　AP has missed seeing Mallet in London recently, but writes to praise his satire *Of Verbal Criticism*.

24　AP tries through the influence of Lord Burlington to get the living of Barrowby (in Lincolnshire) for Walter Harte, his young poet friend.

30　Burlington cannot help with the living for Harte; he informs AP that another priest has already been appointed to it.

December

1　(Fri) On this day AP contracts with Lawton Gilliver to publish the *Ethick Epistles and Imitations of Horace*. AP acknowledges Lord Oxford's annual gift of a collar of brawn and states that he expects to publish the *Epistle to Bathurst* at Christmastime (it appears on 15 Jan).

4　Death of Gay, at the Queensberrys' house in Burlington Gardens, London, attended by Arbuthnot and two other physicians. AP may also be present.

5　AP sadly informs Swift of Gay's death, in which 'one of the nearest and longest tyes I have ever had, is broken all on a sudden'. AP fears he will never see Swift again, without Gay's friendship to bring him out from Ireland.

6 AP writes to Martha Blount about Gay's death, which now provokes for him the fear of his mother's demise.

14 AP tells Caryll that the *Epistle to Bathurst* is in press but retarded by various accidents. AP comments on Gay's posthumous papers and the play *Achilles*, which had just been accepted for performance. He notes that Martha Blount had been taken ill immediately upon learning of Gay's death. AP is now back at home, after several days in London.

23 Gay buried in Westminster Abbey, after lying in state at Exeter Exchange in the Strand. The pall-bearers include AP, the Earl of Chesterfield and General Dormer.

1733

January

13 (Sat) AP sends back some of the Savile papers to Lady Burlington, with suggestions for her to follow in assembling publishable volumes. He has just received from her a painting (by her?) for the new room in his villa.

15 AP's third (second to appear) *Moral Essay, Of the Use of Riches, An Epistle to the Right Honorable Allen Lord Bathurst*, is published this day. Soon after, AP sends a copy to Caryll, saying, 'it is not the worst I have written, and abounds in moral example, for which reason it must be obnoxious in this age. God send it does any good! I really mean nothing else by writing at this time of my life.' Later Swift informs AP that an Irish edition is published, and wishes that he had had the opportunity to fill in the blanks for specific names which the Irish printer has left.

16 Aaron Hill, to whom AP has also sent a copy of the *Epistle*, writes back with thanks and a barbed praise.

31 AP has just returned home from ten days in London. While staying at Lord Oxford's, he has suffered a severe fever; while AP is recovering, Lord Bolingbroke visits and suggests he write a parody of Horace's first satire of the second book, which he does in two days. AP now writes to Caryll to predict the satire's imminent publication, to solicit a position (through Caryll's influence) for his attorney nephew Henry Rackett, and to request that Caryll send him some venison.

February

5 (Mon) AP has just read (in manuscript) Robert Dodsley's play
   The Toy Shop, which he pronounces more suitable for the
   reader than for the stage. Nevertheless, he will recommend it
   to John Rich, manager of the Covent Garden theatre. (The
   play is first performed in February 1735.) Curll publishes an
   unauthorised *Life of Mr Gay*; amongst other references to AP
   he advertises that a *Life of Pope* is preparing for the press.

10 Gay's third ballad opera, *Achilles*, produced posthumously at
   Covent Garden. The 'Prologue. Written by Mr Gay' is
   probably by AP (see Ault, p. 207). The play has nineteen
   performances in its first season. The text is published on 1
   March.

15 AP's earliest Horatian imitation, written at the suggestion of
   Lord Bolingbroke, appears on this day. The full title includes
   his own name but not Fortescue's: *The First Satire of the Second
   Book of Horace, Imitated in a Dialogue between Alexander Pope of
   Twickenham . . . and his Learned Council. . . .*

16 In a long letter to Swift, AP speaks of the disposition of Gay's
   posthumous writings (in the hands of the Duke of
   Queensberry), and sends his inscription for Gay's tomb,
   which Queensberry is erecting in Westminster Abbey. AP
   also speaks of the recently published satire from Horace
   (which he has sent to Swift with the *Epistle to Bathurst*), which
   he claims to have written in two mornings, upon the
   suggestion of Bolingbroke, while he is ill in London in late
   January. AP also includes a very brief account of the moral
   scheme of the epistles, and the information that he has
   completed a draft of the *Epistle to a Lady*. His mother is now
   very much diminished in capacity, which confines him mostly
   to home.

18 AP writes to Jonathan Richardson asking him to conceal his
   authorship of the *Essay on Man*, the first epistle of which will
   appear two days later. On the same day he writes to Fortescue
   about the *Horace* imitation recently published: 'I fancy it will
   make you smile, but though when I first began it, I thought
   of you; before I came to end it, I considered it might be too
   ludicrous, to a man of your situation and grave acquaintance,
   to make you Trebatius. . . .'

20 On this day appears AP's *Essay on Man. Address'd to a Friend.*
   Part I, published in folio anonymously under the imprint of

John Wilford, a printer used by AP here for the first time. AP retains the copyright. Several variant issues of part I of the poem are published on and shortly after this date.

March
1 (Thurs) Publication of James Bramston's *The Man of Taste. Occasion'd by an Epistle of Mr Pope's*. Gay's opera, *Achilles*, published in book form. The Prologue is probably by AP.
2 AP now back at Twickenham after three days in the country near Windsor and some four days in London, where he stays at Lord Oxford's house. While there he has a chance to see the contrast between public reception of the *Essay on Man* and that of the *Horace* imitation: 'a glut of praise succeeds to a glut of reproach'. *Achilles Dissected*, published this day, claims that AP and friends finished *Achilles* after Gay's death and have overloaded it with obscenity. Also appearing is *The First Satire of the Second Book of Horace, Imitated in a Dialogue between Mr Pope and the Ordinary of Newgate . . . by Mr Burnet* (possibly by Curll?).
6 *The Sequel of Mr Pope's Law Case; or Further Advice Thereon* is advertised; this may be the satire in which AP's friend Nathaniel Pigott is abused as the 'Learned Council' (in *The First Satire of the Second Book of Horace*) and to which AP refers in his letter to Fortesque of the 8th.
8 AP now engaged in having the new Palladian portico built onto his house. He writes to Caryll on the recent reception of his works, including the *Horace* imitation, 'which has met with such a flood of favour that my ears need no more flattery this twelvemonth'. He goes on to write, concealing his authorship, that 'the town is now very full of a new poem intitled *an Essay on Man*, attributed, I think with reason, to a divine. It has merit in my opinion but not so much as they give it.' On the same day appear advertisements of Lady Mary Wortley Montagu's attack on AP, published on the 9th. AP sees them and informs Fortescue that she has fulfilled his prophecy in *The First Satire of the Second Book of Horace*, ll. 83–4. To Fortescue too AP speaks of the *Essay on Man* as if by another: 'in many places it is Sett up as a Piece for excelling any thing of mine, & commended, I think more in opposition to Me, than in their real Judgment it deserves'.
9 On this day appears *Verses Address'd to the Imitator of the First*

Satire of the Second Book of Horace, the famous vituperative attack on AP by Lady Mary Wortley Montagu and Lord Hervey. AP is charged with being a 'dull Copist', a 'wretched little Carcass', with 'the Emblem of thy crooked Mind, / Mark'd on thy Back, like *Cain*, by God's own Hand'.

12   Unaware of AP's authorship, Leonard Welsted writes to praise the anonymous poet of the *Essay on Man*. AP eventually reproduces the letter in the 1743 *Dunciad*.

18   Writing to Fortescue, AP begs his 'absolute and inviolable Silence' on the authorship of the *Essay on Man*, of which the second epistle will appear on the 29th. He claims also that he will never reply to Lady Mary Wortley Montagu's libel on him. AP is still at Twickenham, seeing to the final touches on the new portico for his house. He expects to see Mallet in town in four or five days, and asks Mallet to postpone publishing his *Of Verbal Criticism*, for fear of prejudicing the benefit night of Theobald's play *The Fatal Secret*. And he also asks Mallet to give a little more money to John Dennis, who is in straitened circumstances.

20   AP still finishing work on his new portico, which he expects will be ready in three weeks. He has just written, in about two days, another Horatian satire, probably *The Second Satire of the Second Book of Horace* (published July 1734).

21   AP going into London on non-poetical business.

23   AP assigns copyright for one year only to Lawton Gilliver for the first three parts of the *Essay on Man*; the first part has appeared on 20 February.

24   Publication of Bezaleel Morrice's *On the English Translations of Homer. A Satire* (reprinted and revised from 1721).

29   Appearance in folio format of *An Essay on Man. In Epistles to a Friend. Epistle II*, again without AP's name, under the imprint of John Wilford. Variant issues are quickly published and selections from the epistle appear in the *Gentleman's Magazine* for April.

30   On this day appears the anonymous poetic *Epistle to the Little Satyrist of Twickenham*, which argues that AP's writing of satire insults his early genius.

31   Swift writes to AP from Dublin with advice about the management of Gay's estate and posthumous writings; he wishes that *Achilles* (lately published in Ireland) had not appeared, as it does Gay's reputation harm. He reports on

the reception of *The First Satire of the Second Book* in Ireland: 'the work of two mornings, is reconed here . . . to be worth 2 years of any Poets life except yours'. Swift is planning a visit to England starting in August and lasting through the winter to the spring, when he says he will take AP back to Dublin with him.

April

3 (Tues) Anonymous publication of *A Proper Reply to a Lady* [Mary Wortley Montagu], *Occasion'd by her Verses Address'd to the Imitator of the First Satire of the Second Book of Horace*, another shot in the AP–Montagu–Hervey controversy.

10 Under fire from all sides, and widely satirised and petitioned, Walpole withdraws his Excise Scheme from consideration in Parliament.

12 Appearance of David Mallet's *Of Verbal Criticism: An Epistle to Mr Pope*, his response to Theobald's Shakespeare.

13 Publication of the anonymous *Advice to Sappho*, yet another pamphlet poem on the AP–Montagu–Hervey dispute.

17 The *London Evening Post* advertises that the third part of the *Essay on Man* is published this day, although it does not appear to have been issued until later in the month or possibly in May.

18 Publication of Bezaleel Morrice's *Essay on the Universe: A Poem*, in which he ecstatically greets the appearance of the *Essay on Man*, not knowing it to be by AP.

20 About this date, AP responds to Swift's letter of 31 March, commenting on Lord Hervey's and Lady Mary's recent libel and on their standing as court wits. He notes that he has finished writing his *Second Satire of the Second Book of Horace*; he has said the same thing to Caryll on 20 March. And he tells Swift that Gay's papers are partly in his hands, and he will attempt to maintain Gay's reputation by publishing judiciously from them.

May

1 (Tues) Swift writes to AP about an unauthorised London edition of a poem called *The Life and Character of Dr S. Written by Himself*, which has reached him in Dublin. He wants AP to tell all his friends that it is a spurious piece, not by him. Swift

is still worried over the disposition of Gay's posthumous writings and wishes AP to be more active in the matter.

8　According to Mack (*TE*, III, i, 3), the *Daily Journal* advertises that epistle III of the *Essay on Man* is published this day.

10　Published this day, Giles Jacob's *The Mirror: Or, Letters Satyrical, Panegyrical, Serious and Humorous* accuses AP of abusing all his contemporaries in *The Dunciad*.

12　The *Essay on Man* praised in the *Weekly Miscellany* as throughout 'equally beautiful and noble'.

16　Hill writes to AP with belated thanks for the author's presentation copy of *The First Satire of the Second Book of Horace*; he also inquires about the theatre patent, which has passed from Davenant ultimately to John Rich.

17　Griffith (I, 242) gives this date for the publication of epistle III of *An Essay on Man*, again anonymously issued from the press of John Wilford. Variant issues of this epistle and the first two continue to flow from the press.

22　AP promises to find out about the Davenant patent for Hill.

28　AP thanks Swift for conveying Lord Orrery's praise of his 'Epitaph on Mr Gay', given by a man of virtue. AP has received from the printer the spurious *Life and Character* of Swift, with its dedication to AP, about which AP has been misled.

29　*Ingratitude: To Mr Pope*, published this day, repeats the AP–Chandos story in familiar terms of abuse: the satire is a 'Scandalous Libel . . . with all the Malice and Virulency imaginable to Defame and render Odious the Character of his best Benefactor'.

31　Publication of *Mr Taste's Tour from the Island of Politeness, to that of Dulness and Scandal*, as if by AP but by an anonymous hack who is taking advantage of the Chandos controversy. On this same day appears *The Neuter*, a satirical poem dedicated to Lady Mary Wortley Montagu, which attacks AP for stooping to the methods of Grub Street in *The Dunciad*.

June

In the *Gentleman's Magazine* for this month appears the first printing of the first version of AP's 'Epitaph of Gay' (beginning 'A manly wit . . .').

2　(Sat) AP has just had a visit at Twickenham from John Caryll and has been in London for two days. Sir Clement Cottrell, a

Twickenham neighbour, is visiting him at the moment. AP's mother is now very much diminished in her faculties, and getting worse.

7 Death of AP's mother at age 91, after a very long decline of health. AP is upset but resigned to this: 'all our Passions are Inconsistencies, & our very Reason is no better. But we are what we were Made to be' (*Corr.*, III, 374). On this day appears Paul Whitehead's *The State Dunces: Inscrib'd to Mr Pope*.

10 AP asks Jonathan Richardson to provide a death portrait of his mother: 'there is yet upon her countenance such an expression of Tranquillity, nay almost of pleasure, that far from horrid, it is even amiable to behold it. It wou'd afford the finest Image of a Saint expir'd, that ever Painting drew.'

11 In the evening, AP's mother is buried in the Twickenham parish church; pall-bearers are six of the poorest and oldest women in the parish, with a like number of men to carry the coffin. Many of AP's friends attend the funeral.

16 AP's mother's funeral reported at length in the *Universal Spectator*.

23 AP's authorship of the *Essay on Man* publicly revealed in a short anonymous poem in the *Weekly Miscellany*. AP himself does not put his name to the poem until publication of volume II of his *Works* in 1735.

25 AP now more troubled than he would admit by his mother's death. He is settling his affairs and plans to be away from Twickenham to recover: 'as it is a great and New Æra of my life, I must pause awhile to look about me' (*Corr.*, III, 375).

July

During this month (and the next) AP spends most of his time away from Twickenham, at Lord Burlington's in Chiswick, probably at Bolingbroke's Dawley Farm, for at least four days with Lord Cobham at Stowe, at least two weeks in Essex, and at Cirencester with Lord Bathurst. He seems also to have been at Southampton with Lord Peterborough.

1 (Sun) The June number of the *Gentleman's Magazine*, published about this date, prints an early version of AP's 'Epitaph on Mr Gay'. The final version will eventually appear on Rysbrack's monument to Gay in Westminster Abbey.

6 Part II of Paul Whitehead's *The State Dunces: Inscrib'd to Mr Pope* published.
8 Swift's long letter of this date includes his comforting remarks on the death of AP's mother.
15 AP now visiting at Gosfield in Essex, home of Mrs Knight (sister of James Craggs), where he is working on the fourth epistle of the *Essay on Man*.

August
9 (Thurs) To Hugh Bethel, AP writes from Bolingbroke's Dawley Farm, recounting his travels in the previous month. He expects to go soon to Southampton with Lord Peterborough. By this date much of the work on epistle IV of the *Essay on Man* has been done; AP mentions his compliment to Bethel at l. 126.
16 AP back briefly at home, preparing to set out on a small journey with Lord Oxford.
25 Supposed date of composition of AP's first epigram 'On Seeing the Ladies at Crux-Easton Walk in Woods by the Grotto' ('Authors the world of their dull brains have trac'd').
27 AP in London, probably at Lord Oxford's, trying to see Caryll at Ladyholt in the next few days.

September
1 (Sat) AP exhausted, physically and emotionally, as he tells Swift: he is 'sick of writing any thing, sick of myself, and (what is worse) sick of my friends too. The world is become too busy for me, everybody so concern'd for the publick, that all private enjoyments are lost, or disrelish'd.'
4 AP has just received (at Twickenham) a piece of venison from Caryll. He intends to visit Caryll at Ladyholt in five days' time.
9 AP probably at Guildford, stopping at an inn on his way to Caryll at Ladyholt.
24 AP now at Bevis Mount, Lord Peterborough's estate near Southampton. He is next going either to Lord Bathurst's at Cirencester or to London on publishing-business; he prefers the latter. During the time at Bevis Mount, he and Lord Peterborough make a side-trip to Winchester, visiting Winchester College.

October

At some point during the middle of this month, AP arrives at Lord Oxford's London house, at the finish of his summer rambles. He has just spent three weeks with Lord Peterborough at Bevis Mount. While there he is working on a possible collection of his letters and perhaps finishing off the fourth epistle of the *Essay of Man*.

11 (Thurs) On this date, AP seems to have sent Curll a letter (as if from 'P. T.') offering details of his ancestry and early life, for Curll's projected biography of him.

20 AP now back at home, from where he thanks Lord Oxford for the use of his London house. Lord and Lady Oxford are at Wimpole.

23 AP now putting the finishing touches to the *Epistle to Cobham, Of the Knowledge and Characters of Men*, and to the fourth epistle of the *Essay on Man*. He tells Caryll what the conclusion to the latter will be.

November

1 (Thurs) AP has sent Lord Cobham a more-or-less finished copy of the *Epistle*. Cobham now writes back with praise and thanks, and a suggested revision. Anonymous publication of *The Art of Scribling, address'd to All the Scriblers of the Age. By Scriblerus Maximus.*

5 AP publishes his imitation of Donne's fourth satire, which he titles *The Impertinent, Or a Visit to the Court.*

7 Aaron Hill sends AP a copy of his translation of Voltaire's play *Zara* (performed in 1736), asking AP to read it, and to recommend it to Bolingbroke, who might be able to get it produced.

8 AP has adopted some of Cobham's suggested revisions in the *Epistle*. Cobham now writes to approve them.

10 Lord Hervey's verse letter *An Epistle from a Nobleman to a Doctor of Divinity* published this day, claims that AP is merely a translator and plagiariser.

13 AP acknowedges receipt of Hill's translation of the Voltaire play. AP has just seen James Thomson, who has brought him a new poem (title not known). Otherwise he is putting the final brushstrokes to the fourth epistle of the *Essay on Man*, which will soon be printed. He is thinking already of a fine edition of the whole poem.

15 On this date, AP (presenting himself again as 'P. T.') writes to Curll, offering a large collection of AP's letters, in an attempt to get Curll to publish them with the proposed life of AP.
30 In response to Hervey's *Epistle from a Nobleman*, published on the 10th, AP projects a prose 'Letter to a Noble Lord' as a reply to Hervey's personal attack. (The letter is never published in AP's lifetime; Warburton includes it in AP's *Works* in 1751.)

December
5 (Wed) AP sends Lady Burlington a copy of verses supporting him (possibly *Tit for Tat; or Vice Versa*, advertised for publication the week after 4 Dec).
6 Lord Hervey writes to Stephen Fox, describing AP in a violent fury over Hervey's *Epistle from a Nobleman*.
18 A performance of *The Provoked Husband* is held for the benefit of John Dennis at the Haymarket Theatre. AP's 'Prologue, for the Benefit of Mr Dennis' may have been heard first on this occasion.

1734

January
During this month appears Lewis Theobald's edition of Shakespeare's *Works* (7 vols). Throughout the notes Theobald criticises AP's editing: in the Preface he asserts that 'it is not with any secret Pleasure, that I so frequently animadvert on Mr. *Pope* as a Critick; but there are Provocations. . . . His Libels have been thrown out with so much Inveteracy, that, not to dispute whether they *should* come from a *Christian*, they leave it a Question whether they *could* come from a Man.'
1 (Tues) AP is about to send Caryll a whole cargo of books, including the *Essay on Man*, authorship of which *he* still has not revealed. AP still contends that he will not engage Lord Hervey in satiric warfare.
4 Anonymous publication of *A Most Proper Reply to the Nobleman's Epistle to a Doctor of Divinity*, another pamphlet in the AP–Hervey dispute.
6 AP is about to send Swift copies of the *Epistle to Cobham* and the fourth epistle of the *Essay on Man*, both before publication. He has just read Swift's *On Poetry, A Rhapsody*, and possibly

also *An Epistle to a Lady, who Desir'd the Author to Make Verses on her in the Heroick Style*. AP decides he will not publish his reply to Hervey, 'A Letter to a Noble Lord', which he had written in November and has now suppressed on the advice of friends. Death of John Dennis occurs this day.

10 Probably on this date AP is visiting Jonathan Richardson in London during the morning, then lunching with William Cheselden, the surgeon. Also on this day, AP assigns copyright for the fourth part of the *Essay on Man* to Lawton Gilliver for one year.

16 Gilliver issues AP's *Epistle to the Right Honourable Richard Lord Visc^t Cobham*, with AP's name on the title page. The sub-title reads, *Of the Knowledge and Characters of Men*. Several variant issues are published immediately.

24 *An Essay on Man. In Epistles to a Friend. Epistle IV* appears anonymously, again under the imprint of John Wilford.

30 Mary Barber, one of the printers of Swift's *Epistle to a Lady*, is arrested on information contributed by Matthew Pilkington (whom Swift has earlier recommended to AP), who has revealed the author's and printer's identities.

February

1 (Fri) In this month's issue of the *Gentleman's Magazine*, the recently published *Essay on Man* receives a commendatory letter ('the whole Composition is all over Beauty') and poem.

7 Publication of the second version of *Tit for Tat*, an answer to the AP–Hervey controversy. The first version appeared on 4 December 1733.

8 Publication of Lady Mary Wortley Montagu's *The Dean's Provocation for Writing the Lady's Dressing-Room*, attacking Swift and his poem.

12 On this day appears *An Epistle to the Egregious Mr Pope*, another verse satire on AP's ingratitude, plagiarism, stature and family background.

28 AP visiting the Blounts. He has just sent a boxed oil painting to Caryll's daughter.

March

7 (Thurs) Yet another response to the AP–Hervey dispute published: *An Epistle from a Gentleman at Twickenham to a Nobleman at St James's*.

April

Towards the middle of this month, AP probably sees George Berkeley, the philosopher, just before his departure to Ireland as Bishop of Cloyne, when he is at Lord Burlington's house at Chiswick. They will not see each other again.

12 (Fri) Bolingbroke reports to Swift that AP is at present in London. Bolingbroke also criticises the actions of Matthew Pilkington, whom Swift had earlier recommended to AP.

19 AP finally discovers that the oil painting he has sent to Catherine Caryll is at Nathaniel Pigott's house. He is just now sending John Caryll a copy of the fourth epistle of the *Essay on Man*. Having now finished supervising the application of stucco to his house, AP is contemplating a visit to Bevis Mount, Lord Peterborough's house.

May

During this month, AP arranges through Fortescue to loan his sister £300. Writing to Mallet (*Corr.*, III, 408), he advises that he has arranged for Lawton Gilliver to publish Walter Harte's *Essay on Reason*, so as to take advantage of the success of his own *Essay on Man*. He has also determined to spend the summer rambling in the country, visiting friends.

2 (Thurs) Lawton Gilliver issues the first edition of the four epistles of *An Essay on Man* as a single poem; for the first time in the complex publishing-history of the poem, Gilliver's and not Wilford's, name appears on the title page. The whole poem is here dedicated to Bolingbroke.

5 First of four performances of Gay's last comedy, *The Distress'd Wife*, at Covent Garden.

8 Robert Dodsley sends AP a manuscript copy of his 'Lines to Lady Margaret Harley' (who is about to be married). AP is asked to approve them, and make any necessary alterations.

June

14 (Fri) Early in the morning fire breaks out at the French Ambassador's rented house near AP's at Twickenham.

15 AP goes home (from London) to inspect the damage at the French Ambassador's house (owned by AP's friend, Lord Denbigh).

16 AP returns to London and hopes to see Fortescue at about

8 p.m. at his house in Bell Yard near Lincoln's Inn, but Fortescue has not returned from the country.

17 AP has just returned to London. He is now about to depart for Lord Cobham's at Stowe, in company with General Dormer and the Hon. George Berkeley. He expects to stay a week there and then go on to Lord Bathurst's at Cirencester.

25 AP at Lord Bathurst's at Cirencester. On his way he has stopped at the Dormers' house at Rousham.

July

2 (Tues) AP still at Cirencester; he has been in ill health for ten days. He writes to Lord Oxford, tactfully rejecting Mrs Caesar's suggestion that he write verses on Lady Margaret Harley's forthcoming wedding.

4 Gilliver issues *The First Satire of the Second Book of Horace . . . To which is Added, The Second Satire of the Same Book.* This is the first edition of the latter poem.

6 Bolingbroke tells Swift that AP is about to move on to Lord Peterborough's at Bevis Mount from Cirencester. Then he will get back to Bolingbroke at Dawley Farm. AP has been working on an imitation of Horace, *Sermones* I.ii (eventually to be *Sober Advice from Horace*). Of AP's *Moral Essays*, Bolingbroke says, 'they will do more good than the sermons and writings of some who had a mind to find great fault with them'.

7 AP still at Cirencester, where he has been in precarious health, suffering colds and headaches which prevent extensive reading or letter-writing.

11 Marriage of Lady Margaret Harley (daughter of Lord Oxford) to the Duke of Portland.

15 Having heard (at Cirencester) of Arbuthnot's grave decline in health, AP writes to him (at Hampstead). He is still intending to go on soon to Lord Peterborough's house at Southampton.

17 In reply to AP's letter of the 15th, Arbuthnot urges, as a 'Last Request, that you continue that noble *Disdain* and *Abhorrence* of Vice, which you seem naturally endu'd with, but still with a due regard to your own Safety; and study more to reform than chastise'.

25 AP staying with Lord Charles Bruce (Lord Burlington's brother-in-law) at Tottenham, for a day. Tomorrow he goes to Amesbury, to see the Queensberrys, then to Southampton on the following day.

26 Date of AP's supposed letter to Arbuthnot containing his elaborate defence of personal satire; the letter is probably a construction based on a letter of 2 August.

28 AP now at Lord Peterborough's at Southampton. During his long stay here he is probably working on the Horatian imitation which will become *Sober Advice from Horace*, finishing the *Epistle to a Lady*, and assembling the sections of what is to become the *Epistle to Dr Arbuthnot*.

August

 2 (Fri) Writing from Southampton (in a genuine letter), AP defends to Arbuthnot his preference for personal rather than purely general satire: 'General Satire in Times of General Vice has no force, & is no Punishment.'

 4 Now having heard of Lady Margaret's marriage to the Duke of Portland, AP writes to Lord Oxford with belated congratulations.

 6 AP intending this day to visit the Duchess of Montague at Beaulieu, in company with Lord Peterborough. Writing to Hugh Bethel, AP asks if he has seen *The Second Satire of the Second Book of Horace*, which the poet addresses to Bethel.

11 AP, with Lord Peterborough, has just returned to Bevis Mount after his first sea voyage. This has been a voyage around the Isle of Wight. Together the two men went ashore. Later they explored Netley Abbey (south-east of Southampton), and sketched the ruins.

25 AP still with Lord Peterborough at Bevis Mount; together they plan to make some excursions into Hampshire. AP's letter to Arbuthnot of this day makes the first reference to the *Epistle to Dr Arbuthnot*, which he has been putting together over the past several months. In it, 'the Question is stated, what were, & are, my Motives of writing, the Objections to them, & my answers. It pleases me much to take this occasion of testifying (to the public at least, if not to Posterity) my Obligations & Friendship for, & from, you, for so many years.'

30 Swift writes to Lord Oxford noting that he has not heard from AP for months: 'His Time hath indeed been better employed in his Moral Poems, which excell in their kind.' As for the recent *Second Satire of the Second Book of Horace* in which Swift is mentioned (ll. 161–4), 'I could willingly have excused

his placing me not in that Light which I would appear . . . but it gives me not the least offence, because I am sure he had not the least ill Intention, and how much I have allways loved him, the World . . . is convinced' (*Corr.*, III, 429).

September

1   (Sun) AP still at Lord Peterborough's at Bevis Mount, although he had earlier intended to be gone by the end of August. He asks Lord Oxford to send Lord Peterborough a copy of the four-volume set of Swift's *Works*, if they have been published yet (they eventually appear in November). He now intends to go to London 'next week'.

3   In a letter to Arbuthnot, AP speaks of the now-finished *Epistle* to him: 'which I hope may be the best Memorial I can leave, both of my Friendship to you, & of my own Character being such a one as you need not be ashamd of that Friendship. The apology is a bold one, but True: and it is Truth and a clear Conscience that I think will set me above all my enemies. . . .' On the same day AP dines (in Hampshire) with John Conduitt (Isaac Newton's nephew) and his wife.

12   On or before this day Gilliver issues AP's *Second Satire of the Second Book of Horace* for the first time as a separate edition.

15   AP now back home at Twickenham, from where he immediately visits Lord Bolingbroke at Dawley Farm. In a letter to Swift he says he will collect his past works (since the 1717 *Works*) during this winter for publication in a second volume. In three days he intends setting out for a month at Bath with Lord Bolingbroke.

17   AP has just visited Dr Arbuthnot at Hampstead, and has found him in better health. He now expects to move on to Bath (where he will meet Lady Suffolk and Martha Blount), arriving there on the 22nd.

28   AP now at Bath, having arrived there with Lord Bolingbroke. Taking the waters has agreeably improved his health. His circle of friends at Bath includes Lord Lovel, Lord Burlington, and Lord Chesterfield. The *London Evening Post* erroneously reports that AP is 'dangerously ill' in Bath.

October

Either in this month or late in September, the *General Dictionary, Historical and Critical* publishes a life of Atterbury and includes his letter of 23 November 1731 to AP. In Bath, AP learns of this and immediately acts to persuade the *Dictionary*'s editors to cancel the leaf with the letter, so as to minimise his contact with the Jacobite bishop.

4 (Fri) AP writes to Hugh Bethel that newspaper rumours about his health are groundless, but that his headaches prevent him from writing more than a few lines.

15 AP finally back at home in Twickenham after his four months' ramble. Lord Bolingbroke has been his companion on the return journey from Bath.

November

Robert Dodsley's commendatory *Epistle to Mr Pope, Occasion'd by his Essay on Man* appears during this month.

1 (Fri) Swift writes to AP with general complaints about his health and loss of memory and specific praise for the *Essay on Man*: 'I confess I did never imagine you were so deep in Morals, or that so many new & excellent Rules could be produced so advantageously & agreeably in that Science from any one head' (*Corr.*, III, 439).

2 Having intended while in London to see Fortescue in the evening, AP is forced by illness to return to Twickenham.

10 AP informs Lord Oxford by letter that, although he has been in London on three separate occasions (once for six days) since returning home from Bath, they have yet to meet.

23 AP has been away visiting friends in the country. On his return this day, he finds a copy of William Duncombe's tragedy *Junius Brutus* for him to read, and tickets for the opening night (the 25th). For lack of time, AP reads only the Prologue, and sends the play back to Duncombe with the tickets, pleading prior engagements.

27 First three volumes (I, III, IV) of Swift's collected works published in Dublin by George Faulkner.

December

11 (Wed) AP attending at Court, in London.

12 Intending to dine in London with Fortescue, AP is ill with a throat ailment.

15 AP still in London (at Lord Oxford's?) and ill with his throat ailment. He hopes to get back to Twickenham this evening.

19 In a letter to Swift, AP declares his fatigue with the grand

moral work he has been committed to during the past four years. He claims exhaustion of his philosophical resources in writing the poems, but he says he is still working on revisions of the *Epistle to Dr Arbuthnot*; the poem may now already be in press as AP writes this.

28 Publication of AP's *Sober Advice from Horace, to the Young Gentlemen about Town*. The title-page characteristically states that the poem is 'Imitated in the Manner of Mr Pope, Together with the Original, as restored by the Revd R. Bentley', thus continuing both AP's authorial subterfuges and the attack on the pedantic scholarship of Bentley. The publisher is T. Boreman, who reputedly paid AP 60 guineas for the copyright.

30 AP informs Lord Oxford that he has been unable to secure for him an advance copy of the *Epistle to Dr Arbuthnot*. He also coyly disowns authorship of 'that impudent satire', *Sober Advice from Horace*, although it is genuinely his.

31 AP has been ill with a cold for ten days. He writes to Lord Oxford of his continuing poor health and of the *Sober Advice*, 'which I warn you not to take for mine, tho' some people are willing to fix it on me. In truth I should think it a very indecent Sermon, after the *Essay on Man*.'

1735

January

2 (Thurs) Lawton Gilliver issues AP's *Epistle from Mr Pope to Dr Arbuthnot* on this day, his last major attack on the dunces until *The Dunciad* reappears in 1742.

3 Lady Mary Wortley Montagu writes an angry letter of complaint to Arbuthnot over AP's epistle to him, which she terms a 'Lampoon', recommending that AP turn from libelling to a more honest livelihood.

6 The fourth volume (II) of Swift's collected works published in Dublin by George Faulkner. The edition is a great success both as a subscription project and in general sales.

28 Jonathan Richardson and his son publish their *Explanatory Notes and Remarks on Paradise Lost*, in which Bentley's edition of the poem is attacked.

February

4 (Tues) Publication of *An Epistle to Alexander Pope, Esq.*, an anonymous poem attacking AP as a Jacobite, plagiarist, and traitor.

8 Gilliver issues Walter Harte's poem *An Essay on Reason*; according to later commentators, AP inserted many good lines in this work. On the same day the same publisher brings out AP's *Of the Characters of Women: An Epistle to a Lady*, the fourth of the *Moral Essays* to be published. AP sends a copy immediately to John Caryll, but conceals Martha Blount's (Caryll's god-daughter's) identity. He also refuses to send Caryll a copy of *Sober Advice from Horace*, citing its obscenity.

18 In London, AP writes to Caryll of the Bentley affair ensuing from *Sober Advice*, in which Richard Bentley's son has threatened to horsewhip AP if he discovers him as the author of the poem. In the same post, AP sends Caryll a copy of Harte's *Essay on Reason*.

19 AP remains in London, staying with Lord Cornbury, near Oxford Chapel, Henrietta Street.

26 AP visits Arbuthnot on his deathbed.

27 Death of Arbuthnot, aged 68, at his house in Cork Street, London.

March

1 (Sat) Publication of *A Letter to Mr Pope, Occasioned by Sober Advice from Horace*, by Thomas Bentley, nephew of Richard Bentley, whom he defends here. AP is attacked for using Horace to abuse others, for obscenity, for illogic and vanity in the *Essay on Man*; AP is simply 'the purest Wag-prick' (*CH*, p. 28). AP, still in London following Arbuthnot's death, writes a letter of condolence to the doctor's son, George.

3 AP back at Twickenham, depressed at the death and illness of friends; Lord Peterborough is now incurably ill. He asks Lord Oxford to send him a bound book of copies of his letters. At this point he may actually be reading proof of the printed edition of his letters which will appear in May.

4 Burial of Arbuthnot in St James's Church, Piccadilly.

22 AP engaged in making improvements to his garden, which include a hot-house for his banana trees and a stone obelisk with an inscription in memory of his mother. At present he is visiting London.

April

During this month, AP spends a considerable time in London, where he passes half his days in attendance on the dying Lord Peterborough at Kensington.

9   (Wed) AP's letter to Samuel Buckley this day indicates that he is acting as his own bookseller for the about-to-be-published second volume of his *Works*; he urges Buckley, also a bookseller (as well as editor), to take 150 copies of the issue. AP is at present staying with Lord Oxford in the Dover Street house.

23   On or just before this day, Lawton Gilliver publishes *The Works of Mr Alexander Pope*, volume II. The volume collects the *Essay on Man*, the four *Moral Essays*, the *Epistle to Dr Arbuthnot*, epitaphs, some small poems, *The Dunciad*, and two of the Horatian imitations. Volume I, which has no relation to this volume, was the *Works* of 1717.

May

In the *Gentleman's Magazine* for this month appears AP's epigram 'Wrote by Mr P. in a Volume of Evelyn on Coins, Presented to a Painter by a Parson' ('T—m W—d of Ch–sw–c, deep divine').

6   (Tues) AP, at Twickenham, has just received a copy of John Hughes's *Poems* from William Duncombe. He now sends Duncombe a copy of his *Works* via Robert Dodsley, who has just set up as a bookseller.

12   On the morning of this day is published a two-volume edition of AP's correspondence. AP has secretly manoeuvred Edmund Curll into being the publisher of this edition so as later to discredit him. In the afternoon Curll issues a second edition of the work, *Letters of Mr Pope, and Several Eminent Persons*, thus inaugurating one of the most complex and sensational publishing-episodes of AP's career. AP eventually publishes an authorised edition of his letters in 1737. On the same day AP writes to Caryll with feigned anger at Curll's edition of the letters. He now intends to send Caryll a presentation copy of his *Works*, the second volume.

14   On this day and the next, Curll is examined in the House of Lords for advertising that letters to and from peers (which were privileged) are included in his editions of AP's correspondence.

20   In the *Daily Post-Boy*, the *Daily Journal* and the *Grub-Street Journal*, AP advertises that Curll's editions of the letters

contain many forgeries and other letters illegally obtained. He offers a reward for information clearing up the tangled affair.

22 AP's advertisement of the 20th is reprinted in the *Post-Boy*.
23 Appearance of a third edition of AP's letters by Curll, *Mr Pope's Literary Correspondence for Thirty Years; from 1704 to 1734*.
28 Publication of yet another edition, the fourth, of AP's correspondence. Thomas Cooper's name appears on the title page; he is acting for AP.

June
1 (Sun) Between this date and the 10th, two more editions of AP's letters emerge.
3 In the *St James's Evening Post*, Curll advertises (falsely) that he has obtained a packet of Atterbury's letters to AP from Paris.
10 The *Daily Journal* advertises publication of a pamphlet called *A Narrative of the Method by which the Private Letters of Mr Pope have been Procured and Published by Edmund Curll*. The pamphlet is probably by AP.
12 In the *London Evening Post*, AP's front-man, Cooper, posts a reward of £10 for a sight of any of Atterbury's or Bolingbroke's letters to or from AP, and advertises his own edition of AP's literary correspondence.
13 Lord Peterborough, somewhat recovered from his severe illness, is taking the waters at Bath. He sends AP a cask of mum, a beer imported from Brunswick.
16 Another pirated edition of AP's letters appears, together with one published by Thomas Cooper. Following his report of the 3rd, Curll now announces that he intends to publish the (fictitious) packet of Atterbury's letters to AP in a second volume of AP's correspondence.
17 AP informs Lord Oxford about the latest events in the Curll controversy over the Atterbury letters, and requests that he send him a bound copy of manuscript verses and autograph letters of Wycherley from the Harleian Library.
22 About his date, AP informs Fortescue that Curll has served a process (or writ) against Cooper in connection with the letters, and asks him to judge what can be done to oppose it.
24 *The Poet Finish'd in Prose. Being a Dialogue Concerning Mr Pope and His Writings*, published by Curll, presents an extraordinary

range of charges against AP, including his fear of being raped by Lady Mary, his preference for onanism, and his refusal to hire tall servants.

26 Publication of Edmund Curll's 'Third Edition' of *Mr Pope's Literary Correspondence for Thirty Years*, only six weeks after his first edition. This is the first volume; the second appears on 14 July.

July

12 (Sat) In the *St James's Evening Post*, Curll addresses a letter to AP in which he promises to publish the second volume of AP's *Literary Correspondence*, including the non-existent letters of Atterbury, on the 14th; he also claims a third volume is actually in press.

13 AP is in London (at Lord Oxford's) in the midst of the letters controversy. He goes to see Fortescue for legal advice, but Fortescue is out. What AP wants is to see Curll's 'pirated' second volume seized and destroyed, in favour of Cooper and Gilliver's edition. He returns to Twickenham in the evening, where he writes to Samuel Buckley. He requests Buckley to insert an advertisement (in AP's name) in the *London Gazette* in which AP decries the false editions of his letters (Curll's) and announces his intention to publish an authorised edition himself.

14 Curll issues volume II of his *Mr Pope's Literary Correspondence* (the 'Third Edition'). Besides the letters, he includes reprints of numerous pieces of AP's verse and prose.

17 AP tells Caryll that he intends to take a ramble soon and stay three weeks at Lord Cobham's.

21 AP suffering frequent headaches, perhaps from the stress of the recent letters controversy with Curll.

22 Curll writes to Broome asking for any of his letters to AP or AP's to him that he might be willing to put into the third volume of the *Literary Correspondence*.

26 Curll produces in *Fog's Weekly Journal* a long prejudiced explanation of the letters affair, advertising the second volume and the forthcoming third. In revenge, Curll has now begun to use 'Pope's Head' as his business sign.

31 On or just before this day, Gilliver issues another edition of AP's *Works*, volume II, in quarto and octavo formats.

August

2   (Sat) AP admits to Fortescue that there is as yet no *legal* proof that Curll is involved in the pirating of the letters. He therefore asks him to bring an information against *Fog's Journal*, which on this same day issues a public retraction of Curll's defamatory advertisement of 26 July. AP is this day at Fortescue's Richmond house, where he is supervising some renovations. In the evening he will dine with his neighbour, Lord Ilay.

4   Broome writes a conciliatory letter to AP, enclosing Curll's letter to him (see 22 July), which he refuses to answer.

6   Two of Lord Cobham's nephews, George (later Lord) Lyttelton and Gilbert West, are visiting AP at Twickenham. AP is planning to go to Lord Cobham's in about ten days.

18 AP has just been summoned to Southampton to see Lord Peterborough before he goes to France. He fears this will be their last meeting. AP has been suffering a slight fever in the past week. Thomas Cooper issues yet another variant edition of AP's letters.

20 Lord Peterborough sends AP another letter begging him to visit Bevis Mount before he leaves for France in a fortnight. On or just before this date, the first Dublin editions of AP's letters begin to appear.

23 AP has still not set off for Southampton, but has been supervising more renovation work on Fortescue's Richmond house. While there he has been much entertained, and writes to Fortescue (who is in Devon) that he wishes for solitude. He will set off for Lord Peterborough's as soon as he finishes the letter.

25 Having arrived at Southampton, AP gives Martha Blount a long epistolary account of Lord Peterborough's serious condition, and of the relatives and visitors who are there to take their last leave of him.

26 By this date, Lintot is already printing copy for the first volume, in octavo, of AP's miscellaneous works. The volume appears in January 1736.

27 AP informs Lord Oxford of the scene at Southampton and hopes that they can meet briefly in London before AP sets off for Stowe.

28 A new booksellers' edition of AP's letters appears, with additional letters.

29 AP just about to leave Bevis Mount.

September
1 (Fri) Driving in a coach about three miles from Oxford, in Bagley Wood, AP comes upon an overturned coach, and gives up his own coach to an injured woman. He walks the three miles into town, stopping at the Golden Cross Inn, from where he sends a note to Joseph Spence. Spence then entertains him in his college rooms for several hours. In the evening, he sets out for Colonel Dormer's at Rousham, on his way to Stowe.
20 On or about this date Curll issues volume III of *Mr Pope's Literary Correspondence*, with new letters, and some poems and three pamphlets reprinted in it.
22 Broome writes AP another conciliatory letter, trying to restart the correspondence which ceased six years ago.

October
2 (Thurs) In his reply, AP accepts Broome's statements (see 22 Sep) and agrees to forget past difficulties between them. AP is now at home after returning from Stowe. On the way back he has spent three days in Oxford, much of the time with Spence.
4 In the evening, the Prince of Wales visits AP at his house at Twickenham, staying three hours before returning to Kensington.
7 AP declines to act formally as a judge in Edward Cave's poetry contest for the *Gentleman's Magazine*, although he informally indicates a preference for one of the short-listed poems.
8 As he tells the Earl of Orrery, AP is planning to affix Lord Cornbury's commendatory verses on AP to the octavo edition of his poems now printing. In the event, AP waits until the 1739 reprint to do this.
21 At this time, AP is engaged in obtaining subscriptions for Samuel Wesley (the younger)'s *Poems on Several Occasions*; AP gets Lord Peterborough, Hugh Bethel, Dr Delany and Swift, amongst others, for the list.
25 Lord Peterborough dies in Lisbon shortly after his arrival there.
29 Broome writes from his parish (at Pulham) to accept AP's

conciliatory explanation of the *Odyssey* matters which have estranged them.

November

10 (Mon) Lord Peterborough's body is landed at Southampton upon arrival from Lisbon.

18 AP asks Broome to return AP's letters to him, as he has been asking all his friends. He has just sent Broome a copy of the second volume of his *Works*.

20 Lord Peterborough buried at Turvey, in Bedfordshire.

24 Death of AP's publisher, Jacob Tonson, Jr, at age 52. His uncle, Jacob Tonson, Sr, is still alive at 80.

December

1 (Mon) Broome effectively refuses to return AP's letters, but he asks AP to help him get Lintot to reprint his miscellany, and sends AP a poem ('Death') which he has written some years since.

4 AP writes a letter of condolence to Jacob Tonson, Sr, on the death of his nephew.

15 Henry Woodfall presents his bill to Lintot for printing 3000 copies of the first volume of AP's works in small octavo. The edition begins to appear in January.

1736

January

12 (Mon) AP lets Broome know that he has been unable to talk to Lintot (who has been ill) about reprinting Broome's poems, but hopes to shortly. He has also just arranged for a cancellation of Broome's name in *The Dunciad* (III.328) in the 1736 edition just now publishing. For his present editorial project of the 'authentic' edition of his letters, AP requests that Broome send him any of his earlier letters.

14 First volume of a small-octavo *Works* of AP published by Lintot in collaboration with Lawton Gilliver. It is a reprint of the 1717 *Works* and is intended for the first volume of a new pocket edition of AP's *Works*.

15 The *London Evening Post* reports that the *Essay on Man* (in Silhouette's French translation) 'is in great Esteem at Paris, and in the Hands of all the polite People there'.

February

3   (Tues) Death of Bernard Lintot, AP's sometime publisher.

7   Swift writes to AP in great concern over reports of the latter's poor health: 'I have no body now left but you: Pray be so kind to out-live me, and then die as you please, but without pain. . . .'

March

25   (Thurs) By this date Broome has still not responded to AP's letter of 12 January, and AP now writes to tell Broome of Lintot's death. AP sends Swift yet another possible plan for what might follow the *Essay of Man*: he projects a four-epistle poem dedicated to Swift. Curll issues volume IV of his unauthorised edition of *Mr Pope's Literary Correspondence*. As with the third volume, this contains poems as well as letters.

26   Writing to Fortescue, AP further elaborates a possible edition of his letters, including a published proposal for them which will set the record straight (from *his* viewpoint), in light of Curll's continuing publication of volumes of *Mr Pope's Literary Correspondence*.

31   On this day appears Mr Bridges' poem *Divine Wisdom and Providence; An Essay Occasion'd by the Essay on Man* (with a prose preface). Bridges questions the orthodoxy of AP's poem.

April

2   (Fri) AP's letter of this day to Orrery is concerned with Swift's bad health at the moment, but he is evidently also anxious to obtain the return of his letters to Swift in case Swift should die.

7   Date of AP's first extant letter to Ralph Allen. Allen has just visited AP at Twickenham and has apparently offered financial assistance for an edition of his letters.

13   AP sends Fortescue, now back in London after a tour of judicial duty at Monmouth, a copy of what is probably the printed proposal for the *Letters*, which will be subscribed for. He prepares Fortescue for finding subscribers to the edition.

16   Having recently received several accounts of Swift's dreadful state of health, AP begs Lord Orrery to get hold of anything of his letters or writings which Swift may have, so that AP's

enemies cannot obtain them. He also sends Orrery a copy of the *Letters* proposal.

22 After a long silence, Swift finally assures AP that his letters are safely sequestered in a locked cabinet, and that Swift's executors will deliver them to AP at the appropriate time. Swift complains that his constantly recurring deafness and other ailments prevent him from visiting England.

27 Marriage of the Prince of Wales.

29 AP sees Atterbury's son-in-law in London to obtain permission for nine paintings to be copied for Ralph Allen, who is redecorating his house at Bath.

30 AP is now contemplating a fortnight's visit to Lady Peterborough at Southampton in late May. In a letter to Ralph Allen of this date he includes the first version of his epigram 'To One who Wrote Epitaphs' ('Friend! in your Epitaphs I'm griev'd').

May

1 (Sat) About this date, Henry Lintot issues a third volume of *The Works of Alexander Pope*.

2 Viscount Townshend writes to Samuel Buckley on Glover's *Leonidas* and AP's *Second Epistle of the Second Book of Horace* (which he says he has read ten times): 'whatever is produced perfect in its kind in this age, I see, must come from Twickenham'. He urges Buckley to get AP to visit him this summer at Raynham.

3 Lord Burlington writes to invite AP to dine with him in London with Lord Bruce on the 6th.

4 The folio pamphlet of *Bounce to Fop. An Heroick Epistle from a Dog at Twickenham to a Dog at Court* is simultaneously published in London and Dublin. The poem is likely to be a collective work by Swift and AP (Ault, pp. 342–7). The poem also appears in the May issues of the *Gentleman's Magazine* and the *London Magazine*.

5 AP invites Fortescue to dine with him (at Twickenham) either today or on the 7th.

7 AP to dine at Lord Burlington's London residence, together with Lord Bruce, who has come into town from Wiltshire.

10 AP writes to Lord Orrery in Dublin, only barely suppressing his anxiety over Swift's continued withholding of his letters.

17 AP writes to Mrs Knight at Gosfield, enclosing a copy of the

epitaph he has written for her husband, the 'Epitaph on John Knight' ('O fairest Pattern to a failing Age!').

22   King George leaves for Hanover, where he will meet his new mistress, Madame von Walmoden. The departure may influence AP's ironies in the poem he is about to begin at Bevis Mount, *The First Epistle of the Second Book of Horace* (the epistle 'To Augustus').

30   AP just setting off from Twickenham for his fortnight's stay with Lady Peterborough at Bevis Mount. He invites Fortescue and his family to stay at Twickenham while he is away.

June
During the latter part of this month AP is supervising the rebuilding of the shell temple in his garden, which had collapsed in the previous year.

 5   (Sat) AP's long letter of this date (from Bevis Mount) to Ralph Allen justifies his forthcoming edition of the *Letters*, and gives details of the subscription.

16   AP at home, just returned from Bevis Mount. He writes to Hugh Bethel asking him to send soon the names of subscribers (for the *Letters*) he has procured. AP explains that he has recently lent his sister £150 but she has lost in her continuing legal proceedings.

26   *Read's Weekly Journal* and five other papers announce that a monument to Gay is to be put up in Westminster Abbey, with the epitaph to him by AP, in a second version (as printed in vol. II of AP's *Works*, 1735), beginning 'Severe of Morals'.

July
 8   (Thurs) The *London Evening Post* reprints the report of 26 June on Gay's monument, but includes a third version of AP's 'Epitaph on Gay', beginning 'Severe of Morals, but of Nature mild'.

17   In its issue of this day, the *Daily Gazetteer* provides the first printing of AP's 'Epitaph on John Knight' in a description of the monument erected in the church at Gosfield. Publication in the *St James's Evening Post*, the *General Evening Post* and the *London Evening Post* follows later in the day.

18   AP writes to accept payment of subscription monies which Ralph Allen has arranged from a Bath bookseller, James Leake, for the forthcoming *Letters* edition.

30　AP has just received the 50 guineas subscription money remitted to him by Ralph Allen. He now invites Allen to visit him at home before the middle of August, as he will be in Windsor Forest from the 15th to the 18th of the month. The first sheet of the *Letters* is going to press in a week's time.

August

Possibly during this month AP is almost drowned. Helping a young woman into a boat from the stairs at his Twickenham house, the two of them plunge into the river (*Corr.*, IV, 28), and are rescued with great difficulty.

14　(Sat) Lord Bathurst invites AP to visit him soon at Cirencester, and encloses architectural plans for new structures to adorn the park surrounding the great house.

16　AP writes to Fortescue of his intention to set out for Lord Bathurst's in a week's time. He expects also to visit Bath.

26　AP still at home, but preparing to go to Cirencester; he is awaiting the arrival of Martha Blount. In the end, he does not go to Cirencester.

September

During this month, AP's tiny epigram 'To the Earl of Burlington' ('You wonder Who this Thing has writ') is published for the first time, in *Grub-Street Journal* no. 352).

8　(Wed) Ralph Allen has just been visiting AP at Twickenham. Following his departure AP's health declines, and he becomes prey to constant headaches. AP now intends spending a week or two on a second visit to Southampton, to help Lady Peterborough with the gardens at Bevis Mount. Just now AP is helping Nathaniel Hooke by obtaining subscriptions for Hooke's four-volume *Roman History*. In a letter to Allen of this day AP includes a copy of his *Universal Prayer* ('Father of All, in every Age'), written some twenty years earlier but not to be published until 1738.

14　AP writes to Hugh Bethel's brother, Slingsby Bethel, to obtain 'some good dry madeira' and to foward the names of any subscribers he may have collected for AP's *Letters*.

21　AP has just returned home from a brief ramble to an unknown destination, and is now about to set off for Bevis Mount, where he hopes to complete writing what is probably *The First Epistle of the Second Book of Horace*. He also intends to put the finishing touches to Lord Peterborough's garden while there.

30 AP still at Twickenham, now intending to leave for Bevis Mount on 4 October. He sends Slingsby Bethel some receipts for subscriptions to the *Letters*.

October

4 (Mon) AP still in Twickenham, but probably just about to depart for Bevis Mount. He will not visit Bath, nor, as he informs Lord Orkney, can he come to Cliveden, but will work on designs for the gardens over the winter.

7 AP now in Southampton, staying with Lady Peterborough. He is much preoccupied with the forthcoming *Letters*, and plans to be back in Twickenham by the 20th. He expects to travel there via Basingstoke, where he hopes to see a friend, probably Thomas Warton the elder.

17 AP writes to Richard Savage with details of the life and a character assessment of John Gay. The information is to be printed in the account of Gay in the *General Dictionary*, in December. AP asks to read the proof-sheet of this article before it is published.

30 AP, suffering from colic and headache, declines to dine with his friend Mrs Knight.

31 AP assigns copyright to his earlier collection of letters, soon to reappear in volumes v and vi of the *Works* (in octavo format), to Robert Dodsley.

November

During this month, Curll issues yet another volume in his controversial dispute with AP over the letters. His *New Letters of Mr Alexander Pope, and Several of his Friends* in fact contains only two previously unpublished letters.

1 (Mon) Thomas Birch has just received from AP the corrected proof-sheet of his life of Gay for the *General Dictionary*.

2 By this date, the *Letters* edition is half printed.

6 AP tells Ralph Allen that the *Letters* edition is now above three-quarters printed; he intends to bring it out in January.

7 AP writes (from Twickenham) to the Earl of Orrery, begging him to 'take all possible methods' of getting his letters and personal writings away from Swift and into the Earl's custody.

11 The *London Evening Post* advertises Curll's *Letters Written by Mr Pope and Lord Bolingbroke, to Dean Swift, in the Year 1723*, containing only two letters. AP may have fed the letters anonymously to Curll in an effort to encourage Swift to return his letters. Curll includes the two letters in the fifth volume of *Mr Pope's Literary Correspondence* (June 1737).

27 AP writes to Lord Burlington (at Bath). He has been seeing much of William Kent lately, and passes on news of the man to Burlington.

December
Early in the month, AP returns home from London, in company with Lord Burlington.

 2 (Thurs) Swift's long letter of this day to AP lists his illnesses and their mutual friendship with many men of wit and genius, and praises AP's moral poems: 'the Subjects of Such Epistles are more useful to the Publick, by your manner of handling them than any of all your Writings . . . Posterity will enjoy the Benefit whenever a Court happens to have the least relish for Virtue and Religion'. Birch's life of Gay, as compiled with the assistance of Aaron Hill and AP, is published in the *General Dictionary*.

22 At some point prior to this date the Prince of Wales accepts the whelp which AP has offered in *Bounce to Fop, An Heroick Epistle*. George Lyttelton writes of this to AP, together with news of their noble friends at Bath.

30 Responding to Swift's letter of the second, AP begs Swift directly to send him his letters, citing Curll's recent publication of two from Bolingbroke and him to the Dean. With this letter, AP may have sent part or even all of the translation of *The Second Epistle of the Second Book of Horace*, and the lines to Swift from *The First Epistle of The Second Book of Horace* (ll. 221–4).

1737

During this year J. P. de Crousaz, a Swiss professor, publishes his long *Examen de l'Essai de M. Pope sur l'Homme*, in which he calls the poem 'Spinozist' for its alleged deistic basis. Basing his analysis on an inaccurate translation of the poem, Crousaz considers that AP threatened the continuation of the Christian religion. His *Examen* is based on Silhouette's faulty French prose translation of the poem.

January

14 (Fri) In a letter to Lord Orrery AP uses Curll's publication of the two letters to Swift as evidence of the need to recover his letters from Swift, which he urges Orrery to pursue. On the advice of friends, AP has now decided to leave out his miscellaneous prose works and publish only his letters in the forthcoming edition: 'Indeed, it is a mortifying prospect, to have one's most secret opinions, delivered under the Sacredness of Friendship, betrayed to the whole World, by the unhappy Partiality of one's own best Friends in preserving them.'

February

During this month AP arranges for the delivery of Jonathan Richardson's line engraving of AP's head in profile, to be used for the title-page of the *Letters*.

5 (Sat) Lord Orrery sympathises with AP's request of 14 January, but has been unable to approach Swift alone about the letters, although he too fears Swift's declining memory will complicate their return.

8 The *London Gazette* advertises, 'speedily to be published', the quarto, large-folio and small-folio sizes of AP's works in prose – 'an Authentic Edition of his LETTERS'. This is a notice to the subscribers, but the edition does not appear for some time yet.

9 Swift thanks AP for the translations he has sent in December, but does not respond at all to AP's request for the letters.

11 AP melancholy about the death of old friends and the poor health of those surviving: to Hugh Bethel he proclaims that 'I am now arrived, to that part of Life, when I cannot afford to bear the Hazard of a Friend; & every Attack which Sickness makes on such an one, shakes me to the very Heart' (*Corr.*, IV, 57).

March

3 (Thurs) AP ill and at home, but he arranges with Richardson for the delivery of the plates for the profile and engraving for

the title-page of the *Letters* together with the headpiece and initial letter of the Preface.

4   AP still ill, at home, with a severe fever which keeps him confined to his chamber, but he writes again to Lord Orrery on the subject of the letters Swift holds. This time he adds the information that Curll obtained his two pirated letters from Ireland, so that Swift may appear to be at fault here.

9   Publication of *Horace his Ode to Venus* (AP's translation of *Odes* IV.1 ('Again? new Tumults in my Breast?').

18   From Cork, Lord Orrery now writes to Swift, enclosing a copy of AP's letter of 4 March, and reminds the Dean that recently he has verbally agreed with Orrery himself to send AP the letters. Orrery also writes to AP to tell him that Swift has agreed to send him the letters, and sends him a copy of the letter to the Dean.

23   AP now writes a melancholy letter to Swift, in which, however, he does not mention directly the letters issue, but does emphasise his fear that *this* letter and others like it could be published by the likes of Curll. On the same day, Mrs Knight, AP's friend and recently widowed sister of James Craggs, marries Robert Nugent. Nugent thus gained, besides a wife, a seat in Parliament, a parish in Essex and £100,000.

24   Ralph Allen married (for the second time), to Elizabeth Holder of Bath, at St Martin's-in-the-Fields, London. AP assigns copyright of the authorised folio and quarto *Letters* to Robert Dodsley.

28   AP just now recovered from his month-long illness, although his eyes remain affected. As he tells Orrery, he is now relieved that Swift has agreed to hand over the letters; he will now pursue his previous plan of publishing them as a monument to their friendship. The *Letters* is now completely printed, but AP awaits the passage in Parliament of a bill to secure books as property and prevent piracy. (The bill does not pass.)

April

During this month (and March?) AP makes a number of trips to London to attend to the publishing of the *Letters*. While there he stays at Lord Cornbury's house near Oxford Chapel.

19   (Tues) AP has arranged to dine with Samuel Buckley on this day in company either with Lord Carteret or Lord Cornbury.

28   Robert Dodsley issues the folio first edition of *The Second Epistle of the Second Book of Horace, Imitated by Mr Pope* ('Dear

Col'nel! Cobham's and your Country's Friend!'). Gay's monument in Westminster Abbey, bearing AP's 'Epitaph on Gay' and Gay's epitaph on himself ('Life is a Jest, and all Things shew it, / I thought so once, but now I know it'), is unveiled.

30 Publication of *Eugenio: Or, Virtuous and Happy Life*, a poem dedicated to AP.

May

14 (Sat) With publication of the *Letters* imminent, AP arranges to send to Bath the subscribers' copies, together with three special sets for the Allens. In his letter to Allen he notes that the book-property bill has been defeated in Parliament, and that he has not yet received his letters from Swift.

17 Lord Orrery (in Dublin) again assures AP that he will have his letters from Swift, and that Orrery himself hopes to bring them to England. However, he has been unable to persuade Swift to leave Dublin for an English visit.

19 Two years after the first Curll editions of his letters, the authorised *Letters of Mr Alexander Pope, and Several of his Friends* finally appears in quarto and folio sizes published by Gilliver, Dodsley, and two others. Shortly after this date, AP sends a copy of the edition to Hugh Bethel and arranges to see him in London, at Sir William Codrington's house in Arlington Street.

21 AP is just sending off subscribers' copies of the *Letters* to Ireland (via Chester). To Orrery he sends a letter and special presentation copies of the *Letters* and of *The First Epistle of the Second Book of Horace*, with an identical pair of copies for Swift. Finally, he begs Orrery to complete the business of returning his letters.

25 First publication of AP's *First Epistle of the Second Book of Horace, Imitated* ('To Augustus') in a folio edition issued by Thomas Cooper. The poem is addressed to George II, who bore the christened name of Augustus. The tribute to Swift (ll. 221–8) apparently causes the Privy Council to consider taking AP into custody for seditious writing (Mack, *Life*, p. 683).

31 Swift's important letter of this day to AP indicates that he prefers a poetical memorial rather than a epistolary one from AP; that he will not venture out of Ireland because of his

affliction of deafness; and that he will convey to AP about sixty letters in all: 'None of them have any thing to do with Party, of which you are the clearest of all men, by your Religion, and the whole Tenour of your Life.' He has also read *The First Epistle of the Second Book of Horace*: 'My happiness is you are too far engaged, and in spite of you the ages to come will celebrate me, and know you were a friend who loved and esteemed me' (*Corr.*, IV, 72).

June
1 (Wed) During this month Curll publishes volume v of *Mr Pope's Literary Correspondence*.
2 Lord Orrery has discovered a six-year gap in AP's letters to Swift, which may have been created by friends stealing the letters. He will try to recover the lost letters. Swift's health, he worries, is worse and worse, as his deafness and giddiness increase.
8 By letter to Ralph Allen at Bath, AP makes further arrangements for sending subscribers' sets of the *Letters* there, and explains the reasons for his gift to the Allens of the special folio edition.
14 Lord Orrery has spent much time searching out the missing letters but the search has been in vain. He has not yet got the other letters from Swift either, but will, he assumes, obtain them just before he sets off for England.
17 AP has just sent Jonathan Richardson a large paper copy of the *Letters*, in gratitude for engraving AP's head for the title-page.
29 AP invites Jonathan Richardson and his son to visit Twickenham, staying until tomorrow noon. Otherwise AP has been busy entertaining, attending to legal business, and seeing callers.

July
5 (Tues) Death of the barrister and AP's friend and neighbour at Whitton, Nathaniel Pigott, aged 76. Probably shortly after this AP sends Pigott's son a prose epitaph to be engraved on Pigott's monument.
18 Writing to Richardson, AP encloses a copy of the 'Sonnet Written upon Occasion on the Plague' ('Fair Mirrour of foul Times! whose fragile Sheen'), which he says was found

written on a glass window in the village of Chalfont, in Buckinghamshire. The poem is his hoax imitation of Milton. AP has been in Oxfordshire and Buckinghamshire for the past ten days. Thomas Birch prints the poem in his edition of *A Complete Collection of the . . Works of Milton* in 1738, but judges it to be only an imitation of Milton.

21   AP expects to be back at home by this date, having returned from Oxford; at Twickenham he will rendezvous with Jonathan Richardson.

23   By this date Lord Orrery is established in London and has delivered the manuscript of Swift's *History of the Four Last Years of the Queen* to Dr William King and the long-hoped-for packet of letters at last to AP.

24   Lord Orrery spends the day with AP at Twickenham.

26   AP writes to Ralph Allen with a possible proposal for a visit to him in the autumn. AP has hopes of going to Bevis Mount, unless 'an affair I cannot put off' takes him to Oxford; then he will travel to Bath via Lord Bathurst's at Cirencester.

31   A daughter, Princess Augusta, born to the Prince and Princess of Wales, at St James's Palace, in defiance of the Queen's order to have the confinement at Hampton Court. The Prince holds a separate court after this date.

August

1   (Mon) Publication of the second edition of Spence's *Essay on Mr Pope's Odyssey*.

20   AP directs Robert Dodsley to provide a complimentary copy of the *Letters* to Mrs Pendarves.

28   AP has been rambling in the country for about a month, visiting Southampton (Lady Peterborough at Bevis Mount), Portsmouth (where he fails to get to the Isle of Wight) and Oxford. He has now just arrived at Lord Bathurst's at Cirencester, where he is advising on some architectural and gardening designs. He intends to move on, after a week, in the direction of Bath, to see Ralph Allen.

September

10   (Sat) The King orders the Prince of Wales to leave St James's Palace, after a long succession of arguments over disobedience.

25   AP now back at home in Twickenham. Since his stay at Lord Bathurst's at the end of August, he has been to see Ralph

Allen at Bath, and travelled back to Oxford before returning home. In a letter to Bethel, he comments on the recent dissension between the King and the Prince of Wales, now estranged.

October
11 (Tues) AP now recovered from an illness which has been bothering him for the past several weeks.

November
12 (Sat) AP orders more madeira, five dozen bottles, and a dozen of claret from Slingsby Bethel; he has yet to pay for his earlier order.

14 AP seems to be spending this week in London on business, staying with Lord Cornbury.

18 AP is with his solicitor, William Murray (later Earl of Mansfield), about to file suit against a printer who has pirated an edition of the *Letters*; he writes to the solicitor for the Stationers' Company, Nathaniel Cole, for additional information and advice before proceeding.

20 Death of Queen Caroline. About this time, influenced by his friendship with the Prince of Wales, AP composes his epigram 'On Queen Caroline's Death-Bed' ('Here lies wrapt up in forty thousand towels / The only proof that C*** had bowels').

23 AP still in London, at Lord Cornbury's, perhaps interested in the events following the Queen's death. He tries to arrange a meeting with Samuel Buckley, for the 26th.

24 AP writes to Allen on the death of the Queen: 'the Death of great Persons is such a sort Surprize to *All*, as every one's death is to *himself*. . . . We begin to *esteem*, & *commend* our Superiours, at the time that we *pity* them, because *then* they seem not above ourselves.' Bill filed in Chancery for AP with Dodsley as plaintiff, and the pirate printer of the letters (James Watson) as defendant (*CIH*, p. 494).

25 Nathaniel Cole writes to AP that he has received Murray's draft bill of complaint and supplies information for two essential dates (*CIH*, p. 494).

30 Dodsley tells Nathaniel Cole that the pirate printer Watson has agreed to give up his impression into the hands of Mr Knapton (an authorised printer) and that he will give security not to invade any property of AP's in the future, if proceedings

against him are stopped. On this same day Watson also points out to Knapton that AP's books have been improperly registered with the Stationers' Company, which allows him to pirate the work, which he will continue to do, unless he is compensated for his printing-costs in his stolen edition (*CIH*, p. 496).

December
14 (Wed) Watson sends in an account of the printed sheets of his pirated edition of the letters, and an account of his costs (*CIH*, p. 497).
21 A news report in the *London Evening Post* advises that AP is now receiving proposals for the inscription of the new monument to Shakespeare in Westminster Abbey. By this date £300 has been raised at a theatrical benefit towards the cost of the monument.
22 Watson rejects Nathaniel Cole's proposal for compensation because he will lose £40 and have to pay a £100 bond against further piracy (*CIH*, pp. 498–9).

1738

During this year Crousaz rewrites his interpretation of the *Essay on Man* using Du Resnel's new French translation of the poem into verse. His new piece is the *Commentaire sur la traduction en vers . . . de l'Essai . . . sur l'Homme.*

January
5 (Thurs) AP goes to Richardson's in Queen's Square to sit for a portrait, which is for a Dr Mead.
23 Gilliver issues *The Sixth Epistle of the First Book of Horace Imitated. By Mr Pope* ('Not to Admire, is all the Art I know') in folio and octavo sizes.

February
4 (Sat) By this date Watson, the pirate printer, has agreed to hand over his pirated edition to Dodsley (*CIH*, p. 500).
28 Volume I of Nathaniel Hooke's *Roman History* is advertised (in the *Daily Gazetteer*) as available to the subscribers on this day.

March
1 (Wed) Publication of *An Imitation of the Sixth Satire of the Second Book of Horace* ('I've often wished that I had clear / For life, six hundred pounds a year'). The poem was originally written by Swift in 1714, and appeared in print in 1727. Here AP adds the second half of the poem.
7 Publication of AP's *First Epistle of the First Book of Horace Imitated* ('St. John, whose love indulg'd my labours past'), printed by Dodsley and sold by Cooper.

April
2 (Sun) AP responds sympathetically to Lord Orrery's letter concerning a recent relapse of Swift's health which may have caused Orrery to overreact.
6 AP attends the first-night performance of James Thomson's adaptation of *Agamemnon*, a play he has read and criticised in manuscript for Thomson. After possible revisions initiated by AP after this performance, the play is moderately successful, and lasts a further eight nights. On the same day the *Daily Gazetteer* publishes a satiric verse attack on AP and Bolingbroke, one of many such published in government organs between March and the end of the year.
26 Agreement finally signed by James Watson, the printer, with £100 bond, under the terms of which he is to deliver his pirated edition to Dodsley, to undertake never to print any of AP's works in future, and to receive £25 compensation for printing-costs.
28 AP asks Ralph Allen if he objects to having his name in a poem, *One Thousand Seven Hundred and Thirty-Eight*, which will be published next month. On the same day he writes a polite brief letter to his namesake (no relation to AP), who is a Presbyterian minister at Thurso, in the far north of Scotland.

May
11 (Thurs) Aaron Hill, writing from Buxton, Derbyshire, writes AP a long, tedious letter which is largely a treatise on 'Propriety in the Thought and Expression of Poetry'; the poetry dealt with is chiefly AP's.
12 AP registers copyright for himself for the poem *One Thousand Seven Hundred and Thirty-Eight*.

13 Samuel Johnson's *London* published, his adaptation of Juvenal's third satire.
16 Folio edition appears of AP's *One Thousand Seven Hundred and Thirty-Eight. A Dialogue Something Like Horace*, later to be known as the *Epilogue to the Satires, Dialogue I* ('Not twice a twelvemonth you appear in Print').
21 AP's fiftieth birthday.

June
 4 (Sun) A son, Prince George, is born to the Prince and Princess of Wales. He becomes King George III in 1760.
 9 AP has just returned from a long ramble in the country (destinations unspecified), and answers Hill's letter of 11 May.
15 Writing to the Countess of Hertford, Isaac Watts wishes that AP ('that bright Genius & that supreme Poet') could leave off writing satire and turn to 'Lyric Odes' (*CH*, p. 247).
17 Another long letter from Hill to AP mixes praise of AP's qualities and self-defence of Hill's. Hill notifies AP that he is about to send Lord Bolingbroke his manuscript of *The Roman Revenge*, which he wishes to dedicate to him.
20 Expecting Bolingbroke to arrive soon from France, AP promises to convey Hill's manuscript to Bolingbroke.
22 Dodsley publishes *The Universal Prayer. By the Author of the Essay on Man*. AP's poem was originally written in 1715, and is revised here throughout.
25 Hill now asks AP to read his play, and suggests that he will likewise send on the 'Essay on Propriety' for AP's approval.

July
 6 (Thurs) AP informs Ralph Allen that he will not get to Bath this summer.
 8 Lord Bolingbroke arrives in London from France.
15 AP has now read Hill's manuscript twice, but defers giving his opinion to Hill until Bolingbroke has read the play. AP expects Bolingbroke at Twickenham in a few days. After arriving, Bolingbroke entrusts AP with a copy of *The Idea of a Patriot King*, asking him to print a few copies for friends.
18 Dodsley issues the folio first edition of AP's *One Thousand Seven Hundred and Thirty-Eight. Dialogue II*, later to be the *Epilogue to the Satires, Dialogue II* ('Tis all a Libel – Paxton (Sir)

will say'). This marks the end of the Horatian period in AP's career. For the next four years he publishes almost nothing.

21 Bolingbroke is now at Twickenham, at AP's house, where he will stay for the next nine months while he tries to sell Dawley Farm. Both AP and Bolingbroke write to Hill with fulsome praise of Hill's tragedy. At some point between the 8th and the 21st, windows in AP's house are smashed by an unknown person (a political operative?) while AP and Bolingbroke are dining, probably in company with Lord Bathurst.

31 Hill writes to both AP and Bolingbroke with a tedious display of thanks for having read the play and of praise for AP's *Epilogue to the Satires, Dialogue II*: 'it carries the acrimony of *Juvenal*, with the *Horatian* air of ease and serenity'. For the past six days AP has been suffering from a severe cold. He tells Hugh Bethel that Lord Bolingbroke's presence will keep him from any extended rambles this summer.

August

8 (Tues) Swift writes to AP on the *Epilogue to the Satires, Dialogue II*, 'to equal almost any thing you ever writ' (*CH*, p. 332).

15 Lord Bolingbroke ill with a fever at AP's house.

17 Lord Bolingbroke somewhat recovered from the fever, but not well enough to go out. AP asks Lord Burlington for some of his pineapples to aid in the recovery, and to send Mr Scot (Burlington's gardener) to assist him in building a stove for the Twickenham house.

19 AP asks Ralph Allen to send for Lord Bolingbroke's use a supply of bottled Bath waters.

24 A prose attack on AP appears in the *Daily Gazetteer*.

26 A verse attack on AP appears in the *Daily Gazetteer*.

29 Hill writes to AP, yet again, about his tragedy, but decides not to have him read it a fifth time.

30 AP replies (politely) to Hill that both he and Bolingbroke will favour him with rereading of the play.

September

1 (Fri) Hill now sends his revised version of the tragedy to AP for assessment.

6 Bolingbroke (and AP) optimistic that Dawley Farm will soon be sold, as two or three offers are forthcoming.

8 Just before this date Lady Burlington sends AP copies of the prose and verse attacks on him in the *Daily Gazetteer*. AP jokingly replies on this date that this is her attempt to bear malice to him or else to imitate (badly) his works.

12 AP returns Hill's play with his and Bolingbroke's criticisms, suggestions and praise.

25 AP, back at Twickenham after a short stay in London, now writes to Lord Orrery over an unsettling letter from Swift (written 8 Aug) about the letters; he hopes Orrery will shed light on the matter. AP returns a copy of a Swift poem Lord Orrery has sent him, probably a version of *Verses on the Death of Dr Swift*.

29 Second volume of Gay's *Fables* published, six years after his death; the work is seen through the press by AP, who has been editing it during the past months. On the same day AP declines to write an epilogue for Hill's play, noting that he has also refused, in the past year, to write epilogues for James Thomson and David Mallet.

October

4 (Wed) Lord Orrery writes to AP with assurances about Swift's conduct in the letters matter.

10 AP cancels the supply of Bath waters from Ralph Allen, as Lord Bolingbroke is to be away from Twickenham.

12 Writing for his friend Lyttelton, AP asks Swift to find a place for William Lamb, the son of Lyttelton's nurse, in the choir at St Patrick's (see 19 Apr 1739).

19 AP informs Lord Orrery that he has decided to cease his attempts to get all of his letters back from Ireland. He also regrets that Lord Orrery has not been approached to buy Dawley Farm, which has been conditionally sold to a merchant from London.

24 Publication of the satirical *Supplement to One Thousand Seven Hundred and Thirty-Eight. Not Written by Mr Pope*.

28 William Kent calls at Twickenham to examine the garden he has designed for AP.

November

2 (Thurs) About this time AP is making final adjustments to the Horatian poems to be issued in a quarto edition in January.

Writing to Ralph Allen he notes changes in Allen's character from *Epilogue to the Satires: Dialogue II*.

5   AP tells Hill that James Thomson and David Mallet will probably bring their tragedies (competing with Hill's) to the stage in the middle of the winter, so that Hill's can now be submitted to the theatre-managers.

8   Hill, with AP's blessing, has by now sent his play for consideration to Charles Fleetwood, manager at the Drury Lane Theatre.

9   The *Daily Gazetteer* publishes an attack on AP and Bolingbroke in response to AP's praise of the latter in *Epilogue to the Satires: Dialogue II*, l. 139.

21   Another attack on AP and Bolingbroke published in the *Daily Gazetteer*.

22   The *Daily Advertiser* promotes Curll's publication of Crousaz's *Commentaire* on the *Essay on Man* in a new translation by Charles Forman. The translation is friendly to AP but Curll's Preface tries to convert it into a critical satire on the poem.

23   J. P. Crousaz's *Examen de l'Essai de Monsieur Pope sur l'Homme* (1737) appears in an anonymous English translation (possibly by Elizabeth Carter) as *An Examination of Mr Pope's Essay on Man*. AP informs Lord Bathurst that Bolingbroke has called off the sale of Dawley Farm to the London merchant, citing the latter's miserly offers on house, contents and land. Lord Cornbury has been visiting AP at home this day.

24   The Duchess of Queensberry visits AP at Twickenham.

25   AP arrives in London and stays overnight, probably at Lord Cornbury's.

26   Early in the morning, AP visits Kent, who is not up. AP then returns later, and the pair go to Jonathan Richardson's, where they view several pictures intended for Lord Bolingbroke. In the evening AP dines with William Murray (later Earl of Mansfield) and his wife, and gets very drunk.

December

During this month, William Warburton issues his first letter of defence for AP against Crousaz's attack on the *Essay on Man*. This and the five subsequent monthly letters (though to April 1739) appear in *Works of the Learned*, but are later reworked in Warburton's full-scale *Critical and Philosophical Commentary on Mr Pope's Essay on Man*, published in 1742.

8 (Fri) AP conveys to Hill James Thomson's willingness to let Hill's tragedy be seen first at Drury Lane, if Fleetwood, the manager, accepts it, and also to provide any assistance he can.

9 By now Hill begins to suspect, despite AP's praises, that his play will not be accepted at Drury Lane.

19 Yet another attack on AP and Bolingbroke published in the *Daily Gazetteer*. AP writes to Lord Burlington on the recent attacks on him in the press: '*All* Great *Genius's have, & do suffer the Like.* Pray just tell my Lady Burlington that it is in the same manner I comfort myself against the Dreadful Papers She has Sent me.'

25 AP writes to Fortescue (who is at Bath) with apologies for seeing him not at all this year, because his connections to Lord Bolingbroke do not accord with Fortescue's Walpolean politics.

30 The *Daily Gazetteer* publishes still another attack on AP and Bolingbroke.

1739

January

9 (Tues) AP invites the Allens for a winter visit to Twickenham, in February.

11 Publication of *Poems and Imitations of Horace. By Mr Pope*, the first collection of the Horatian poems in one volume. Dodsley and Gilliver issue this in quarto format to match earlier volumes of the *Works*.

15 Hill sends AP a copy of the fifth edition of his *Northern Star*, with a revised Preface which eliminates the attack on AP. Hill reports that Mallet's tragedy will go first at Drury Lane.

22 AP in London again, whence he came after being briefly at Dawley, then London, then Twickenham. He enlightens Hill on the muddled state of affairs at Drury Lane. AP's letter of this day to his nephew, Michael, outlines the massive financial problems in the Rackett family, and urges him to agree to the sale of the Hallgrove estate; with the proceeds the nephew could then purchase a commission in the army.

26 Hill decides to withdraw his play without its being acted. AP is now in London. William Kent reports that he is paid a visit

by AP in the evening, 'about eight a clock in liquor & would have More wine, which I gave him'.

29 Dodsley and Cooper issue a small-octavo edition of AP's *Works*, volume II. It contains no new pieces but adds five complimentary poems by anonymous authors, one of them possibly Dodsley himself.

February

2 (Fri) Date of AP's first extant letter to William Warburton, written in thanks for Warburton's defence of the *Essay on Man* in *Works of the Learned*, begun in December 1738.

6 AP now commuting between Twickenham, London and Dawley Farm. He is at present at home, but goes up to London shortly to spend a week at Erasmus Lewis' house in Cork Street.

13 AP attends the first night of David Mallet's tragedy *Mustapha* at Drury Lane.

14 AP advises Aaron Hill to try his tragedy at Covent Garden, after its rejection by the manager at Drury Lane.

16 AP still in London. He tries to reserve a box (through Mallet) at the sixth night of Mallet's *Mustapha*.

21 Hill's last extant letter to AP: he gives a character of Samuel Richardson (at this time printer of the *Daily Gazetteer*, which had been attacking AP), and also declares his annoyance over the treatment of his play at Drury Lane.

March

13 (Tues) William Ayre's *Truth. A Counterpart to Mr Pope's Essay on Man* appears, the first epistle only. On the same day is published *Characters: An Epistle to Alexander Pope, Esq.*, written by one of Walpole's hacks, in which AP is charged with treasonous behaviour under Bolingbroke's influence.

27 Publication of William Dudgeon's *View of the Necessitarian or Best Scheme*, a response to the AP–Crousaz controversy over the *Essay on Man*. AP visiting Lady Suffolk at Marble Hill. He has not yet settled back into his Twickenham routine, but intends to do so soon.

April

During this month, AP is requested by Beau Nash to provide an inscription for Nash's obelisk to the Prince of Wales at Bath; he declines at this time. The Prince of Wales in this month conveys

through George Lyttelton that he wishes to donate some urns or
vases for AP's garden. Early in the month AP is kept at home by
an attack of rheumatism.

11 (Wed) AP thanks Warburton for the third and fourth
   instalments of his defence of the *Essay on Man* in the February
   and March issues of *Works of the Learned*, which he has just
   read: 'for You have made my System as clear as I ought to
   have done & could not'. He hopes Warburton will put the
   letters together into a book and AP hopes to procure a
   translation into French for all or part of the work.

12 AP evidently in London, at Lord Oxford's, where he awaits
   Lord Bolingbroke's departure for France.

13 Lord Bolingbroke executes the deeds of sale for Dawley Farm.

14 With the sale of Dawley Farm complete, Lord Bolingbroke
   sails from Greenwich for France, leaving AP bereft of the last
   of his important early friends.

17 With Bolingbroke gone to France, AP is now back home at
   Twickenham. He has been suffering from a rheumatic attack,
   but invites the Allens to stay with him.

19 Swift writes to his friend Alderman Barber asking him to tell
   AP that he has found a full vicar-choralship in the choir at St
   Patrick's for Lyttelton's nurse's son (William Lamb) as
   requested in October 1738.

28 Swift's letter of this date introduces his cousin Deane Swift,
   who carries the letter to AP on a visit to London.

May

1 (Tues) Dodsley and Cooper issue the small-octavo edition of
  The Works of Alexander Pope, volume II, part II, containing six
  poems published for the first time. (The title page bears the
  date 1738.) These include the famous 'Epigram Engraved on
  the Collar of a Dog' ('I am his Highness' Dog at Kew; / Pray
  tell me Sir, whose Dog are you?') and *The Seventh Epistle of the
  First Book of Horace, Imitated in the Manner of Swift* (' 'Tis true,
  my Lord, I gave my word'), and AP's mock epitaph on
  himself ('Heroes and Kings! your distance keep'), which
  Warburton later has engraved on a monument to AP at
  Twickenham church, seven years after AP's death. A fourth
  piece appearing here, 'Cloë A Character' ('"Yet Cloë sure
  was form'd without a Spot" – '), later is incorporated as
  ll. 157–80 of the *Epistle to a Lady* (see Ault, pp. 266–75).

5 Allen conveys the news that Lord Oxford has another great
Dane for AP, again named Bounce, and urges AP to send for
it immediately.

15 About this date, having reversed his earlier declaration, AP
sends Beau Nash an inscription for the obelisk to the Prince
of Wales at Bath.

17 AP's long letter outlines to Swift Lord Bolingbroke's plans for
a retired country life in France at Fontainebleau. At the
moment AP is at Lewis' house in London. He notes that the
Duchess of Marlborough has recently been paying him court,
and that he has written but ten lines since last year, an
insertion for a new edition of *The Dunciad*.

18 By this date AP has received his gift of stone (?) urns for the
garden and several marble busts for the house from the
Prince of Wales. AP himself has made a present of the puppy
Bounce to Ralph Allen. He has just seen William Fortescue in
town.

19 AP now visiting at Lord Orrery's residence in London, in
company with Dr William King.

26 AP thanks Warburton at the conclusion of his series on AP's
Essay on Man in *History of the Works of the Learned*.

June
In this month's issue of the *Gentleman's Magazine* appears AP's
'Cloë: A Character' (see 1 May).

13 (Wed) Publication of William Ayre's *Truth . . . Epistle the
Second*, opposing AP's 'Opinions of Man as an Individual'.

22 Martha Blount dines at Twickenham with AP.

23 AP invites Fortescue to dine with him tomorrow, but
Fortescue is still away.

27 About this date AP leaves Twickenham for a ramble in
Buckinghamshire and Oxfordshire.

July
3 (Tues) AP at Lord Cobham's at Stowe, where the Duke of
Argyll drops in to see him, as well as George Grenville, Lord
Cobham's nephew.

4 From Stowe, AP directs to London a haunch of venison for
Martha Blount.

7 AP still at Stowe, but planning to be at George Lyttelton's
father's house at Hagley (near Stourbridge), Worcestershire,

in the next couple of days, eventually moving on to Rousham, where the Dormers live, and Cornbury.

9 AP stays at the Duke of Argyll's residence at Adderbury, formerly the home of John Wilmot, Earl of Rochester. The occasion gives rise to AP's 'On Lying in the Earl of Rochester's Bed at Atterbury'.

19 AP seems to have stayed with the Duke of Argyll at Adderbury this night on the way back to Rousham.

26 AP now at the Dormers' residence at Rousham; tomorrow evening he expects to meet Fortescue's fellow-judge, Sir Francis Page, at dinner and in a few days will go to Cornbury, where he is to advise on garden alterations.

August

In their issues for this month the *London Magazine* and the *Scots Magazine* both print for the first time AP's 'On Lying in the Earl of Rochester's Bed at Atterbury'.

1 (Wed) AP arrives home at Twickenham after a month's absence, tired and sore.

16 AP dines with Charles Jervas, who is now in declining health. AP's own health is still poor after his month's ramble, and now he begins to have kidney trouble.

September

In its issue for this month, the *Gentleman's Magazine* prints (anonymously) AP's 'On Lying in the Earl of Rochester's Bed at Atterbury'.

14 (Fri) Nathaniel Hooke, who has spent the month of August as Ralph Allen's guest, is now visiting AP, trying to encourage AP to visit Allen in the coming winter. AP agrees and writes to Allen. At the moment, he is revising either his letters to and from Swift or the *Martinus Scriblerus* material, perhaps both.

20 Writing from Twickenham, AP asks Warburton to have his printer send a copy of the instalments of the defence of the *Essay on Man* so that AP can have them properly translated into French.

October

15 (Mon) AP recommends a candidate to Lord Burlington for the now-vacant living of Eyam, Derbyshire, which is held by him.

19 Britain declares war against Spain.
31 AP had intended to go up to the City on business, but his appointment is changed to Highgate and he declines to travel that far.

November
2 (Fri) On this day AP probably visits the City, and may perhaps dine with Fortescue as he returns.
3 Charles Jervas dies in London. In his will AP receives a legacy of £1000 if he outlives Jervas' widow (which he does not).
14 Publication announced of William Warburton's *Vindication of Mr Pope's Essay on Man, from the Misrepresentations of Mr de Crousaz*. On this day or possibly the next, AP arrives at Ralph Allen's house at Bath. Shortly afterwards he arranges to see the son of Lord Bolingbroke's secretary, John Brinsden.
19 AP probably now settled at Bristol, where he is taking the waters for his health. He writes a long description of the town to Martha Blount.
20 AP recommends Fortescue to purchase Warburton's *Vindication*, just published; whether AP has a copy by this date is not clear.
22 AP now at Bath, having tired of Bristol; he is staying with the Allens and taking the waters mixed with those of Bristol, but does not go into the city.
27 Writing in *The Champion*, Henry Fielding praises AP's works, which 'will be coeval with the Language in which they are writ' (*CH*, p. 235).

December
1 (Sat) AP still with the Allens at Bath. In response to an earlier letter, AP writes to Henry Brooke at length of his beliefs, and sends him a copy of Warburton's *Vindication*.
15 AP remains at Bath, and so offers John Brinsden the use of his Twickenham house while away.
17 AP writes a palliative letter to Mallet, who is annoyed at comparisons between his play *Mustapha* and that of Roger Boyle, Earl of Orrery, whose *Dramatic Works* were published earlier in the year by AP's publisher, Robert Dodsley.
25 AP at Ralph Allen's for Christmas. Date of AP's last extant letter to Lord Oxford.

26 The Revd William Borlase has just shipped to AP a box of mineral samples from Cornwall, for display in the walls of the grotto at Twickenham.

27 AP writes humorously to Martha Blount, who has complained of being entertained too much: 'to be all day, first dressing one's body, then dragging it abroad, then stuffing the guts, then washing them with Tea, then wagging one's tongue, & so to bedd; is the life of an Animal'.

1740

January

Early in the month AP's friend William Kent, is appointed (to succeed Jervas) as Face Painter to His Majesty the King. In this month the London *Daily Post*, *Evening Post* and the *Daily Gazetteer* all advertise that Thomas Osborne has for sale copies of AP's *Iliad*, although this seems to be an infringement of copyright. The advertisements appear also in February and March.

1 (Tues) AP still at Bath, staying with the Allens. AP writes to Fortescue concerning his next step in the long-running lawsuit of his sister, Magdalen Rackett.

4 As AP writes to Warburton about inaccuracies in the *Vindication* which should be changed in the next edition, the second edition of the work is advertised (in the *Daily Journal*) as appearing this day. AP notes that Silhouette's French translation of the *Vindication* is complete, so he awaits Warburton's advice before allowing it to be published.

5 AP requests that Fortescue perform 'the good office I desired to Mrs. Jervas . . . for I would not have her think me a Brute'. AP is somewhat embarrassed by the legacy of £1000 Jervas has left him if he survives the widow.

10 Prompted by the recent receipt of a six-page letter from Sir William Cleland, AP worried about his mounting debt of correspondence.

17 AP has just this morning received from Warburton an advance copy of *A Seventh Letter, which finishes the Vindication of Mr Pope's Essay on Man*, which deals with the fourth epistle. When he gets back to Twickenham, he will revise the French translation of the *Vindication* (by Silhouette) and add the *Seventh Letter* to it.

19 Writing to Lord Burlington, AP gives an account of the medical treatment he has received at Bath: 'The Kitchen, Backside, & Yard requird Scowring, & I hope to have done it so effectually, as to present you at my Return with a most Clean Creature.' Having heard just now of Kent's appointment, he recommends the same 'to cleanse His Pencil, & purify his Pallat, from all that greasy mixture & Fatt Oyl they have contracted'.

23 AP writes to Fortescue offering to release him from service as his executor, to prevent political embarrassment, as Fortescue is a Whig supporter and appointee. (Fortescue is not so named in AP's final will.)

29 Henry Lintot tries to explain by letter how Thomas Osborne has copies of *The Iliad* for sale. AP notes that the procedure followed by Lintot results in a fraud, and is evidently thinking of legal action to regain his property.

February

10 (Sun) AP arrives in London, from Bath.

11 AP, in London but on the way home, arranges to meet Jonathan Richardson at Mr Murray's house in Lincoln's Inn Fields, in the evening.

12 AP departs London for Twickenham, early in the morning.

18 AP now in London, where he complains to Hugh Bethel (by letter) of the irregular dining-hours, which have upset his health again. He reiterates his unease at having been left a conditional legacy of £1000 from Jervas.

23 Lord and Lady Orrery report from Ireland that Swift is more and more under the power of his guardian, Mrs Martha Whiteway.

25 AP back at Twickenham.

27 Death of Alexander Hume, second Earl of Marchmont, and succession of his son, Hugh, to the title.

29 AP sends condolences and praises to his friend Hugh Hume, on his father's death; Hugh, Viscount Polwarth, is now third Earl of Marchmont.

March

The *Gentleman's Magazine* issue for this month includes 'On the Benefactions in the Late Frost' ('Yes, 'tis the time! I cry'd, impose the chain!'), probably by AP.

1 (Sat) AP intends to see both Dr William King (Principal of St Mary Hall, Oxford) and the Earl of Marchmont in London this day.

9 In Twickenham, AP receives the great trunk of minerals sent to him from Cornwall by William Borlase. His letter to Borlase shows he has already begun to plan their placement in the grotto.

25 AP just returned to Twickenham from a week in London. The weather is miserable, he has been suffering from colds, and cannot get on with the spring planting in his garden or the decoration of his grotto.

26 Nathaniel Hooke visits AP at Twickenham. AP writes to Mrs Knight's husband, Robert Nugent, with thanks for a volume of his *Odes and Epistles*, and for sending word that Mrs Whiteway has more of AP's letters to Swift which she says she will return. He has been carefully reading Nugent's 'Ode to Marchmont'.

April

2 (Wed) From Bath, Robert Nugent now conveys by letter to Mrs Whiteway AP's wish that she send his letters, *via* Nugent, who will be back in London next week.

14 An anonymous *Satirical Epistle to Mr Pope* published.

16 AP invites Warburton to meet him in London, and then be carried down to Twickenham for a few days. Their first actual meeting occurs within ten days of this letter.

18 AP visiting unnamed friends in Windsor Forest for a few days, before Warburton arrives in London.

19 AP writes with abundant thanks to Ralph Allen for a recently received cargo of Bristol water, cider and building-stone.

21 Warburton arrives in London, late at night. He meets AP perhaps on the 23rd, and AP begins by showing him off to his noble friends, including Lords Oxford and Bathurst, and George Lyttelton.

26 AP invites Warburton to dine with him this afternoon at Lord Bathurst's, in St James's Square.

28 Probable date of AP and Warburton's departure together for a week at Twickenham.

30 Replying to AP's letter of 9 March, Borlase sends another large basket of mineral specimens for the grotto decoration.

May

Perhaps in this month, or possibly in June, AP sends a copy of their printed correspondence to Swift, claiming it to be the only copy in public hands (*Corr.*, IV, 242–3). This is the so-called 'clandestine volume', which AP has had printed so as eventually to force Swift to return his letters so that they may be printed by him (see *CIH*, pp. 97–8).

2   (Fri) Possible date of AP and Warburton's return to London. AP lodges with his friend William Cheselden, the surgeon.

3   In Dublin, Swift signs his last will. AP is bequeathed only a miniature, and not (as earlier promised) his papers.

5   AP shifts his lodgings to Erasmus Lewis' house, as the Cheseldens have gone to the country.

7   George Lyttelton asks to dine with him and Warburton tomorrow evening at eight.

15 Warburton now back in London after another week's stay with AP at Twickenham. During this time he has met the Duke of Argyll and Lord Cobham, and together he and AP have read over some of the Scriblerus material which AP has been revising. AP has just received another cargo of minerals from Borlase for his grotto, to which his thoughts now turn.

16 AP writes to Henry Lintot about the publication of the new *Dunciad*, asking him not to part with his legal share of the work except to AP himself. On this same day, Mrs Whiteway writes to AP about the disposition of Swift's works, some of which AP has asked for to print in their forthcoming correspondence. She also claims to have several more of AP's letters which she will send soon.

23 Probably on this day, Warburton and AP say farewell, in London; AP has had another appointment for dinner, so they must meet afterwards.

24 Probable date of Warburton's departure from London, for Cambridge. AP goes back to Twickenham.

27 AP invites Ralph Allen to send his gardener soon, so that he may assist with the grotto.

June

2   (Mon) After this date AP probably spends a few days in London attending again to his sister's lawsuit, which William Murray is helping him with.

8 By this date the decoration of the grotto is half finished. AP thanks Borlase for his continuing contributions of minerals, and promises to put Borlase's name into the decoration. The letter gives a full description of the grotto.

17 Work in the grotto now stopped for lack of materials; AP sends Ralph Allen's gardener back to Bath.

18 AP responds elegantly to Mrs Whiteway's letter of 16 May, which promises to convey more of AP's letters back to him.

24 AP at Twickenham. He has been and is now reading Warburton's *Divine Legation of Moses* (1738), a copy of which Warburton has given him during his recent visit. Warburton's *Seventh Letter, which finishes the Vindication of Mr Pope's Essay on Man* published.

July

During this month, Curll publishes *The Tryal of Colley Cibber*, a satire which indicts both Cibber and AP for misuse of their talents.

14 (Mon) AP dines with Lord and Lady Oxford. Later that night he writes his 'Lines to King George II' ('O all-accomplish'd Caesar! on thy Shelf'). But the Caesar is not in fact George II but Mary Caesar, a dinner guest this day and an old friend of AP.

17 Writing to Ralph Allen, AP speculates about visiting Bath in September, but not before, and pleads his declining health: 'I am in no pain but my Case is not curable, & must in course of time as it does not diminish, become painful first, & then fatal.' The problem is that his deteriorating spine and rib-cage are slowly crushing his heart and lungs. He also is just now receiving another cargo of Allen's stone for his grotto, 'the last of the laborious Baubles of my life'.

29 George Faulkner writes to AP from Dublin asking for permission to print a collection of Swift's letters, also including AP's to Swift; he has seen the 'clandestine volume' AP sent to Swift in May or June.

August

2 (Sat) AP now in London, having been compelled by a continuing painful kidney and urinary-tract problem (a partial stoppage of the urethra) to seek medical attention from Cheselden, the surgeon. AP has seen Patty Blount in town.

AP is operated on by Cheselden, for a stoppage (an inch from the pubic bone in the urethra). The surgical probe is very painful and must be repeated to make the passage wider. AP informs Hugh Bethel that the most painful part is having to urinate now after the operation.

4   About this date, AP discusses ownership of the *Key to the Lock* with Charles Bathurst, who will be printing AP's *Works in Prose*, volume II, in 1741.

14 In light of Faulkner's letter of 29 July, AP now writes to Robert Nugent, thanking him for help in the Swift-letters affair, and hoping that the publication will not be completed. He now distrusts Mrs Whiteway's intentions as to the letters.

16 AP sends his negative reply (not extant) to Faulkner via Robert Nugent, in hopes that it will arrive more quickly than through the ordinary post.

29 AP has gathered more materials for publication, as he informs the printer, Charles Bathurst. These include Scriblerus material, and some of Swift's pieces, for the volume of *Works in Prose* which will appear in April 1741.

September

3   (Wed) AP has been rereading Robert Nugent's 'Ode to Marchmont' in the past few days. AP's letter of this day to Bolingbroke mentions the latter's proposed interpretation of the *Essay on Man* (which was never written). AP includes with his letter a copy of his 'Verses on a Grotto by the River Thames at Twickenham' ('Thou who shalt stop, where *Thames'* translucent Wave'), a poem on which he has just been working. AP also gives Lord Orrery a detailed summary of the Swift-letters affair, finally asking him to edit out any unfavourable passages if Faulkner does go ahead with publication.

5   AP in London.

8   AP visits Martha Blount in London.

9   Probable date of visit by the Duchess of Marlborough to AP at Twickenham.

17 AP now intending to go to Bath at the end of October. He is better after his August surgery. Now he works on his grotto.

26 AP has decided not to have a repeat of his August surgery because of the subsequent pain and soreness, opting for a dietary treatment instead.

27   In Ireland, Lord Orrery requests that he see the printing of
     AP's and Swift's letters before Faulkner issues the volume. In
     an undated letter shortly after, Faulkner agrees to this and
     promises to bring the proofs to Orrery at Caledon.

October
During this month, AP is increasingly worried about the current
political situation, in which he supports the opposition. His long
patriotic letter to Marchmont urges him to come to London to lead
the opposition to Walpole.

3   (Fri) AP well enough, but not to travel. He summarises for
    Allen the Swift-letters affair, which 'has fretted, & imployed
    me a great deal' to no satisfactory end.

4   AP writes Faulkner to demand a reading of the Swift letters
    before publication. On the same day Orrery sends AP a copy
    of his letter of 27 September, Faulkner's answer, and word
    that he will try to keep Faulkner's original copies of the
    letters. Faulkner visits Orrery this day at Caledon.

6   Orrery recounts to AP the visit of Faulkner, who has brought
    only the printed copy of the letters, which he will hold back
    from publishing at the moment.

7   Mrs Whiteway's letter to Lord Orrery details her part in the
    letters affair, including her attempt to dissuade Faulkner from
    publishing, although Swift is firm about it.

8   Lord Orrery writes to Swift encouraging him to detain or
    suppress publication of the letters. Meanwhile AP notes the
    completion of his grotto, except for some exterior decoration;
    he informs Dr William Oliver (a Bath friend and physician)
    that both his and Borlase's names will be memorialised in the
    grotto.

10 Lord Orrery forwards Mrs Whiteway's letter of 7 October to
    AP, with a gloss on its untruths.

14 AP now proposing to visit Ralph Allen next month and stay
    until February; he expects Nathaniel Hooke will accompany
    him.

15 Dr Oliver volunteers to obtain more mineral samples for AP's
    grotto, and looks forward to seeing him at Bath next month.

17 AP's troubled letter to Orrery goes over the letters matter,
    and also indicates he is resigned to the eventual publication,
    since he has received Faulkner's first two printed sheets of
    them.

18 Orrery sends back to Faulkner the printed letters, so that they can now be sent to AP. AP, at Twickenham, notifies Charles Bathurst that his note of mistakes to be rectified for a future reprint of the AP–Swift *Miscellanies* is available at Dr Cheselden's house.

24 Publication of James Miller's *Are These Things So? The Previous Question from an Englishman in his Grotto, to a Great Man at Court*, in which a symbolic poet of virtue, modelled on AP, addresses the Great Man, modelled on Walpole. The pamphlet provokes a rash of further supporting and opposing replies in the following three months (see Mack, *Garden and City*, p. 97).

25 Charles Bathurst dines with AP at Twickenham. AP writes to Orrery yet again with deductions about the letters and further plans for action if and when the letters are published.

27 Orrery hopes that AP will have received the parcels of letters from Faulkner as directed by Orrery (see 18 Oct). AP suffering from eye troubles, but is able to make suggestions to Warburton for a proposed Latin translation of the *Essay on Man*. He now says that the Scriblerus material must be delayed to see if the AP–Swift letters appear.

November
 4 (Tues) AP has just returned home from visiting his sister at Hallgrove (Bagshot, Surrey) in Windsor Forest. He is still seeing to her long-running lawsuit. He intends to visit the Allens in a little more than a week's time. After this date he goes up to London on more legal business, to William Murray's. AP also directs Faulkner to send the printed letters to him at Bath.

 8 Having heard from Faulkner that the letters are not now to be conveyed to AP, Lord Orrery tells Faulkner that he will take charge of them, and then writes to AP that he will quietly send them on for AP's alterations, which can then appear to be Orrery's changes.

11 Business and his fear of the bumpy journey keep AP in London (at Murray's), so that he cannot meet Allen's prearranged carriage at Newbury, Berkshire.

12 Lord Orrery has now read the letters and declares them of negligible interest, but tells AP that their publication cannot be stopped completely. He will send the printed letters on as soon as he gets them from Faulkner

13 Faulkner sends the printed letters to Orrery.

14 Orrery now sends the printed letters in nine parcels to AP; Faulkner does not know that he does this.

15 Faulkner checks to see that the letters have arrived safely. Lord Orrery writes back that they have. On this same day, AP writes to Orrery to say that he has not yet received the letters, supposed to have been sent on 27 October.

17 AP (at Twickenham) explains to Ralph Allen why he delays his trip to Bath, but notes that he will now soon go there with Dr Arbuthnot's son George.

19 Lord Orrery now writes to Faulkner, pretending that he alone will read the letters, when he has in fact sent them to AP.

December

2 (Tues) AP informs Ralph Allen that he will at last set out for a Bath visit in ten days, with George Arbuthnot. He hopes to meet Allen's carriage at Newbury on the 13th.

3 Another letter from AP to Lord Orrery on the Swift letters: AP now imputes publication interests in London to Mrs Whiteway. AP plans a special answer to Faulkner once he has seen the book.

6 AP in London, where he visits Lord Bathurst and William Murray.

10 AP at Twickenham. He has finally received the 'book' (nine parcels of sheets) of the letters, and is pleased that the contents are 'trivial and familiar', as he tells Lord Orrery. AP has found annotations in Swift's hand in the proof-sheets. Work is continuing meanwhile on his own authorised version of his letters, which will ultimately appear before Faulkner's Dublin edition.

11 Probable date of George Arbuthnot's arrival at AP's house.

12 AP and George Arbuthnot depart Twickenham. They stay the night at Reading.

13 A carriage (perhaps Ralph Allen's) meets AP and George Arbuthnot at Newbury, around noon, taking them to Marlborough, Wiltshire, where they stay the night.

15 Henry Lintot purchases the full copyright of *The Dunciad*; legally the property should revert to AP in 1742.

20 Orrery now responds to AP's letter of the 10th, promising to get the proof-sheets (which AP now has and must return to Orrery) back from AP after the volume has been published.

24 Orrery's letter to AP theorises on exactly how the letters came to be published. His letter to Mrs Whiteway demands the letters she months ago promised to send to AP, and asks her who has been stealing letters from Swift's papers.

27 AP, well settled at Bath for almost two weeks, writes twice to Lord Orrery. The first letter lists his grievances both about the original letters and about their printing by Faulkner. The second letter is to be shown to Mrs Whiteway and Faulkner, promising to prosecute if an edition is published in London. AP also returns to Orrery five packets containing proof-sheets.

29 At Bath, AP visits Dr Oliver, drawing a sketch of his grotto for him. Writing to Orrery yet again, AP now asserts that he will publish a narrative of events in the letters matter if the book is published in London; he does not in the end follow through with this.

30 AP's letter to Orrery of this day is the narrative of events in the letters controversy. Mrs Whiteway's letter gives *her* narrative of events from the Dublin perspective and offers to return the letters.

1741

January

During this month, AP's 'Verses on a Grotto by the River Thames at Twickenham' has its earliest printing in the *Gentleman's Magazine*.

2 (Fri) Lord Orrery accepts Mrs Whiteway's offer of returning his letters as well as those for AP, and sends his agent to collect them. He repeats his suspicions about the theft of the letters. Alderman John Barber, an old friend of AP's, dies this day; his will leaves AP a small bequest. AP is still at Bath, with the Allens, as the year begins.

3 *The Publick Register; or, The Weekly Magazine* (Dodsley's periodical) prints the 'Epigram (On Lopping Trees in his Garden)' ('My Ld. complains, that *P——* (stark mad with Gardens)'), probably by AP.

7 Orrery's agent returns to him with the two packages of letters, one for him and one for AP.

8   Lord Orrery lets AP know that he will deliver the packet of letters (from Mrs Whiteway) personally.

9   AP writes to congratulate Lord Marchmont on his recent agreement (after an earlier refusal) to work for the opposition in Parliament.

10 AP's 'Epitaph. On Himself' ('Under this marble, or under this sill') appears in the *Publick Register*. 'Verbatim from Boileau' ('Once (says an Author, where, I need not say)') in the same issue may also be AP's. Lord Orrery now tells Mrs Whiteway that he will not give back the printed sheets of the letter book (which are probably just arriving back from AP) until given a command by Swift or AP.

12 On or shortly after this date Lord Orrery receives the parcels of printed sheets of the letters back from AP, whom he notifies of their arrival, and thanks for the narrative of events, to which further details can be added when they meet.

17 Anonymous publication of AP's 'Prologue, for the Benefit of Mr Dennis', in the *Publick Register* no. 3.

23 AP writes to thank Lord Orrery for his help (in the letters matter) and that of Mrs Whiteway, to whom he will show the letter.

25 AP writes to David Mallet about Richard Savage, whom he has been secretly supporting for some time with small donations of cash.

29 AP requests Orrery to have Faulkner send him a copy of the Swift–AP letters book when published.

31 AP advises Henry Lintot to seek out Gilliver's partial share in the *Dunciad* copyright, stating that he is willing to do revisions for a new edition by Lintot of the poem.

February

2 (Mon) AP asks Charles Bathurst for his response to changes in the proposed reprinting of the AP–Swift *Miscellanies*; AP is withdrawing some material for his *Works in Prose*, volume II, to join the *Memoirs of Martinus Scriblerus*.

4 AP still at Bath, but just about to leave for London.

11 On or just before this date AP leaves Bath for London. He has been reading Richardson's *Pamela* 'with great Approbation and Pleasure, and wanted a Night's Rest in finishing it' (*Corr.*, IV, 335).

March

12 (Thurs) AP invites Lord Orrery (returned from Ireland) to Twickenham for the day, but the weather proves unfavourable.

15 AP has spent time at Twickenham, and is now in London seeing to the sale (by Slingsby Bethel) of his South Sea Company annuities. He stays at William Murray's house in Lincoln's Inn Fields.

17 AP still in London at Murray's. He corresponds with Nathaniel Cole over Lintot's claims, probably over the *Key to the Lock* (1715), which AP wants to reprint in his prose volume.

22 AP visiting Lord Orrery in Duke Street, Westminster, where they write a joint letter to Swift. AP mentions his 'pain' over the recent letters matter, but does not reveal his real part in the controversy.

April

During this month, Jacob Tonson publishes George Ogle's collection of *The Canterbury Tales of Chaucer, Moderniz'd by Several Hands*; the three-volume set includes AP's version of *The Wife of Bath's Prologue*.

14 (Tues) AP at Twickenham, where he tells Warburton that a complimentary copy of the *Works in Prose*, volume II, awaits him in London.

16 Publication in folio and quarto formats of *The Works of Mr Alexander Pope, in Prose*, volume II, containing many new letters of AP to Swift and the *Memoirs of Martinus Scriblerus*, amongst much reprinted work. This represents the authorised version of the letters, published two months ahead of Faulkner's Dublin edition prompted by the 'clandestine volume' of 1740.

17 AP has arranged for folio copies of the *Works in Prose*, volume II, to be sent to Ralph Allen and Dr Oliver. He is now about to embark on an investment of £1000 in the Sun Fire Office shares, with Allen's help. The grotto and its decoration are at last finished.

May

14 (Thurs) AP describes to Allen the final aspects which will complete his garden: an arch at the entry and the stone urns on the lawn. He presages a lawsuit with Curll for pirating the AP–Swift letters.

21 AP arranges for a complimentary copy of the *Works in Prose*, volume II, for Robert Nugent to be left at Murray's in London; this in return for services in the letters affair.

26 William Warburton's second volume of *The Divine Legation of Moses* published.

27 AP in London at William Murray's house, where he expects to meet Warburton, who is about to arrive in London. Not finding him, AP departs for Twickenham in the afternoon.

28 AP back at Twickenham but expects to go into Berkshire tomorrow. This evening he probably sees Lord and Lady Cobham nearby. Warburton arrives in London late in the evening.

31 Warburton spends the day with AP at Twickenham.

June

4 (Thurs) AP probably in London this day, to see Warburton and to bring suit in Chancery against Curll for his piracy of the AP–Swift letters.

5 AP writes Allen that he and Warburton are going up to Oxford, and that they may get as far as Cirencester (Lord Bathurst's), where they hope to see Allen. The visit to Oxford is apparently to collect honorary degrees which (rumours have it) will be voted to them both.

6 Warburton and AP going back to Twickenham together.

13 AP has earlier requested a naval preferment for his waterman; George Lyttelton now tells him that Lord Baltimore has arranged for the preferment to be granted.

14 Date of Curll's sworn responses to AP's suit in Chancery.

15 On this day or the next, AP leaves Twickenham for Oxford and Cirencester. He tells Charles Bathurst that on his return he will rework the *Miscellanies* for their reprinting.

16 Death of Edward Harley, second Lord Oxford, AP's old friend, at age 52.

17 Decision brought down in Chancery in AP's favour: its basis is that a letter remains the property of the writer, not the recipient, and there is no right to publish without the writer's permission.

20 In Dublin, George Faulkner finally issues his edition of *Letters to and from Dr J. Swift*, with reprinted letters by AP. A pirated London edition is immediately put out by Curll, *Dean Swift's Literary Correspondence, for Twenty-Four Years; from 1714 to*

1738, which also includes AP's 'Epitaph On Himself' ('Under this Marble, or under this Sill').

July
14 (Tues) AP sends word to Allen of a gift to him from Twickenham, two pineapples. He reports the partial success of his court injunction against Curll's piracy of the letters.
17 AP visits the sculptor Roubiliac in London; he is making statuary heads for Ralph Allen's Prior Park house.
23 AP declares to Charles Bathurst that he has a month's leisure time and would work on revising the AP–Swift *Miscellanies* if Bathurst should decide to reprint soon. On this day he receives six tons of building-materials from Ralph Allen which he requested on 14 May. This is for the grotto's garden entrance. With his thanks for this, he also asks Allen to use his influence in getting an army commission for Nathaniel Hooke's son.

August
11 (Tues) AP in London, to see Hugh Bethel.
12 AP back at Twickenham, having missed seeing Fortescue, who has gone to Devon. AP asks him to send a hogshead of scallop shells for the grotto. On the same day, having just received some ideas from Warburton (about the *Dunciad* revision?), AP writes to him also to say that he will not accept an honorary degree from Oxford unless Warburton gets one.
13 Hugh Bethel departs London for Italy, because of his asthma. AP sends a gift of pineapples from his garden to the Duchess of Marlborough in anticipation of his dining with her on the 16th.
15 The Duchess of Marlborough has just sent AP a present of venison – a whole buck. He proposes that she return to Twickenham with him tomorrow after they have dined, so as to view the grotto.
16 AP probably dines with the Duchess of Marlborough at her house at Wimbledon.
28 AP sends Allen an inscription for one of his statues at Prior Park. Workmen are still paving the porch of the grotto, having worked already for a fortnight. Nathaniel Hooke is staying with AP.

September

5 (Sat) AP has now provided work for the printer whom Charles Bathurst has employed to do the reprinted *Miscellanies*. He writes to Bathurst to recover some of the profits for the *Works in Prose*, volume II, or possibly for an advance on the *Miscellanies*.

20 AP's letter to Warburton is the earliest mention of the project to annotate all of AP's poems. He also mentions the completion of *The Dunciad*. AP now intending to go to Ralph Allen's at Bath in a month's time.

21 Death of AP's friend Sir William Cleland, two months after being sacked by Walpole as Commissioner of Taxes in England.

24 AP tells Ralph Allen that he will arrive in Bath about the middle of October, when the last alterations to the grotto are complete.

October

1 (Thurs) AP now proposes the 19th as the day he will set out for Bath, since Allen will be in London then.

19 David Garrick's debut in the London theatres, in the role of Shakespeare's Richard III (see Mack, *Life*, p. 760).

22 AP still at Twickenham. He tells the Duchess of Marlborough that Hooke (who has been working on the Marlborough papers) and his wife are to live in the Twickenham house while he is at Bath.

23 The Allens come to see AP at Twickenham; all three will travel to Bath tomorrow. AP possibly attends Garrick's fifth night in the title role of *Richard III* (but see Mack, *Life*, p. 750).

27 AP reaches Bath with the Allens by this date.

29 AP expecting to receive (with George Arbuthnot's help) his £100 legacy from Alderman John Barber, which he intends to give to Anne Arbuthnot and Martha Blount to bring them to Bath. He asks Arbuthnot to tell Bathurst not to print Dr Arbuthnot's 'Sermon Preached at the Mercat Cross of Edinburgh' in the *Miscellanies*.

November

The *Gentleman's Magazine* this month advertises publication of *A Commentary on Mr Pope's Principles of Morality, or Essay on Man. By Mr Crousaz*, a translation probably by Samuel Johnson. The work is eventually published with a 1742 title-page, although some copies were available as early as 1739 (*TE*, III, i, xxi).

3 (Mon) AP writes to Lyttelton of friendship: 'I feel every day what the Puritans calld *out-goings* of my Soul, in the Concern I take for some of [my friends]; which upon my word is a warmer Sensation than any I feel in my own, and for my own, Being.'

12 Having heard that Warburton's publisher has died, AP writes to recommend John Knapton as a successor, and also invites Warburton to visit and stay with him at Prior Park.

15 AP now writes to Charles Bathurst to say (not to hurt Bathurst's feelings) that *Warburton* would prefer to use Knapton as his bookseller.

22 AP advises Warburton to go through London (to attend to publishing-business) before coming to Bath, and asks him to bring his notes upon AP's poems: 'They may make a winter Evenings amusement, when you have nothing better.'

December
AP spends all of this month staying with the Allens at Bath. Warburton joins him there, either very early in the month or else at the very end of November. While there he works on *The New Dunciad*, a fourth book to the poem.

1742

January
1 (Fri) AP remains at Bath, with Warburton, at Ralph Allen's. He writes to Bethel, who is in Italy, with political and poetical news; he has been writing *The New Dunciad*, or book IV of *The Dunciad*: 'I little thought 3 months ago to have drawn the whole polite world upon me . . . as I certainly shall whenever I publish this poem. An Army of Virtuosi, Medalists, Ciceronis, Royal Society-men, Schools, universities, even Florists, Free thinkers, & Free masons, will incompass me with fury. . . . But a Good Conscience, a bold Spirit, & Zeal for Truth, at whatsoever Expence, of whatever Pretenders to Science, or of all Imposition either Literary, Moral, or Political; these animated me, & these will Support me.'

6 AP and Warburton reach Avebury, Wiltshire, through deep snow, having now left Bath.

7 AP and Warburton reach Newbury, Berkshire; the winter weather still severe.

9 AP at home at last, with Warburton.

10 AP goes up to London on business connected with Nathaniel Hooke's son's commission, and possibly with Warburton's problems over the death of his publisher. He may also be drawn by the political upheavals which will lead to Walpole's resignation.

18 AP, in London, writes to the Duchess of Marlborough at Marlborough House, before returning to his home.

19 AP back at Twickenham briefly, where he reports to Allen that Hooke has finished working on the Marlborough papers. Later this same day he returns to London, staying with William Murray, perhaps to assist in Warburton's publishing-affairs.

31 Seeing an impossible situation in Parliament, Walpole decides to resign, thus ending his political life.

February

In the *Gentleman's Magazine* for this month appears 'Tom Southerne's Birth-day Dinner at Ld Orrery's' ('Resign'd to live, prepar'd to die'), probably by AP.

8 (Mon) AP tells Allen that Hooke's work on the Marlborough papers has earned him £1000 plus future considerations. Warburton's affairs with his late publisher's executors are now cleared up, thanks to help from AP and William Murray. AP has at last been able to invest in the Sun Fire Office shares. The owner of the land on which the Twickenham house stands has just died; AP must decide whether to buy the land, plus adjoining cottages, or to move. He is now on the point of deciding to publish *The New Dunciad*.

11 Following the failure of his majority in Parliament, Sir Robert Walpole retires from politics, resigning after twenty years as Prime Minister.

13 About this date Warburton leaves London for Newark, Nottinghamshire, now that his publishing-difficulties are settled.

14 About this date, AP leaves London for Twickenham.

March
During this month, AP attends the London auction of the late Lord Oxford's collection of paintings, coins, medals and curios.

2 (Tues) Nathaniel Hooke's first work with the Marlborough papers is published, *An Account of the Conduct of Sarah, Duchess of Marlborough*. He continues to work on the material during the year.

20 On this day, Thomas Cooper publishes *The New Dunciad: As it was Found in the Year 1741*. This is the first edition of Book IV of *The Dunciad*. A second edition of the work appears before 3 April, and there is some slight revision and addition to the text and notes.

28 AP recommends Hooke's son to Dr William Holmes, Regius Professor of History at St John's, Oxford.

30 AP thanks Sir Hans Sloane in advance for his intended gift of basalt from the Giant's Causeway in Northern Ireland.

31 Warburton selects William Bowyer to publish the new edition of the *Essay on Man* commentary.

April
During this month, the first piracies of *The New Dunciad* appear. AP also is about to sever relations with Richard Savage, whose conduct towards AP has become somewhat irrational.

1 (Thurs) On or about this date Thomas Gray, the poet, writes to his friend Gilbert West in praise of *The New Dunciad*; several sections 'are as fine as anything [AP] has written' (*CH*, p. 333).

3 On this day appears Bezaleel Morrice's *To the Falsely Celebrated British Homer. An Epistle*, which belatedly attacks AP's modern translations as plagiarised.

8 Death of Lord Bolingbroke's father, which will necessitate St John's return from France to see to the estate.

23 AP's letter to Warburton reveals that they are planning jointly to edit Shakespeare (the edition appears in 1747). Shortly after this date Bolingbroke arrives in London from France. AP has apprently now decided to change printers, from John Wright to William Bowyer, for the revised first three books of *The Dunciad*, which are probably either finished or almost so.

24 After several pirated and authorised editions of *The New Dunciad* have appeared, Thomas Cooper reissues a previous issue with a new title-page and calls it the 'Second Edition'.

May

20 (Thurs) From this date forward, Swift is declared not responsible for his own health and safety, and he is taken care of by a committee of guardians.

21 AP at Twickenham after several days in London, where he sees Patty Blount, Lord Bolingbroke and others. On arrival he finds Sir Hans Sloane's gift of basalt from the Giant's Causeway which will adorn the grotto.

27 AP at Twickenham, where he is looking after Bolingbroke, ill with a fever.

June

5 (Sat) AP asks Warburton to review (again) the 'Essay on Homer' for correction because a new edition of AP's translation is to appear.

10 Bolingbroke improving, but ill health has kept him at AP's for some days.

12 AP and Bolingbroke go to Jonathan Richardson's studio in Queen's Square, where the artist is to make a last portrait sketch before Bolingbroke's departure for France. AP has just received a shipment of Bristol water from Ralph Allen, and expects more building-stone soon.

14 His father's estate settled, Lord Bolingbroke returns to France.

16 With Bolingbroke gone, AP is back at home, where he writes to Slingsby Bethel about further investments and also sends him a copy of *The New Dunciad*.

18 AP tells Warburton that he will be in London or at home for the next month, then travel to Ralph Allen's at the end of August.

30 AP has been entertaining guests at home for the past five days (possibly Gilbert West and family).

July

3 (Sat) Charles Bathurst issues a four-volume reprint edition of Motte's *Miscellanies* (first volume published in 1727), with works by Swift, Gay, Arbuthnot and AP, calling it the 'Fourth Edition'.

15 Earliest advertisements for the forthcoming *Letter from Mr Cibber, to Mr Pope*, published by W. Lewis, whom AP has also used as a publisher.

18   AP has just read over Warburton's corrections to the Preface and Essay for the new edition of the Homer translations.

19   AP tells Allen that he must delay his visit because the Duchess of Marlborough has asked him to stay at Windsor Lodge with her.

23   AP aware of the imminent publication of Cibber's *Letter*; he sends Lord Orrery a letter containing his 'Epigram. On Cibber's Declaration that he Will Have the Last Word with Mr Pope' ('You will have the *last word*, after all that is past?').

24   Cibber's famous *Letter from Mr Cibber, to Mr Pope* appears on this day. His anecdotal *Letter* reviews their past relations, and charges AP with various literary misdemeanours, and includes the story of his rescuing AP from a brothel, where he had found 'this little hasty Hero, like a terrible *Tom Tit*, pertly perching upon the Mount of Love!'

27   Lord Orrery has just received a copy of Cibber's *Letter* from his bookseller; and thinks (having read AP's epigram) of collecting all of AP's epigrams.

30   AP has been away from home, probably visiting in the country; he invites Jonathan Richardson to spend tomorrow evening and night at Twickenham.

August

3   (Tues) Appearance of a pamphlet attack on Colley Cibber, *A Blast upon Bays; Or, A New Lick at the Laureat*, probably by AP in response to Cibber's *Letter*.

4   AP in London briefly, on legal business.

5   AP goes to Lord Burlington's at Chiswick, where Jonathan Richardson probably meets him to view the paintings in the house. In the evening AP and Richardson probably take the latter's coach back to Twickenham.

7   Warburton's *Vindication of Mr Pope's Essay on Man*, revised from its first appearance in the periodical *History of the Works of the Learned*, is published as a *Critical and Philosophical Commentary on Mr Pope's Essay on Man*.

19   Published this day, Lord Hervey's *Letter to Mr Cibber, on his Letter to Mr Pope* contributes more general abuse of AP to the Cibber–AP dispute.

21   A further pamphlet in the AP–Cibber dispute, Hervey and Cibber's verse letter *The Difference between Verbal and Practical Virtue*, repeats earlier charges of AP as libellist and usurer.

24   AP at Twickenham, where he has been kept for several days
by the illness of his guest, Lord Chesterfield. A further
shipment of building-stone from Ralph Allen has arrived for
the grotto. The Allens are now in London.
27   The Allens are now visiting AP at Twickenham. Lord
Chesterfield, recovering from illness, has left, and Warburton
just arrived. The latter will accompany the Allens to Bath.
31   *Sawney and Colley, A Poetical Dialogue* is published this day.
This vicious verse pamphlet attacks both Cibber and AP,
whose mother is called a whore and he illegitimate. On this
same day, writing in *The Champion*, Henry Fielding strongly
defends AP as a satirist with correct principles and motives.

September
1   (Wed) AP replies to Louis Racine, whose poem *La Religion*
(published earlier in the year) attacks the *Essay on Man*, on his
religious principles: 'my Opinions are intirely different from
those of Spinoza; or even Leibnitz; but on the contrary
conformable to those of Mons. Pascal & Mons. Fenelon: the
latter of whom I would most readily imitate, in submitting all
my Opinions to the Decision of the Church'.
2   AP in London, partly on Warburton's legal business; he fails
to meet the solicitor acting for the bookseller's estate.
12   Probable date of John Knapton's visit to AP at Twickenham,
further to the Warburton legal business.
13   By this date the Allens and Warburton have been at Bath for
several days. AP sends Allen a copy of a letter to Richard
Savage and instructions for sending the poet a 5-guinea
postal order.
19   Lord Chesterfield takes AP from Twickenham to stay for two
days with the Duchess of Marlborough at Windsor Lodge.
23   AP still at Windsor Lodge (where Hooke is still working on
the family papers), detained by the Duchess of Marlborough.
Lord Chesterfield has gone on to see Lord Cobham at Stowe.
30   Publication of *The Scribleriad. Being an Epistle to the Dunces, on
Renewing their Attack upon Mr Pope*, by 'Scriblerus'.

October
Early in the month, AP finally leaves Windsor Lodge and journeys
to Bath, where he stays with the Allens.

13 (Wed) AP, at Bath, sends an inscription to the Duchess of Marlborough for Rysbrack's bust of Admiral Vernon.

16 In the *Universal Spectator* this day, Cibber's 'Tom Tit' story is transformed into a satiric cartoon, with AP perching on the whore's lap.

25 Louis Racine replies warmly and apologetically to AP's letter defending his religious principles.

November

1 (Mon) Warburton has just left Bath for Newark, travelling via London. On the way, he injures his leg. AP is making changes to the printed proofs of *The Dunciad*.

6 Warburton has been in London attending to AP's legal business over recent piracies of *The Dunciad*. AP is still sorting out details in the poem, as *The Dunciad* is being printed off.

13 AP (in Bath) now dealing directly with the printer Bowyer, who is attending to more small changes in *The Dunciad*.

18 AP's friend William Murray is made Solicitor-General.

27 AP still at Bath, but just leaving for home. He writes to Warburton of a scheme for making him the editor of *The Dunciad* in its new edition: 'I have a particular reason to make you Interest your self in Me & My Writings. It will cause both them & me to make the better figure to Posterity.'

30 Late at night AP arrives home at Twickenham, very weary.

December

During this month a lengthy libellous poem against AP is published; *The Blatant Beast* gathers most of the previous charges against AP, who is a 'Distorted Elf! to Nature a Disgrace,/Thy Mind envenom'd pictur'd in thy Face'.

4 (Sat) AP now in London, where he writes again to enlist Warburton as official editor of *The Dunciad*. He is staying with William Murray.

8 Hooke is still working for the Duchess of Marlborough at Windsor Lodge; AP sees his confinement as a sort of slavery. AP tells Allen that he hopes to persuade Martha Blount to stay at Allen's Hampton Manor (near Prior Park); he remains in London.

27 The printing of Bowyer's new edition of *The Dunciad* is now complete; piraters of the fourth book have now ceased and handed over their unsold copies to AP's solicitor. The freehold

of AP's Twickenham property has now been offered to him, and he thinks he will continue to live there. He is now staying in private lodgings in London.

28 AP back at home; William Murray is staying with him. He sends hearty thanks to Warburton for the *Dunciad* assistance, and announces he is sending the *Essay on Man* to Bowyer to be printed with Warburton's *Commentary*.

1743

January
 1 (Sat) About this date AP goes up to London for a fortnight to see Ralph Allen and stay with him.
11 Publication of *The Egotist: or, Colley upon Cibber*, a pamphlet possibly by Cibber himself.
13 AP still in London. He writes to enlist Lord Orrery's help to obtain from Oxford an honorary degree for Warburton.
18 AP back at Twickenham. He soothes Warburton's suspicions about plagiarism in the notes to Thomas Hanmer's new edition of Shakespeare. *The Dunciad* is now completely printed, but AP decides to delay publication, probably so that copyright can revert to him.
21 Samuel Richardson writes to George Cheyne to suggest that, although *The Dunciad* is a skilled satire, AP might employ 'his admirable Genius better than in exposing Insects of a Day' (*CH*, p. 340).

February
 9 (Wed) AP at Twickenham after a brief visit to London. He is still furious over the delay in granting Warburton an honorary degree from Oxford, which he tells Lord Orrery is 'a Demonstration of the Malignity of Dulness, which is never so rancorous as under the Robe of Learning'.
15 Cibber's *Second Letter from Mr Cibber to Mr Pope* published, an advance reponse to some lines from the forthcoming *Dunciad*.
16 AP files a complaint in Chancery against Henry Lintot, concerning property in *The Dunciad*, and sues Jacob Ilive for pirating the fourth book of *The Dunciad*.
21 Publication of the anonymous short poem *Mr Pope's Picture in Miniature*, a comprehensive summary of previous anti-AP charges.

March

3 (Thurs) In response to his inclusion in *The Dunciad*, John Henley attacks AP in his prose pamphlet *Why How Now, Gossip Pope? Or the Sweet Singing-Bird of Parnassus Taken out of its Pretty Cage to be Roasted*.

12 AP has seen Lord Oxford (the 3rd Earl, cousin of the late Edward Harley) some time ago in London, but for the past eight days has been 'locked up' at home working on more additions to the grotto.

13 Lord Marchmont is visiting AP.

20 AP gives Hugh Bethel an account of his health, which is declining due to asthma and dropsy, and of his estate at Twickenham, which he must yet decide to purchase.

22 AP receives his year's interest from £700 invested through Slingsby Bethel. He continues ill with 'a very bad cold & feverish complaint'.

24 AP tells Warburton that Bowyer has begun to print the quarto edition of the *Essay on Criticism* but that *The Dunciad* cannot be published yet because of the dispute over copyright. AP wants Warburton to carry on with his edition of the *Epistles* and the *Essay on Criticism*. He is still suffering from shortness of breath and fever.

April

During the early part of the month, Lord Bolingbroke arrives in England for a short visit, during which he will spend part of a week with AP, whose health is poor at this time.

12 (Tues) AP tries to arrange for a visit to Ralph Allen's for Martha Blount.

14 AP informs Ralph Allen that Martha Blount will not now be at Bath for another two or three weeks.

May

21 (Sat) AP in London, where he has just received from Warburton the first three sheets of the commentary on the *Essay on Criticism*. He has been with Lord Bolingbroke either in London or at Twickenham for the past five weeks. AP has also just read Warburton's brief commentary prefacing Charles Jervas' translation of *Don Quixote* (published in Apr). AP notes that his lawsuit with Lintot over *The Dunciad* is finished, and that publication can go ahead.

25 Lord Bolingbroke departs from Greenwich for France, early
in the afternoon.

June
Probably late in this month AP journeys to Bath to stay with the
Allens at Prior Park. Martha Blount and Warburton are also there
as visitors.

25 (Sat) AP's 'Epitaph on Mr Rowe' ('Thy Reliques, *Rowe*! to this
sad Shrine we trust') appears in *The Universal Spectator* and in
Common Sense, not long after the poem is engraved on Rowe's
monument in Westminster Abbey.

July
During most of this month AP is at Bath with the Allens, Martha
Blount, and Warburton. He sees Lord Chesterfield occasionally,
and follows his physician's prescriptions.

11 (Mon) Following the Duchess of Buckingham's death (in
Apr), AP now writes to a friend of Hugh Bethel's to deny real
authorship of a 1729 *Character of John Sheffield, Late Duke of
Buckinghamshire*, which he said he has only edited from the
Duchess' manuscript.

23 AP still suffering from asthma, which makes movement
difficult. He writes to George Arbuthnot that they will have
to stay together in the Allens' big house at Prior Park, rather
than in a smaller house in Hampton (now called Bathampton).
Arbuthnot is to arrive shortly.

August
At the very end of July or the first day of this month, a
misunderstanding arises over accommodation with the Allens at
Prior Park when George Arbuthnot arrives. He refuses to impose
on the Allens, AP supports him and wants to stay at Allen's small
house at Hampton, there is a quarrel and AP then goes off to
spend four or five days with Lord Bathurst at Cirencester. Martha
Blount remains with the Allens for those days, but is apparently
made to feel unwelcome. Writing to her (*Corr.*, IV, 464), AP asserts
that at Prior Park 'I never will set foot more – however well I
might wish the Man, the Woman is a Minx, & an impertinent
one.'

5 (Fri) Death of AP's old adversary John, Lord Hervey, at age
46.

6　AP probably passing through Bath, where his address is care of Lord Chesterfield, on the way back from Cirencester and on the way to Bristol.

12　AP at Bristol, with George Arbuthnot, where he has arrived by water down the River Avon. To Lord Orrery he writes, 'I have just heard of the death of Lord Hervey. Requiescat in pace!' (*Corr.*, IV, 466).

16　AP writes to Hugh Bethel (just returned from Italy) about financial arrangements and annuities he wishes to provide for Martha Blount, as he feels 'the gradual approaches of Decay in many ways'.

18　AP still at Bristol but just on the point of returning to London in hopes of seeing Hugh Bethel.

20　AP probably sees Dr Oliver in Bath; Arbuthnot is with him. But he avoids seeing Allen, likely out of embarrassment over the accommodation quarrel.

21　Probable date of AP's departure by coach towards London.

28　AP back in Twickenham for the past several days; he has missed seeing Bethel in London.

September

4　(Sun) AP at home with house guests, including the Arbuthnots. By this date he has sent two letters of reconciliation to Ralph Allen.

5　AP probably goes up to London with Arbuthnot (where he will stay), perhaps on publishing-business; he intends to see Bowyer, the printer. Warburton is also in London or just about to arrive.

13　AP writes another friendly letter to Allen in an attempted reconciliation.

29　During the past fortnight AP has been into Oxfordshire with Lord Cornbury, spent two days at Rousham, then gone to Oxford, arriving back at home on this day, after a brief visit to the Duchess of Queensberry in London. While at Oxford he has looked in at the University Press, where he sees a single sheet of Hanmer's Shakespeare edition.

October

5　(Wed) AP writes to Hugh Bethel, having missed him in London, with news and a statement of his declining health.

7　AP tells Warburton he has just given the *Essay on Criticism* (with commentary) to Bowyer for printing and ordered the advertising for *The Dunciad*. He also settles Warburton's fears over the Hanmer Shakespeare edition, which he does not think plagiarises any of Warburton's notes.

11　The *Daily Gazetteer* advertises that the four-book *Dunciad* (in quarto) will now be published on the 29th of this month. Publication is delayed until AP has regained copyright.

13　William Kent's will, drawn this day, bequeaths to AP a 'Raphael Head Busto and an Alabaster Vase'. Dodsley and Cooper publish a separate edition of AP's 'Verses on a Grotto by the River Thames at Twickenham' (originally in the January 1741 number of the *Gentleman's Magazine*), together with Dodsley's translations of the poem into Latin and Greek and 'The Cave of Pope. A Prophecy'.

15　About this date, Lord Bolingbroke arrives in England for a long stay, remaining until after AP's death.

28　AP at Twickenham where he orders from Slingsby Bethel some madeira for Martha Blount. He sends a copy of the new *Dunciad* to Hugh Bethel via Slingsby.

29　The final version (in royal quarto) of *The Dunciad* appears: *The Dunciad in Four Books. Printed According to the Complete Copy Found in the Year 1742. . . .* In this edition Colley Cibber replaces Theobald as hero of the poem. To the end of the poem AP adds here the passage beginning 'In vain, in vain, – the all-composing Hour'.

30　AP in London, where he writes a conciliatory letter inquiring about Ralph Allen's recent illness.

November

3　(Thurs) AP with Lord Marchmont at Battersea for a few days. He instructs Bowyer to watch out for piracies of the *Dunciad*, and complains obscurely that the *small* octavo of the *Dunciad* is not being properly prepared.

6　Christopher Smart, now an undergraduate at Pembroke Hall, Cambridge, writes to request permission to translate part or all of the *Essay on Man* into Latin.

8　AP again by letter inquires solicitously about Ralph Allen's illness.

15　Warburton is working steadily on the commentary for the *Moral Essays*, some of which AP is now sending back. AP intends to publish a small number of the Warburton–AP editions of the *Essay on Criticism* and *Essay on Man*.

17 AP writes yet again to inquire about Ralph Allen's health. AP has just recently seen Lord Bathurst and spent much time with Lord Bolingbroke. He is still occasionally at Twickenham, but may spend the winter in London at Lord Orrery's house in Duke Street. Mostly he lives at Lord Bolingbroke's in Battersea, where he, Lord Marchmont and Bolingbroke can talk without interruption.

18 AP replies to Christopher Smart, telling him to try a Latin translation of the last epistle of the *Essay on Man* or else the *Essay on Criticism*.

23 From Battersea, AP writes to Slingsby Bethel to acknowledge receipt of some madeira for Martha Blount (now in London), and to Ralph Allen, whose wife is now quite ill. Their breach of friendship now seems to be healed.

December

8 (Thurs) Ralph Allen's wife recovered; AP writes to Allen to clear up the last details of misunderstanding. He continues to commute between Battersea and London, staying seldom at home. His asthma seems worse and prevents any long journeys: 'I have nothing to do but to remove from one warm Fireside to another . . . & and from one Friends Side to another.'

12 AP has Spence witness his signature to his will. The other two witnesses are AP's neighbours Lord Radnor and Dr Stephen Hales. AP leaves his manuscripts and papers to Bolingbroke, and memorial gifts to many friends. The majority of the estate goes to Martha Blount (see Mack, *Garden and City*, pp. 263–5).

1744

January

3 (Tues) AP confined by his asthmatic condition at William Murray's house in Lincoln's Inn Fields.

12 AP at Battersea, somewhat healthier. He spends almost all his time with Lords Marchmont and Bolingbroke. To Warburton he writes, 'My present Indisposition takes up almost all my hours, to render a Very few of them supportable:

yet I go on softly to prepare the Great Edition of my things with your Notes.' He has decided to publish a small number of the *Essay on Man* and the *Essay on Criticism* in this edition, but Bowyer has advised delay. He has also just heard of Cibber's next abusive pamphlet: 'He will be more to me than a dose of Hartshorn; and as a Stink revives one who has been oppressed with Perfumes, his Railing will cure me of a Course of Flatteries.'

19   *Another Occasional Letter from Mr Cibber to Mr Pope*, Cibber's last attack on AP, appears; in addition to repeating earlier charges, Cibber alleges that AP has veneral disease. On the same day the *Daily Gazetteer* advertises that the *Essay on Man* with Warburton's commentary is to be published in a few days, and Samuel Richardson, writing to Aaron Hill, complains about the misuse of AP's talents in *The Dunciad in Four Books*: 'I admire Mr. Pope's Genius, and his Versification: But . . . I am scandaliz'd for human Nature, and such Talents, sunk so low' (*CH*, p. 345).

20   AP still at Battersea, where he acknowledges Allen's delivery of a bank bill.

27   AP back at home, because he sleeps better in the country. He has now gone over Warburton's commentaries on the *Epistle to Cobham* and the *Epistle to Bathurst*, urging him to go on the the *Epistle to a Lady* and the *Epistle to Burlington*, then to the *Epistle to Dr Arbuthnot*.

February
During this month, the first volume of Warburton's annotated edition of AP's *Works* appears. It is *An Essay on Man: Being the First Book of Ethic Epistles*, printed together as a pamphlet with *An Essay on Criticism*, both pieces with Warburton's commentary and notes. In the same month King George invokes by royal proclamation the 1688 Act forbidding Catholics to live within ten miles of London, in the face of a possible Jacobite invasion from France. AP complies with the Act.

 6   (Mon) AP in London for a few days, staying with Lord Orrery in Duke Street, Westminster. He seems to be arranging some of his financial affairs, perhaps for the benefit of Martha Blount.

 8   AP still in London, where he spends much of the day dining at Burlington House with Lords Burlington and Orrery.

9 Both AP and Lord Orrery ill after yesterday's dining at Burlington House. Perhaps shortly after this AP goes to have blood let by his friend Cheselden, the surgeon at Chelsea Hospital.

15 Lord Bolingbroke (who has borrowed Lord Marchmont's chariot) takes AP to Battersea.

16 On this day (or possibly the 15th), AP has a violent fit of his 'asthma' and almost stops breathing. Cheselden comes from Chelsea Hospital to let blood for him; the two go back to the Hospital for a brief stay. Publication of the anonymous pamphlet *Lick upon Lick; Occasion'd by another Occasional Letter from Mr Cibber to Mr Pope*.

18 First advertisements appear (in the *Daily Gazetteer*) for the edition of the *Essay on Criticism* and *Essay on Man* with Warburton's commentary.

20 AP back at home after treatment by both Cheselden and his regular physician, Dr Simon Burton. He has just received the portrait Hugh Bethel has sent of himself, and writes with thanks, but resignedly in what he thinks will be 'my last Winter'.

21 AP tells Warburton that he has spent a little time in the past few days revising the commentary for the *Epistle to Burlington*. He now tells Warburton that he will be the official editor of his works: 'no hand can set them in so good a Light . . . as your own. This obliges me to confess, I have for some months felt myself going, and that not slowly, down the hill.'

23 AP writes to remind Bowyer that the new edition of the *Essay on Man* and *Essay on Criticism* with Warburton's commentary should have been registered by now at Stationers' Hall.

25 AP now at Chelsea Hospital for more blood-letting treatment from Cheselden; the 'asthma' seems better as a result.

March

3 (Sat) AP writes to instruct Bowyer on the printing of the *Epistle to Cobham* with Warburton's commentary (AP issued a few of these to friends just before his death, but his executors suppressed the edition until the Knaptons brought out the *Four Ethic Epistles* (with Warburton's commentary) in 1748).

6 AP urges Ralph Allen to visit him at Twickenham, since due to the royal proclamation he is unable to stay in London, although a brief visit may be possible.

13 Warburton, possibly on this day, dines with AP at Twickenham.
15 AP writes to console Fortescue in the death of his sister.
18 AP sends his sailor nephew, John Rackett, to see Slingsby Bethel, with information on Sir William Codrington's West Indian estates.
19 AP's dog Bounce, in the care of the Orrerys, is attacked by a mad dog, on or just before this date, and is seriously wounded. At Twickenham, AP is confined to his room: 'I drink no wine, & take scarce any meat. Asses milk twice a day. My only Medicines are Millepedes & Garlick, & Horehound Tea' (*Corr.*, IV, 508). He is now arranging to purchase a lease on a house in Berkeley Street (the house is leased ultimately by Martha Blount, who lives there until her death in 1763).
22 On this day and the next (Good Friday) the Allens visit AP at Twickenham.
25 AP writes to Martha Blount about his conversation of the past few days with Ralph Allen over the accommodation quarrel of the previous year. He encloses a copy of his letter to his physician so that she can know the details of his illness.
26 AP invites Lords Marchmont and Bolingbroke to visit him, bringing William Murray with them, in a few days.
30 AP somewhat better; during the past few days he has gone out twice for chariot rides, and is just now going to dine at Lord Burlington's at Chiswick, returning before evening.

April
AP probably spends the whole month at home, confined by his very poor condition and by the royal proclamation against Catholics residing in London. Lords Bolingbroke and Marchmont both see him, as does Warburton frequently.
 9 (Mon) Possibly on this date AP intends to see the Allens at a farewell dinner before they return to Bath, but ill health prevents this.
10 AP writes to Lord Orrery to inquire into the fate of his dog, Bounce, adding in lamentation a couplet adapted from Chaucer's *Knight's Tale*, AP's last known piece of poetry.
14 In conversation with Spence during the week after this date, AP modifies his original *magnum opus* design yet again.

20 AP writes to rejoice in Allen's safe arrival in Bath and to describe his own worsening state of health.

May

1 (Tues) On or about this date is printed Warburton's annotated edition of the *Four Ethic Epistles* by AP, the so-called death-bed edition. The poet is said by Spence to have distributed copies to friends, but the volume is published by the Knaptons with a new title-page in 1748 (see *TE*, iii–ii, xiv–xv).

5 By this date, as he tells Orrery, AP has a new physician, Dr Thompson, whose treatment is purging. AP feels somewhat better and goes out every day in a chariot.

6 AP is ordered by his physician to take several doses of physic, which render him senseless for the entire day.

7 AP at Chelsea Hospital, for a last treatment by Dr Cheselden.

14 AP complains of seeing false colours on objects, as his mental state deteriorates further.

15 George Lyttelton visits AP for a last farewell.

19 Mallet (who has spent yesterday and today with AP) writes to Orrery with a last, detailed description of AP's state as he drifts towards death.

21 AP gets out of his sickbed to dine with Spence, Lord Bolingbroke and John Arbuthnot's daughter, Anne; Bolingbroke remarks 'sure Providence does this to mortify the whole human species' (Spence, i, 267), and weeps while leaning against AP's chair.

28 AP, with Spence, takes the air in his garden for a last time; he sits in a sedan chair for three hours. Mallet comes to take a last farewell, staying for dinner.

29 At the instigation of Nathaniel Hooke, a Catholic priest is sent to give AP the last sacraments, who receives them this morning kneeling on the floor by his sickbed. In the afternoon he takes a final airing at Bushy Park, the royal preserve about two miles south of Pope's villa.

30 AP dies in the evening aged 56 years and nine days. The exact time is not noticed, 'for his departure was so easy that it was imperceptible even to the standers-by. May our end be like his!' (Spence, i, 269).

June

5 (Tues) AP buried in Twickenham church.

14   AP's will proved, in London, in the presence of Lords
     Bathurst and Marchmont, George Arbuthnot and William
     Murray, each of whom receives a token bequest. Lord
     Bolingbroke is named as literary executor; Warburton, Ralph
     Allen and Martha Blount divide his books; Warburton receives
     the property of the literary works and the command to write
     commentaries on them; others who receive small bequests
     are Magdalen Rackett, her three sons, Erasmus Lewis, Gilbert
     West, Sir Clement Cottrell, William Rollinson, Nathaniel
     Hooke, Anne Arbuthnot and John Searle, AP's gardener.
     Most of the estate goes to Martha Blount, the lifelong friend
     of AP.

Principal Persons
Mentioned

Addison, Joseph (1672–1719) Poet, statesman, and essayist for the *Spectator*, *Tatler* and *Guardian*. An early supporter of AP, but later estranged over the *Iliad* translation.

Allen, Ralph (1694–1764) Postmaster, philanthropist, and friend of AP from 1736; the model for Fielding's Squire Allworthy in *Tom Jones*.

Arbuthnot, John (1667–1735) Physician in Ordinary to Queen Anne, 1709–14; author of *History of John Bull* (1712), member of the Scriblerus Club; contributor to *Three Hours after Marriage* (1717); and close friend of AP (see *Epistle to Dr Arbuthnot*, 1734).

Atterbury, Francis (1662–1732) Bishop of Rochester, Jacobite sympathiser, and friend of AP.

Bathurst, Allen, Earl Bathurst (1684–1775) Tory peer (1712), close friend of AP, and addressee of the third *Moral Essay* (*Epistle to Bathurst*).

Bentley, Richard (1662–1742) Master of Trinity College, Cambridge, distinguished classical scholar, but for AP arch-representative of verbal critics; as in *The Dunciad* and *Sober Advice from Horace*.

Bethel, Hugh (died 1748) MP for Pontefract, AP's long-time friend; see the *Second Satire of the Second Book of Horace*.

Blount, Martha (1690–1762) Younger Blount sister, AP's main female friend from youth and his principal legatee.

Blount, Teresa Maria (1688–1759) Elder sister of Martha and early friend of AP; they became estranged after 1721.

Bolingbroke, Henry St John, Viscount (1678–1751) Statesman, Jacobite Tory, philosopher, lifelong friend and mentor of AP.

Boyle, John, Earl of Orrery (1707–62)   Friend and correspondent of both Swift and AP after 1730.

Boyle, Richard, third Earl of Burlington (1695–1753)   Patron, statesman, close friend of AP after 1715; residences at Burlington House (London) and Chiswick.

Broome, William (1689–1745)   AP's assistant translator on the *Iliad* and *Odyssey* projects.

Brydges, James, Duke of Chandos (1673–1744)   Patron of Handel, and friend of Gay and AP.

Burlington, Lord   *See* **Boyle, Richard**.

Burnet, Thomas (1694–1753)   Youngest son of Bishop Burnet, member of Addison's circle, author of several attacks on AP.

Caryll, John (1667–1736)   Squire of West Grinstead, Sussex, early correspondent with AP (from 1710).

Chandos, Duke of   *See* **Brydges**.

Cibber, Colley (1671–1757)   Actor, dramatist, Poet Laureate (1730–57), enemy of AP's from 1717, hero of *The New Dunciad*, 1742.

Cleland, William (1674–1741)   Scottish soldier, government official, friend of AP.

Cobham, Viscount   *See* **Temple**.

Cornbury, Lord   *See* **Hyde**.

Craggs, James the younger (1686–1721)   Secretary of State, involved (with his father) in the South Sea Company scandal, and friend of AP.

Cromwell, Henry (1659–1728)   Elderly minor poet, London friend and correspondent of AP, 1708–12.

Curll, Edmund (1675–1747)   Infamous publisher of piracies and pornography, and AP's constant adversary, 1714–41.

Dennis, John (1657–1734)   Dramatist, critic, AP's first and most persistently abusive opponent.

Dodsley, Robert (1703–64)   Poet, playwright, and one of AP's publishers after 1735.

Dormer, James (1679–1741)   Military hero, general, member of the Kit-Cat Club, acquaintance of AP, who frequently visited his house at Rousham.

Douglas, Charles, Duke of Queensberry (1698–1778)   Privy Councillor to George I, and, with his Duchess, Gay's patron in the poet's latter years.

Fenton, Elijah (1683–1730)   Minor poet, scholar; assisted AP with Homer translations.

Fermor, Arabella (1690?–1738)   Daughter of a prominent Catholic family from Ufton Nervet, Berkshire, celebrated beauty, model for Belinda in *The Rape of the Lock*.

Fortescue, William (1687–1749)   Barrister, Whig MP, Baron of the Exchequer, Master of the Rolls, and AP's close friend and legal adviser.

Frederick Louis, Prince of Wales (1707–51)   Disobedient son of George II and father of George III; he was friendly to AP in the 1730s.

Gay, John (1685–1732)   Poet, playwright (*The Beggar's Opera*), charter member of the Scriblerus Club, close friend of AP.

Gilliver, Lawton (died 1748)   Trusted publisher of all AP's major poems 1729–37, including the epistles to Bathurst, Cobham, Burlington, Martha Blount and Arbuthnot, and the *Essay on Man*.

Harley, Edward, second Earl of Oxford (1689–1741)   Son of Robert Harley, bibliophile and collector, friend of AP and Swift.

Harley, Robert, first Earl of Oxford (1661–1724) Chief Tory minister in 1714, statesman, bibliophile, friend of AP.

Harte, Walter (1709–74) Minor poet, miscellaneous writer, friend and admirer of AP.

Hervey, John, Baron Hervey of Ickworth (1696–1743) MP, Walpole-supporter, enemy of AP, subject of 'Sporus' portrait in *Epistle to Arbuthnot*.

Hill, Aaron (1685–1750) Minor poet and dramatist, early antagonist then friendly correspondent of AP after 1728.

Hooke, Nathaniel (died 1763) Historian and long-time Catholic friend of AP.

Howard, Henrietta, Countess of Suffolk (1681–1767) Mistress of George II and AP's neighbour at her Marble Hill house, whose gardens he designed.

Hume, Hugh, Earl of Marchmont (1708–94) Member of the Whig opposition to Walpole, the young 'patriots'; friend to AP after 1739.

Hyde, Henry, Viscount Cornbury (1710–53) MP for Oxford and AP's good friend after 1735.

Jervas, Charles (1675–1739) Portraitist, fashionable painter, close friend and tutor of AP.

Kent, William (1684?–1748) Painter, designer, architect, friend of AP.

Kneller, Sir Godfrey (1646–1723) Portrait-painter, near neighbour at Twickenham of AP, who wrote his epitaph.

Lintot, Bernard (1675–1736) Eminent publisher and bookseller, whose press issued many of AP's works between 1712 and 1736; his son, Henry, carried on the business after 1736.

Lyttelton, George (1709–73)   Lord Cobham's nephew and member of the anti-Walpolian faction in Parliament in the late 1730s.

Mallet, David (1705?–65)   Minor poet and dramatist of Scottish birth, AP's correspondent and friend.

Marchmont, Lord   *See* **Hume.**

Montagu, Lady Mary Wortley (1689–1762)   AP's close friend from 1715 until the early 1720s, thereafter his bitter enemy; in 1718, introduced inoculation for smallpox into England.

Mordaunt, Charles, Earl of Peterborough and Monmouth (1658–1735)   Soldier, gardening-enthusiast, close friend of AP; residences at Bevis Mount and London.

Motte, Benjamin (died 1738)   Bookseller and publisher of *Gulliver's Travels* and the AP–Swift *Miscellanies.*

Murray, William, Earl of Mansfield (1705–93)   MP, later Solicitor-General and Attorney-General, and Lord Chief Justice; AP's friend after 1735 and sometimes legal adviser.

Orrery, Lord   *See* **Boyle, John.**

Oxford, Lord   *See* **Harley, Robert,** or **Harley, Edward.**

Parnell, Thomas (1679–1718)   Irish-born poet, contributor to the *Spectator* and *Guardian*, and member of the Scriblerus Club; AP edited his posthumous poems.

Peterborough, Lord   *See* **Mordaunt.**

Philips, Ambrose (1675?–1749)   Minor poet and dramatist, AP's rival pastoralist.

Pope, Alexander (1646–1717)   London merchant, AP's father.

Pope, Edith (1642–1733), *née* Turner, AP's mother.

Pope, Magdalen (1679?–1749)   AP's half-sister, married Charles Rackett of Hammersmith, *c.* 1694.

Queensberry, Duke of *See* **Douglas**.

Rackett, Charles (died 1728?), of Hammersmith, husband of Magdalen Pope, AP's half-sister.

Richardson, Jonathan (the elder) (1665–1745) Painter, author of many sketched portraits of AP after 1733.

Rowe, Nicholas (1674–1718) Dramatist, first editor of Shakespeare, Poet Laureate, early friend of AP.

Sheffield, John, Earl of Mulgrave, Duke of Buckingham and Normanby (1648–1721) Courtier, statesman, poet, Jacobite sympathiser and friend of AP, who edited his poetical works.

Spence, Joseph (1699–1768) Friend of AP, collector of anecdotes, author of an *Essay on Mr Pope's Odyssey*, Professor of Poetry (1728) and later Regius Professor of Modern History at Oxford.

Steele, Sir Richard (1672–1729) Essayist, politician and dramatist, and sometimes acquaintance of AP; originated *The Tatler*, *The Spectator* and *The Guardian*.

Suffolk, Lady *See* **Howard**.

Swift, Jonathan (1667–1745) Satirist, poet, author of *Gulliver's Travels*, Dean of St Patrick's, Dublin, AP's lifelong friend, correspondent, and fellow Scriblerian.

Temple, Sir Richard, Viscount Cobham (1675–1749) Soldier and statesman, friend of AP; residence at Stowe, Buckinghamshire.

Theobald, Lewis (1688–1744) Dramatist, scholar, AP's rival editor of Shakespeare, hero of *The Dunciad*, 1728.

Tickell, Thomas (1686–1740) Poet, essayist, friend of Addison, rival translator to AP of Homer.

Tonson, Jacob (1656?–1736) Eminent bookseller and publisher; his nephew, Jacob Tonson, Jr, carried on the business.

Trumbull, Sir William (1639–1716)   Former Secretary of State to William III (retired 1698), near neighbour in Berkshire and elderly friend of AP.

Wales, Prince of   *See* **Frederick**.

Walpole, Sir Robert, Earl of Orford (1676–1745)   Politician and Prime Minister (1721–42), acquaintance of AP and (later) frequent object of AP's attacks on Whig government.

Walsh, William (1663–1708)   Poet, critic, courtier, AP's early friend.

Warburton, William (1689–1779)   Bishop of Gloucester; originally AP's anonymous antagonist in early pamphlets, later defender of the *Essay of Man*, and AP's last major friend; edited AP's works (1751), with commentary, as AP's literary executor.

Wycherley, William (1640?–1716)   Poet, playwright (*The Country Wife*), early friend of AP.

Principal Places Mentioned

Amesbury Town in Wiltshire, 10 miles north of Salisbury; country home of the Duke and Duchess of Queensberry.

Bath Fashionable Somerset health resort and spa for polite society; AP visited here frequently in his later years.

Bevis Mount 1 mile north of Southampton's city gates; home (now gone) of Lord Peterborough.

Binfield, Berkshire 9 miles east of Reading; AP and family lived here at Whitehill House, *c.* 1700–15.

Chiswick, Middlesex 8 miles west of London, home of Lord Burlington, and of AP and family, 1716–19.

Cirencester Park Lord Bathurst's house in Oakley Wood, near the Gloucestershire town of the same name.

Dawley Farm South-east of Uxbridge, Middlesex, 15 miles west of London; Bolingbroke's residence from 1725.

Down Hall Matthew Prior's estate in Matching Green, 7 miles north of Epping, Essex; after Prior's death it reverted to Lord Oxford, who had helped Prior buy it.

Easthampstead Berkshire village, 3 miles south of Binfield; home of Sir William Trumbull.

Grub Street Unfashionable London street just outside London Wall near St Giles Cripplegate (the site is now covered by the Barbican development); legendary refuge of third-rate writers and publishers who would attack AP and Swift.

Hammersmith In AP's time, a village 6 miles west of London; AP's family resided here 1692–1700.

Ladyholt Park At South Harting, Sussex, 4 miles south-east of Petersfield, Hampshire; home (now gone) of John Caryll.

Mapledurham House, Oxfordshire   4 miles north-west of Reading; family residence of Martha and Teresa Blount.

Marble Hill   Immediately next to Twickenham on the Thames; location of Lady Suffolk's celebrated house and garden.

Prior Park   Palladian house at Combe Down, 2 miles south of Bath, built for Ralph Allen after 1735.

Richmond, Surrey   In AP's time, a fashionable village opposite Twickenham on the Thames, 11 miles south-west of London.

Riskins   Richings Park, 17 miles west of London, near Slough; home of Allen, Lord Bathurst.

Rousham Park, Oxfordshire   11 miles north of Oxford; home of General James Dormer, remodelled by William Kent, and famous for its naturalistic landscape garden.

Stanton Harcourt, Oxfordshire   8 miles west of Oxford, home of Lord Harcourt.

Stowe, Buckinghamshire   Stately home of Lord Cobham, 4 miles north of Buckingham; AP greatly admired the elaborate gardens and visited frequently after 1725.

Theatre (Haymarket)   Known as the **Queen's Theatre** before 1714 and the **King's** after that year; first London playhouse built in the eighteenth century (1705).

Theatre (Lincoln's Inn Fields)   On Portugal Street, just south of Lincoln's Inn Fields, built in 1714; John Rich was manager; *The Beggar's Opera* played there in 1728.

Theatre Royal (Covent Garden)   John Rich's great project, built in 1732 west of Bow Street on the corner of Covent Garden Market.

Theatre Royal (Drury Lane)   One of the principal London playhouses, just off Drury Lane and Russell Street; Colley Cibber was among the actor–managers here.

Twickenham, Middlesex In AP's time, village on the Thames upstream from London; AP lived here, 1719–44, in his riverside villa (now gone, but the grotto is extant).

Upper Letcombe (Letcombe Bassett), Berkshire (now Oxfordshire) Village 2 miles south-west of Wantage.

Whitehill House Residence of AP and family at Binfield.

Whitton In AP's time, village 1 mile north of Twickenham; home of several of AP's friends, including Nathaniel Pigott.

Wimpole Hall, Cambridgeshire 10 miles south-west of Cambridge; country house of Edward Harley's wife.

Bibliography

In addition to the works cited in the List of Abbreviations (p. xiii), this chronology has drawn upon the following:

Aitken, George A., *The Life and Works of John Arbuthnot* (1892; repr. New York: Russell and Russell, 1968).

Arbuthnot, John, *The History of John Bull*, ed. Alan W. Bower and Robert A. Erickson (Oxford: Clarendon Press, 1976).

Ault, Norman, *The Prose Works of Alexander Pope*, vol. I (Oxford: Basil Blackwell, 1936).

Ehrenpreis, Irvin, *Swift: His Life, his Works, his Times*, 3 vols (London: Methuen, 1962–83).

Gay, John, *Dramatic Works*, ed. John Fuller, 2 vols (Oxford: Clarendon Press, 1983).

——, *The Letters of John Gay*, ed. C. F. Burgess (Oxford: Clarendon Press, 1966).

——, *Poetry and Prose*, ed. Vinton A. Dearing and Charles E. Beckwith, 2 vols (Oxford: Clarendon Press, 1974).

Griffith, Reginald Hervey, *Alexander Pope: A Bibliography*, 2 vols (1922–7; repr. London: Holland Press, 1968).

[Rocque, John,] *The A to Z of Georgian London*, intro. by Ralph Hyde (Lympne Castle, Kent: Harry Margary, 1981).

Rogers, Robert W., *The Major Satires of Alexander Pope* (Urbana: University of Illinois Press, 1955).

Wimsatt, William Kurtz, *The Portraits of Alexander Pope* (New Haven, Conn., and London: Yale University Press, 1965).

Index